The First Year and the Rest of Your Life

Movement, Development, and Psychotherapeutic Change

Ruella Frank
Frances La Barre

Routledge
Taylor & Francis Group
New York   London

Routledge
Taylor & Francis Group
711 Third Avenue
New York, NY 10017

Routledge
Taylor & Francis Group
27 Church Road
Hove, East Sussex BN3 2FA

© 2011 by Taylor and Francis Group, LLC
Routledge is an imprint of Taylor & Francis Group, an Informa business

International Standard Book Number: 978-0-415-87639-1 (Hardback) 978-0-415-87640-7 (Paperback)

Library of Congress Cataloging-in-Publication Data

Frank, Ruella.
    The first year and the rest of your life : movement, development, and psychotherapeutic change / Ruella Frank, Frances La Barre.
        p. cm.
    Includes bibliographical references and index.
    ISBN 978-0-415-87639-1 (hbk.) -- ISBN 978-0-415-87640-7 (pbk.) -- ISBN 978-0-203-85747-2 (e-book)
    1. Nonverbal communication in infants. 2. Interpersonal communication in infants. 3. Motor ability in infants. 4. Infants--Development. 5. Parent and infant. I. La Barre, Frances. II. Title.

BF720.C65F73 2010
155.42'223--dc22
                               2010011681

Visit the Taylor & Francis Web site at
http://www.taylorandfrancis.com

and the Routledge Web site at
http://www.routledgementalhealth.com

Dedication

For my husband, Colin Greer

F. L.

In loving memory of my mentor, Richard Kitzler

R. F.

Contents

Acknowledgments

We are very grateful to our respective psychoanalytic and gestalt communities for many years of lively discussion that contributed to the ideas for this book. The ongoing interest, support, and enthusiasm of our colleagues and friends have been invaluable in developing our work.

Frances La Barre gratefully acknowledges Mark Sossin, for his collaboration and support, and the students in the graduate psychology program at Pace University; Karen Mruk, Judy Levitz, Catherine Lindenman, and students at the Psychoanalytic Psychotherapy Study Center; Rosemary Masters and the members of the trauma group at the Institute for Contemporary Psychotherapy; Frances Sommer Anderson and students at the National Institute for the Psychotherapies; Margaret Dieter and the members of the Ithaca Psychotherapy Group and students of the Adolescent Institute; Regina Miranda at the Laban Institute for Movement Studies; Katya Bloom; Susan Loman at Antioch New England's Dance Therapy Department, Keene, New Hampshire; Rosamaria Govoni, Marilyn LaMonica, and the students at the Institute Art Therapy Italiana in Bologna, Italy; Warren Lamb, Action Profilers International; Frieda Rietzes, Beth Teitleman, and the mothers and babies in the New Mother/New Baby classes at the 92nd Street Y; Jacquelyn Carleton, founding editor of *Energy & Consciousness: International Journal of Core Energetics*; Patrizia Pallara and students at ICP in Washington, D.C.; Serge Prengel of *Somatic Perspectives on Psychotherapy*. Special thanks to Tom Menaker for all the conversation and his unfailing encouragement.

Ruella Frank gratefully acknowledges students of the Developmental Somatic Psychotherapy training programs, Center for Somatic Studies, New York City; Gestalt Associates for Psychotherapy, New York City; Lynne Jacobs, Gary Yontef, and students of Pacific Gestalt Institute, Los Angeles; Gro Skottun, Daan Van Balen, and students of Norsk Gestaltinstitutt, Oslo; Carmen Vazquez Bandin and students of Centro de Terapia y Psicologia, Madrid; Jean-Marie Robine and students of Institut Francaise de Gestalt-therapie, Paris/Bordeaux; Margherita Spagnuolo-Lobb and students of Istituto di Gestalt-H.C.C., Syracusa/Palermo, Italy; Peter Philipson and students of Manchester Gestalt Center, Manchester, England; Lynda

Osborne and students of Metanoia, London; Myriam Munoz and students of Instituto Humanista de Psicoterapia Gestalt A.C., Mexico City; and, of course, Richard Kitzler and the ongoing teaching and learning community that is the New York Institute for Gestalt Therapy, New York City.

In addition, we want to thank our friends and colleagues Dan Bloom, Susan Baronoff, Margaret Dieter, Susan Friedberg, Lynne Jacobs, Joe Lay, Eda Rak, and Gary Yontef for their useful comments on selected chapters and case studies. We thank Mark Sossin for his reading and commentary on the manuscript, for his generosity and support, and for the inspiration we have drawn from his work. We have also been inspired by George Downing's integration of video microanalysis in infant–parent psychotherapy treatment.

Many thanks to Hilke Kaupert for her design of the charts, Sebastian Kaupert for technical and design work with photographs, Eric Breitbart for the photographs in the Postscript, and Anna Hindell for skillfully modeling the movements in that section.

We also want to thank our friends and colleagues who so generously shared the family photographs that appear in the book.

Ruella Frank wishes to thank all the teachers at the Iyengar Yoga Institute of Greater New York, in particular Mary Dunn, James Murphy, Genny Kapuler, Brooke Myers, Matt Dreyfus, and Robin Janus. Frances La Barre wishes to thank the teachers at Kinespirit Riverside, especially Evelyn Hubbell for her expert eye and gentle guidance and also Vicki Volmer for her skillful transmission of the Iyengar method of yoga. Their teaching inspires us in the search to understand the powerful role of movement in healing processes and in development.

We thank our editor, John Kerr, for his skillful reading and commentary, which pushed us to clarify our ideas. Thanks to Emily Pearl for her helpful editorial suggestions on the final manuscript.

Kristopher Spring at Routledge has been wonderfully supportive and responsive to us. We appreciate his encouragement to broaden the book to its present dimensions.

We are especially indebted to our patients for collaborating with us, giving us the opportunity to hone our relational skills and to transform our hypotheses into theory through practice. In particular, we want to thank the parents and babies and the adult patients who have permitted us to tell their stories here. Without them, this book would not have been possible.

We are immensely grateful to Colin Greer, who has continuously and generously given his time to our project. He has closely read and commented on every draft of the manuscript. His help in forming the final manuscript has been invaluable.

We could not have developed our theory and practice without having encountered and studied with Judith Kestenberg, Margaret Rustin, and Bonnie Bainbridge-Cohen. We cannot thank them enough.

Finally, we wish to thank each other. From the first moments of meeting, we each recognized a kindred spirit and quickly began sharing our expertise with one another. Once we began working together, we recognized in each other the enormous patience, persistence, and perseverance that is requisite in thinking, working, and writing with another person. We wrote every chapter together and gave valued comments on each other's case studies. In the process, we truly discovered the definition of teamwork. Our professional collaboration has been illuminating and our friendship an added pleasure.

About the Authors

Ruella Frank, Ph.D., is founder and director of the Center for Somatic Studies, and faculty at Gestalt Associates for Psychotherapy and the New York Institute for Gestalt Therapy. She teaches throughout the United States, Europe, and Mexico, and is the author of articles and chapters in various publications, as well as *Body of Awareness: A Somatic and Developmental Approach to Psychotherapy* (Gestalt Press, 2001), available in four languages.

Frances La Barre, Ph.D., is a psychologist-psychoanalyst in private practice in New York City, where she works with individual adults, children, and couples. She is adjunct professor and co-director of the Parent–Infant/Toddler Research Nursery at Pace University, and a supervisor and faculty member at the Psycho-analytic Psychotherapy Study Center and the Institute for Contemporary Psychotherapy. She lectures and teaches both in the United States and Europe. Her book, *On Moving and Being Moved: Nonverbal Behavior in Clinical Practice* (The Analytic Press, 2001), and articles are known for her unique application of movement studies to psychotherapy.

Foreword

The philosopher Maurice Merleau-Ponty wrote many years ago that "the perceiving mind is an incarnated mind." He compared the bond between soul and body to that between the convex and the concave. He believed, in other words, that the mind–body difference was one of perspective and description, and he left us a philosophy of embodied intersubjectivity. Nonetheless, the clinical losses we suffer through our continued and relentless concentration on the mental and the psychical have been immense. From work with infants and children through the horrors of massive traumatic experience to the encroaching losses at the end of life, we clinicians are now learning anew that we must live, learn, and work through our bodies to reach out and to engage in healing relationships, no matter in what healing traditions we work.

Here two master clinicians, one gestaltist and one psychoanalytic, show us the intricate dance of embodied intersubjectivity, primarily in the first year of life, but also in parenting, in couples, and in individual work. Despite their capacities for multiple focus, they have each and both developed an exquisite sensitivity to embodiment in movement. Like Merleau-Ponty, they invite us to inhabit our own bodies more mindfully in posture and movement as we engage with our patients and thus, as they eloquently tell us, to widen the hermeneutic field, the possibility of understanding. They show us how bodily movement patterns ground all the most basic elements of psychological organization and how specific body experiences become self- and relational experience, and vice versa. I believe this to be the most fruitful use of infant research that I have ever seen and am honored to help to introduce its verbal expression.

Donna Orange

The embodied relationality of development—this is the theme and the achievement of this book. Our experiential worlds cannot exist without our bodies, but to the degree that we lack mindful embodiment, to that degree our experiential worlds are impoverished. Our embodiment *is* our engagement with the world. It shapes our experiential worlds, and in endless recursive cycles, our experiential worlds also shape our embodiment. In this recursive cycle, every nuance of the way we live our bodies and our bodies live us carries our contextual histories, our relational histories, and creates new embodied relational histories in the present moment.

As I write, I suffer the frustration of an impoverishment of language. I write as if our embodiment is distinct from our experiential world. Nothing could be further from the truth. As Kepner (1987) wrote about a similar distinction, that between body and sense of self:

> Our language encourages the distinction between body and "I." We have no single word that allows us to say, "I-body." At the most we might say "my body" in much the same way we might refer to "my car," implying that one's body is property but certainly not *self.* Our language supports the notion that our body is an object: something that happens to me, rather than the "me that is happening." (p. 7)

And yet, when I read this book, I do not suffer the same frustration. The authors have found a means to describe, explain, evoke. I experienced this book as a whole; I lived it through my senses, my bodily movements, my thoughts.

For some time now, gestalt therapists and contemporary analysts have acknowledged *bodymind*, the unity of what has previously been separated into psyche and soma. And there have been efforts from analysts and gestalt therapists to integrate the entirety of our embodiment into a therapeutic praxis, which begs for dialogue that speaks to and from our lived bodymind. We refer to "nonverbal process" and "implicit process," but by and large, such language still leaves us bifurcating spoken words and body words. We struggle to find language that captures how all language, whether spoken orally or not, is embodied language, embodied living. As hard as these progenitors have tried, *the* body remains firmly ensconced as an add-on to our verbal explorations. In its concreteness, our embodiment—without which there be no words—resists easy integration into a process that attends largely to symbolic spoken words.

Now comes something different. These two authors and master clinicians—one from the world of gestalt therapy, one from the psychoanalytic world—bring together the threads that we know belong together, but have not had the means before to integrate. They embed embodiment in an understanding of the radical relationality of the development of our experiential worlds. Thus, we have embodiment, development, and relationality, all under one roof.

The particular forte of Frank and La Barre is attention to bodily movement. They describe and teach about the foundational movements and postures that are the building blocks for our living-in-our-worlds throughout our lives. They paint sensitive portrayals of the interplay of movements between parents and children and also between therapists and patients. From my vantage point as a gestalt therapist, I believe we finally have a developmental theory that is true to our commitments to a nonlinear process theory and to the unity of the bodymind.

I am delighted to have read this book and honored to participate in some small way in its fruition.

Lynne Jacobs

REFERENCE

Kepner, J. (1987). *Body process: Working with the body in psychotherapy* (1st ed.). San Francisco: Jossey-Bass.

Preface

This book is the result of the collaboration between two people—a gestalt therapist and a psychoanalyst—who bring their two different psychotherapeutic traditions in train yet share a common and important understanding. In coming together and with the writing of this book, we have found a way to see past and through our differences of emphasis and technique. We do this by focusing on the details of interaction that allow us to understand the interactive flow within all relationships, in particular the psychotherapy relationship. Because we come from two different psychotherapy cultures, each with its own jargon, we have chosen to use "the language of the body moving" to describe complex theoretical ideas. Rather than offering a series of "how-to" techniques, we instead offer and illustrate our theory—*foundational movement analysis*—to be integrated within any form of psychotherapy.

Each chapter of this book presents theoretical constructs and case examples to demonstrate our theory. These cases also show what, how, and why we do what we do. Our ways of working are particular to us and will not necessarily be consistent with our readers' styles of working, nor should they be. We believe, however, that by coming to understand our nonverbal lexicon and its theoretical underpinnings, psychotherapists will discover their own unique ways of working within this approach and usefully apply it to varied populations—parents and babies, children, adolescents, individual adults, and couples.

Chapter 1

The Significance
of the First Year

In recent years, interest in nonverbal behavior has been growing among psychotherapists of many different persuasions. There is generally greater appreciation of the enhanced understanding of human interaction offered by learning about and attending to the body in action.[1] In this book, we seek to advance this point of view in three ways. First, and above all, we identify a language of movement description that makes observing the nonverbal more accessible to the clinical eye. Second, we show how, in the first year of life, nonverbal repertoires develop within parent–baby interactions and how knowledge of this process can vitally inform psychoeducational and psychotherapeutic work with parents and babies. Third, we elaborate this perspective to demonstrate how the patterns of nonverbal interactions emerging in infancy continue to serve as the foundation of a person's expressive interactive repertoire throughout life.

We emphasize movement in parent–baby interactions during the first year of life because nonverbal behavior is never more evident than at this time, when it is the primary means of communicating. In this first year, emergent core organizing actions can be seen *before* and *as* they become entwined with later developing mental and kinetic processes that add greater complexity. A baby's characteristic movements are immediately seen, sensed, and responded to by each parent's specific movement repertoire, and both

---

[1] The following are several references, among many others, to psychotherapists who focus on nonverbal behavior: Anderson (2008); Aposhyan (2004); Aron and Anderson (1998); Beebe and Lachmann (1998, 2002); Black (2003); Bollas (1983); Boston Change Process Study Group (2002, 2005, 2007, 2008); Boulanger (2007); Bromberg (1998, 2006); Bucci (1997); Butler (1993); Chasseguet-Smirgel (2003); Clemmens (1997); Cornell (2008); Davies and Frawley (1991, 1994); Davoine and Gaudillière (2004); Ellman and Moskowitz (1998); Fonagy, Gergely, Jurist, and Target (2002); Frank (2001, 2004, 2005); Gendlin (2007/1978); Green and Stern (2001); Harris (2005); Kepner (1987, 1995); Kestenberg (1975); Kestenberg-Amighi et al. (1999); Knoblauch (2000); La Barre (2001, 2005, 2008, 2009); Levine (1997); Lyons-Ruth (2000, 2003); Miller et al. (1989); Ogden, Minton, and Pain (2006); Perls (1993); Renik (1998); M. Rustin (1998, 2002); Smith (1985); Sossin and Birklein (2006); D. B. Stern (1997, 2010); D. N. Stern (1985); Tortora (2006); Totten (2003, 2005); van der Kolk, MacFarlane, and Weisaeth (1996).

baby's and parents' movements are continuously developing in their encounters. As their relationship develops and new movement capacities and verbalizing appear, the earlier interactive patterns do not vanish but remain components of each person's expressive repertoire. Similar movements are elaborated in changing situations and purposes, with varying results. The functional adaptations of movement patterns that emerge within the earliest relationships are thus basic to all relationships between adults, including, importantly, the psychotherapy relationship.

Our perspective is based on our years of experience working in several arenas: We work with parents and babies as well as with couples and individual adults, and we train psychotherapists, including both those who work primarily with babies and parents and those who work exclusively with adults. We and the therapists we work with consistently find that studying the life of babies and their parents as it is organized and expressed through movement sheds new light on many aspects of all relationships. Moreover, applying this same perspective to the psychotherapeutic relationship with adults augments understanding of several essential human imperatives that begin at birth and continue thereafter.

In the first year, a baby begins the search for safety, comfort, and pleasure—the quest to survive and thrive—that is elaborated throughout life. Verbal expression can often obscure but never escape the fundamental bodily basis for these action-guiding basic experiences that come to affect later relationships. Recognizing the way movement emerges and develops in the first year—how the baby moves in his or her parents' arms, and how the parents' arms adjust to the baby's movement—helps us better see movement interactions emerging within the adult psychotherapy dyad, those coconstructed moments that relate to the fundamental experience of physical and emotional security and their mental elaborations. Observing baby–parent interactions in the first year, psychotherapists can learn to see and feel the essential ways in which bodies relate to one another and the ongoing fundamental organizing actions of each individual's modes of operating within a session.

Both of us came to our understanding of the importance of the nonverbal in general, and of the preverbal first year in particular, through our individual study and application of a variety of movement theories within our separate adult psychotherapy practices (Frank, 2001; La Barre, 2001). Then, also independently, we found ourselves working with people who, during psychotherapy, reported having difficulties in the first weeks and months of parenting a baby.

We began working together in the fall of 2005. We conducted workshops to introduce parents to the movement theory that we found so useful in our individual practices. In the course of giving these workshops for parents, we confirmed that relational difficulties, which might be the basis for later, more entrenched problems, could be addressed early in the baby's life through the application of movement analysis. Over the course of these workshops, we found that many parents could easily make use of this way of seeing themselves and their baby and could make changes in their own and their baby's movement patterns that were immensely helpful in their developing relationships with their baby. They found, as an added benefit, that movement analysis also informed their relationships with others in their lives. A number of parents, however, could not make salutary use of movement information alone and needed the closer and more intensive focus of psychotherapeutic intervention that also incorporated movement analysis. Thus, there were parents who were already in individual treatment for their own difficulties who could make good use of direct information about their movement patterns as well as other parents who met us first in workshops and who sometimes discovered that they needed treatment to cope with more entrenched difficulties.

In focusing on the first year, we are clearly taking a developmental approach. We recognize that there are ongoing controversies about the usefulness of developmental theory in conceptualizing adult experience. There are also controversies regarding how infant experience should be interpreted or reconstructed (Green & Stern, 2001; Mitchell, 1993; D. B. Stern, 2010). Our view is that while we cannot "reconstruct" early experience from adult memory, action patterns that took shape beginning in the first year and have been refined and reshaped over a lifetime are still alive and active in the present moment and thereby play a significant role in organizing adult experience. In working with adults, we are interested in how their present experiences incorporate images and sensations from the past. Consider that simply asking people to imagine how they might have been held, carried, fed, picked up, and put down as babies—regardless of whether the images they create are accurate—often evokes immediate and profound physical and emotional responses that are certainly relevant to how these individuals connect with themselves and others now.

In the course of this book, we introduce *foundational movement analysis*, a conceptual framework that emphasizes a phenomenological approach to observing and understanding interactive movement patterns within psychotherapy. We stress that seeing the details of movement interaction is always enlightening, and often necessary, to grasp the essentials of relationships and thus promote helpful change. Through case reports, we show first how we use foundational movement analysis in working with parents to help them develop a heightened awareness of nonverbal behavior so that they can recognize the most salient and defining moments between themselves and their babies. Incorporating that awareness into our work with adults, we illustrate how we use this somatic and developmental frame of reference to see and identify similar defining moments in the kinetic patterns continuously emerging between ourselves and our patients.

In developing foundational movement analysis, we have gathered a set of movement identifiers and descriptors, derived from ideas honed in various movement theories and studies of nonverbal research that we regard as essential information for psychotherapists. Here, we intend to make the essentials of movement analysis accessible to clinicians without prior movement training, enhancing psychotherapists' perceptions and understandings of the somatic and kinetic experiences of babies and their parents and of themselves and the adults they treat.

Several different kinds of movement analysis exist, and they are used for different purposes, ranging from developmental neurological assessment all the way to choreographic notation for dancers. In creating our own approach, we have reviewed different systems of movement analysis and adapted elements from three of them: the Kestenberg Movement Profile (Kestenberg, 1975; Kestenberg-Amighi et al., 1999; Kestenberg & Sossin, 1979; Sossin, 1987); Warren Lamb's Action Profiling (Lamb, 1965; Lamb & Watson, 1979); and Bonnie Bainbridge-Cohen's (1993) Body-Mind Centering. We selected particular elements, what we refer to as *fundamental movements* and *movement inclinations*, from these systems because of their particular usefulness in understanding the nonverbal world of infancy and because they are involved in all later arising and more complex movements and actions and, in turn, influence cognitive, emotional, and psychological development.

Foundational movement analysis incorporates, then, two basic lenses for observing movement: fundamental movements[2] and movement inclinations. We summarize here the detailed descriptions that follow in Chapters 3 and 4. The fundamental movements are *yield, push, reach, grasp, pull,* and *release*. These basic movements emerge in the first year and integrate, one with another, in complex interactions with objects and people. These movements constitute interactive dynamics of engaging and are detailed and discussed in Chapter 3. *Movement inclinations* refer to the various ways that movements of any kind can be executed—that is, to their qualities— and to the dimensions of the body in which they take place. The movement qualities are differentiated by their high or low intensity, performed with even or fluctuating flow, and characterized by abrupt or gradual transitions between muscle tensions that are reducing or freeing and tensions that are increasing or binding. The spatial dimensions of the body in which movements are characteristically performed include *horizontal* (side to side), *vertical* (up and down), and *sagittal* (forward and backward). The specifics of movement inclinations, and why we think of them as "inclinations," are described in Chapter 4.

---

[2] "Fundamental movements" are to be distinguished from "Bartenieff Fundamentals" (Bartenieff & Lewis, 1980; Bartenieff & Davis, 1965), a series of exercises that activate and integrate the whole body.

In explicating our approach with parents and infants, and with adults, we draw on our previous work on the usefulness of movement theory in general in clinical practice (Frank, 2001, 2004, 2005, 2009a, 2009b; La Barre, 2001, 2005, 2008, 2009) and on the contributions of others from outside the world of movement theory whose theories and practices effectively converge with our own in recognizing the significance of nonverbal behavior in understanding parent–child and therapist–patient relationships. All of these figures recognize the significance of the body and action vis-à-vis the "mental" sphere in a way that supports our emphasis on movement and the benefits of its close observation. These include contributions by leading figures in infant research,[3] infant observation,[4] attachment theory,[5] trauma theory,[6] and neuroscience.[7] Because the theoretical frameworks of attachment theory, infant research, and trauma theory frequently make use of nonverbal behavior in deriving and explicating their findings, each has usefully drawn the attention of psychotherapists to the importance of nonverbal behavior in the development of overall mental functioning.

We believe our work significantly augments these theories as they pertain to clinical work in two respects. First, we emphasize that nonverbal processes are key to a general theory of communication and interaction and not just applicable in special instances of interaction. Second, we are concerned to show how nonverbal processes remain significant even when verbalization and reflection are already operative. We want here to strengthen the focus on the nonverbal and not move clinicians too quickly away from the specific details of movement and movement interaction. In presenting foundational movement analysis, we aim to augment contemporary theories by emphasizing and showing the importance of movement details in themselves. Here, we stress the utility of investigating how parents

---

[3] Contributions to infant research include those by Ainsfield (2005); Beebe and Lachmann (2002); Beebe et al. (1982); Beebe, Knoblauch, Rustin, and Sorter (2005); Boston Change Process Study Group (2002, 2005, 2007, 2008); Brazelton (1992); Brazelton and Cramer (1990); Buschell and Boudreau (1993); Condon (1982); Condon and Ogston (1971); Condon and Sander (1974); Corboz-Warnery, Fivaz-Depeursinge, Bettens, and Favez (1993); Fivaz-Depeursinge and Corboz-Warnery (1999); Fogel (1993, 2001); Gibson (1989); Lyons-Ruth (2000, 2003); Lyons-Ruth et al. (1998); Meltzoff and Moore (1977, 1995, 2000); D. N. Stern (1985, 1995); Thelen (1984, 1995); Thelen and Smith (1993); Trevarthen (1979, 2004); Tronick (1979, 1989, 2005, 2007).

[4] Contributions to infant observation include those by Bick (1964, 1968, 1986); Bloom (2006); Briggs (2002); Miller et al. (1989); Piontelli (1992); M. Rustin (1988, 1998, 2002); M. J. Rustin (2002); Sternberg (2005); Trevarthen (2004).

[5] A few of the many contributions to attachment theory include those by Ainsworth et al. (1978); Fonagy (2001, 2002); Goldberg, Muir, and Kerr (1995).

[6] Contributions to trauma theory include those by Anderson (2008); Bromberg (1998, 2006); Davies and Frawley (1991, 1994); Davoine and Gaudilière (2004); Goodwin and Atias (1999); Ogden et al. (2006); Sossin and Birklein (2006); van der Kolk et al. (1996).

[7] Contributions to neuroscience include those by Hurley and Chater (2005); Damasio (1990, 2003); Iacoboni (2008); Le Doux (1996); Libet (2004); Moskowitz, Monk, Kaye, and Ellman (1997); Rizzolati and Sinigaglia (2008); Schore (1994); Solms and Turnbull (2000).

and babies, couples, or psychotherapists and patients meet each other in movement within interactions that can either support the establishment of a secure relationship or interfere with it no matter how developed the participants' abilities to reflect.

Research into and theories about infants, for example, have been especially attentive to showing how mental processes arise from nonverbal interaction. Much of this research and theory has reached psychotherapists through the work of Daniel Stern (1977, 1982, 1985, 1995; Green & Stern, 2001). For example, Stern's (1985) pioneering concept of "vitality affects" illustrates that "many qualities of feeling that occur do not fit into our existing lexicon or taxonomy of affects. These elusive qualities are better captured by dynamic, kinetic terms, such as 'surging,' 'fading away,' 'fleeting,' 'explosive,' 'crescendo,' 'decrescendo,' 'bursting,' 'drawn out,' and so on" (p. 54). His work leads him to conclude that "different feelings of vitality can be expressed in a multitude of parental acts that do not qualify as 'regular' affective acts: how the mother picks up the baby, folds the diapers, grooms her hair or the baby's hair, reaches for the bottle, unbuttons her blouse" (p. 54). Further, he says that babies directly experience "sensations, perceptions, actions, cognitions, internal states of motivation, and states of consciousness ... in terms of *intensities, shapes, temporal patterns*, vitality affects, categorical affects, and hedonic tones" (p. 67, italics added).

Our work, using the finely discriminating lexicon we introduce in this book draws clinicians' attention to how we see "intensities, shapes, and temporal patterns" and adds detailed delineation and descriptive capacity to what Stern calls "vitality affects" and other concepts. With a second example, drawn from the infant research of Edward Tronick (1989, 2005, 2007; Tronick, Als, & Adamson, 1979; Gianino & Tronick, 1985), who has also greatly advanced the field's thinking, we further illustrate how foundational movement analysis adds to this perspective. Like other researchers of infancy, Tronick moves from the *physical* elements of dyadic regulation—synchronization, complexity of behavior, mismatching and repair—to the cognitive and emotional processes of meaning making. Thus, Tronick (2007) describes a mother who provides the infant with "regulatory support that permits the infant to achieve a more complex state of organization" (p. 290). Tronick emphasizes the changes that occur in the infant's state of consciousness, a mental state, as a result of the mother's recognition of what the infant needs to achieve and her ability to support the needed change. In our work, we stay with the physical interaction, whose significance is attested to by Tronick's description en route to his conclusion. He says that the mother gives her infant *"postural support* in response to the infant's frustration vocalizations ... [so that] the infant's state of consciousness gains coherence and complexity beyond the infant's endogenous capacities" (Tronick, 2007, p. 290, italics added). We add that parents and psychotherapists need to see the multiple ways and means of postural support because, as we show in our case studies, not just any postural support will do.

In addition, there is, to be sure, a great similarity between our approach and the technique of infant observation (Bloom, 2006; Briggs, 2002; Miller, Rustin, Rustin, & Shuttleworth, 1989; M. Rustin, 1988, 1998, 2002; M. J. Rustin, 2002). The similarity lies in the shared emphasis on the close and detailed observation of parents and infants over time with the aim of understanding the infants' and parents' experiences. Here, also, foundational movement analysis adds significantly to infant observation through its use of a finely tuned lexicon for describing movement that, simply put, helps the practitioner see more detail. As our case examples show, movement observation does not stop at emotion or fix on the search for intentions—it starts with and stays with what happens and how it happens. Interpretation is a separate step that follows at a distance from observation. The observer who is looking for intention or emotion may inadvertently limit what can be seen and heard and prematurely curtail further observation and reflection. In our work, we find that when we maintain our focus on movement, we are always surprised by the expansion of our understanding that occurs. In short, we find it consistently useful to go beyond the recognition of the nonverbal realm's importance as the route *to* so-called higher-order mental functioning alone and to recognize the extent of the significance of movement in itself as *primary, lived communication.*

We share this orientation with contemporary neuroscientists who also emphasize the idea that engagement in the world with flexible movement and action is important itself since movement and action are always a part of perceiving, feeling, thinking, and meaning making (Damasio, 1990, 2003; Iacoboni, 2008; Rizzolati & Sinigalia, 2008; Solms & Turnbull, 2000). These studies confirm that sensorimotor learning is not merely a stepping stone to higher orders of learning and thinking or verbalization. These abilities do emerge later out of action, but they do not then displace sensorimotor engagement or necessarily come to control it, as has been conventionally thought. In fact, on the contrary, we always think with our bodies; that is, with the practiced action repertoires that begin to develop in the first year and through which we perceive, understand, and interact with the world. Yet, this domain of being is hidden from our awareness by our routine ways of functioning and by the lack of concepts and a usable vocabulary that can help us see differently.

In Chapter 2, we continue this discussion by examining how the repertoire of movement identifiers and descriptors that we bring together in foundational movement analysis can usefully shift the psychotherapist's focus, enhancing perception of nonverbal communication by providing the concepts needed to differentiate what is available to see. Chapter 3 describes the movement fundamentals that every physically healthy baby develops and maintains as the basis for all other movements. These fundamental

movements are essentially an infant's first language, immediately embodying, directly communicating, and soon also signifying the baby's needs and
desires. The cases in Chapter 3 illustrate how movement fundamentals not
only become basic modes of moving and self-expression but also constitute
the pragmatic dynamics of engaging; they convey when and how parent
and baby communication goes well and when and how it is derailed. In
Chapter 4, we consider how all movements have an individual stamp manifested in the qualities of movement and in the number and coordination of
dimensions that each person uses. We show and explain these aspects of
movement so that they can be recognized in oneself and others. Further,
we present cases in which mismatches between parents and infants in their
respective movement inclinations threaten mutual understanding and trust
and then, when recognized and worked with, become the basis for growth.

Chapters 5, 6, and 7 focus primarily on adults and introduce the concept of embodied history or those routine movement patterns that evolve
and endure through time. In Chapter 5, our cases illustrate how parents'
inevitable use of their present movement repertoire in their interactions with
their infants can obstruct their capacities to respond as flexibly as necessary
for their children's well-being. We show how parents' misinterpretations of
their infant's actions derive from their own unexamined embodied histories.
Understanding embodied history through the analysis of movement again
fosters well-focused methods of therapeutic interaction. Chapter 6 deals
with cases in which basic movement differences between parents complicated by patterns of embodied history create problems that lead to polar-
izing their different points of view rather than parenting as partners. We
demonstrate how lack of cooperation and coordination between parents
is always embodied and acted and create baby–parent problems by com-
plicating and obstructing parents' movement interactions with their baby.
Understanding the couple's movement characteristics—their use of fundamental movements and their individual movement inclinations—enables
them to better understand and work with each other, form a more functional team, and work better with their baby. In Chapter 7, we illustrate
how we use the insights drawn from the nonverbal interactions of the first
year of life to see and work with the ongoing action that occurs in psychotherapy with adults. Here, we show the kinds of movement patterns that
emerge in treatment and how they reveal the adult's primary functioning
in relation to the effort to find and make safety, comfort, and pleasure in
relationship to others. In our Postscript, we return to the first year and offer
psychotherapists and parents a set of explorations in movement that are
based on the developmental progression of movement in the first year and
on the fundamental movements, inclinations, and dimensions that are with
us throughout life. These explorations give psychotherapists and parents a
better understanding of the life of infants and, from that point of view, their
own bodily experiences.

Chapter 2

Why Movement?

INTRODUCTION

Movement is singularly important as the exclusive language of the first year of life, and it remains central to communication throughout life. When this language is working well, whether between new parents and their baby or between two adults, signals are clearly sent, received, and understood, without any particular attention given to how this occurs. In these instances, the participants' movements communicate fluidly as part of the whole experience and need not be closely examined. But, when signals are routinely misunderstood, lost, or garbled, it is crucial to look at the elements of movement involved. Movement analysis then becomes a highly effective point of focus and intervention.

Parents diaper and feed, rock and jiggle, talk and sing, and make faces with their babies as they try to satisfy their needs. Their actions comprise sequences of movements that we can define precisely and observe in fine detail. With adults, too, precise movement delineation within the psychotherapy session expands the perception of both psychotherapist and patient. Seeing the actions and movements within psychotherapy alerts us to the unformulated and prereflective arena. It is here that we see "where the action is"—how each partner influences and organizes the emerging relationship through the ongoing language of movement. Examining the subtlety of these exchanges requires a conceptual framework and a vocabulary of accurate movement descriptors.

Consider how the details of movement augment our perception of the following interaction observed between a mother and her 6-month-old baby: Without recourse to the details of movement, we might describe this particular interaction with the following statement: "The mother took the spoon away from the baby, and he slumped and looked hopeless, as if he were about to cry." In fact, this is a statement of conclusions, not a full description of what took place. Psychotherapists and parents understandably often focus primarily on what *feeling* a baby is expressing—whether the baby is happy, sad, cranky/angry, and so on—because these feelings seem to be the most obvious indicators of how effectively parents are responding to their baby's biophysical and psychological states. But, in fact, feelings are a later-developing aspect of the experience of physical and kinetic elements of interaction (Damasio, 1990, 2003).

With a closer, more movement-oriented reading of this interaction, we might look at the same baby and parent in this way: The baby is sitting on his mother's left leg, facing a dining table. He moves with smooth, undulating tension changes most of the time. He frequently folds his torso to his left side, at which point his mother pulls him upright with her left arm and wraps him more tightly. The mother is speaking to her older daughter, who sits on her right side. The baby glances at a spoon on the table. His eyes widen, and he drools. His arms and legs, repeatedly and with increasing speed, reach forward and pull back. He suddenly tilts his whole body forward and pats the table with both hands. In spurts of reaching forward, he moves his hands toward the spoon, grasps it with his right hand, and pulls it toward his face and mouths it. The mother stops talking to the child at her right, turns her head quickly toward the baby, and with smooth, even movements, removes the spoon from the baby's mouth and hand and places it out of his reach. The baby briefly freezes, then gradually turns his face away from his mother and tilts it downward. At the same time, his muscle tension lowers, he pulls his chest backward, and his torso drops downward. He grasps and lightly pulls at his sweater with his hands. His eyes glance downward, while his gaze appears diffuse. His cheeks and mouth are slack and drooping. His mother turns away from him, rummaging for something in her bag and talking to her daughter at the same time.

Refining observation through a fine focus on movement in this way greatly enhances the parents' and the psychotherapist's domain of understanding and enlarges the freedom to alter the interaction. Close observation produces a new order of questions about what a baby or adult wants and how he or she wants to be handled or treated. In the case of the mother and baby just discussed, we might wonder about this baby's lack of protest, loss of muscle tone, shrinking down and pulling back. Another baby might cry, lengthen his spine, continue to reach for the spoon, and move with more intensity and a seemingly heightened sense of purpose and protest. We also consider whether this kind of interaction between mother and infant is typical of them or happens only when the mother is distracted. Over time, we note the frequency of mismatches; that is, those moments when aspects of the mother's movements are strikingly different from those of her baby. We also note their duration and the extent of their impact. If they have become established into a predictable routine, we want to think about how the pattern came to be, whether the mother sees it, and how she understands it. All along, we consider how to recognize and introduce movement elements in the session to promote better communication between mother and baby, which in turn leads to greater mutual comfort and satisfaction.

The kind of description we offer allows the mother to see more clearly what her baby is doing in relation to her. She is offered the opportunity to become fascinated with what is, rather than judging what should be. With the movement elements of mother and baby clearly revealed as coemergent, the treatment can become organized around both mother and baby and not inadvertently centered on "fixing" the mother or the baby. The mother can begin to reflect on and understand the baby's experience and to expand the possibility of choices and shifts in her movement behaviors. This in turn will promote a shift in the baby's pattern, which in a circular way will then influence the mother and so on. The shift in the movement dynamics at the heart of their engagement will facilitate the mother taking responsibility for her part in the dialogue without being overburdened by it.

We bring the same level of intensive observation to our work with couples and individual adults. This refined attention to the particulars of the movements involved in an interaction generates much valuable information that reveals how problems are embodied and enacted and what specific movement factors are involved.

There are several aspects to this process. First, we gather detailed specifics of individuals moving together. This process itself may have a number of steps because, as we showed in the case discussed, additional questions may arise as we attend to the details of movement. Second, during this period of movement observation, we actively work to suspend thinking in terms of psychological formulations of what we observe—that is, about intentions, fantasies, interactive attitudes, and such—so that we can uncover more information than we might were we to lead with psychological theories and concepts. While perhaps useful later in understanding what we have seen, these theories can crowd out perception of action and movement and thus limit the clarity of our observations if and when we lead with them. Third, we discover meanings *with* patients that spontaneously arise from the more elaborate picture we have drawn.

In all relationships, of course, what happens between people has deep roots in early associations with those who were most influential in the first years of life. Interactions take shape and become a crucial part of each individual, and they are not easily relinquished or edited. A parent's own early care may have been excellent but not broad enough in scope to encompass the challenges presented by a particular new baby. In that case, a mother, for example, may be able to resolve a parent–baby dilemma relatively easily by making use of suggested options in her movement vocabulary that we demonstrate and teach to help her reengage her child.

The lexicon we present—foundational movement analysis—allows for specific, early identification of those dilemmas that can be solved quickly with suggestions for movement adjustments and for longer-term psychotherapeutic inquiry. For example, with one mother, who complained that she had difficulty soothing her 3-month-old baby, we found that she needed to match the baby's excited and jumpy rhythm before she could employ the smoother, calmer rhythm she imagined would be soothing for her baby. That is, we taught her to meet and follow her baby's movement qualities rather than her idea of what she imagined to be soothing. This shift was easy for her to make once she understood the impact of matching her baby's movements before trying to shift her baby to a different rhythm. Between adults, also, the same kind of shift may be needed in the movements of one or both to effect and convey understanding. For example, imagine that one member of a couple needs to be joined in his lively expression of excitement to feel well met by the other. However, his partner, who has a different way of moving, is often uncomfortable with his enthusiastic displays. Rather than rising to his level of excitement, she remains in her own less-animated state, which dampens her partner's state in turn. Here, both partners need to appreciate their own and the other's different movement patterns and expressions. Then, they can understand their reactions to one another as well as explore possible changes in movement repertoire that would help them better adjust to and accommodate each other.

Relational glitches or miscommunications happen frequently in the course of bringing up a child and between people at all stages of life. Human development is often quite forgiving; there is room for struggle, and some kinds of struggle are necessary for growth. However, when parents cannot see or comprehend nonverbal cues or cannot adapt their actions to their children's needs or when stressful early relational mismatches continue over time with adult partners, there can be an accumulation of missteps: disjunctive patterns of behavior that become fixed, bringing continuing strain, deterioration of fluidity in contact, and escalating difficulties. Next is an extended example of a more entrenched problem that illustrates the mother's restricted movement options and introduces the application of our movement lexicon.

ROSALIE AND EMMY

Rosalie, a large, sturdy, athletic woman in her mid-30s, is seated cross-legged on the floor with her daughter, Emmy, on her lap. Rosalie's shoulders are broad and her back long. She periodically *reaches* upward with her head, *pulls* it slightly backward, and lengthens her spine, emphasizing her uprightness, her *verticality*. Her widespread eyes dart *abruptly* around the room from one object to the next.

Emmy, her 6-month-old daughter, quiet and alert, sits with her back curved, leaning against her mother's torso, facing outward. Her eyes glance softly in front of her, and she shifts her focus *gradually*—it seems to float from the flowers to the bookcase and then to the windows. Emmy's gaze wanders softly from object to object as she slowly turns her head from side to side *horizontally*.

First, we notice some particular differences between Rosalie and Emmy: Rosalie's eyes shift abruptly or dart, while her daughter's head and eyes gradually drift as they explore the room. Also, at least initially, Rosalie is primarily using up-and-down, vertical movement, and Emmy is primarily moving side to side, in horizontal.

Rosalie looks down toward Emmy, *abruptly* lifts her daughter, and changes her position so that she now faces sideways on Rosalie's lap. Emmy twists and *reaches* her head back around toward her original outward-facing orientation. But, Rosalie does not support this movement and presses her baby close to her chest, cupping her right hand around Emmy's head, while her left hand is around Emmy's right-side body. In response, Emmy squirms and turns her head and body back toward the front. Then, she *pushes* against Rosalie's chest with her left hand. Rosalie now *pulls* Emmy closer and makes a soft and sustained noise, "Shhhhhh!" At the same time, Rosalie energetically rocks herself and Emmy from side to side.

First, Emmy appears simply to want to resume her earlier position looking outward from her mother's lap. As Rosalie pulls her away from that position into one closer to her, Emmy objects and pushes away. At 6 months old, many babies want more space to feel comfortable looking around. But, Rosalie seems to have a different interpretation of her daughter's signals or wishes of her own that counter Emmy's.

Emmy vocalizes, "Ah, Ah, Ah!" and in the same rhythm she *abruptly* *pushes* the base of her pelvis down, elongating her spine (*vertically*), and twists and arches (*horizontally*), *reaching* her torso away from her mother. Emmy's *pushes* grow more energetic, and she uses both her arms and legs.

With lots of *high-intensity* energy but also a lilting, *tension-changing* rhythm and tone, Rosalie says, "What's the matter Emmy? Don't you want hugs? Mommy loves you!" as she *reaches* her face down and *pushes* it forward into Emmy's with playfully rough kisses for her. Emmy's now-frowning face is briefly visible before Rosalie *pulls* Emmy's head into her chest once again.

Suddenly crying furiously, Emmy's movements *abruptly* grow to *high intensity*, and this time, as she forcefully *pushes* her hands against her mother, she finds enough leverage to move her torso away from Rosalie. Rosalie's actions grow more *high intensity* in response: She *grasps* onto Emmy, lifts her to face over her shoulder, pats Emmy's back and makes intense hushing sounds and rapid bounces that are now less *gradual* and more sharp and *abrupt*.

Rosalie does not see or understand Emmy's movement signals and the reason for her protest. We imagine that Rosalie believes she is trying to comfort her daughter, but she appears to be doing the very things that Emmy is trying to avoid. At this point, there is a rapidly escalating battle that creates discomfort, upset, and confusion for both Rosalie and Emmy.

When asked what made her shift Emmy's position from her earlier outward-facing position, Rosalie says that she wants her daughter to feel "well attached" to her. She says that she felt disconnected from Emmy and just wanted to cuddle.

Now, the meaning of Rosalie's grasping onto Emmy becomes a little clearer. Being well attached is, of course, a good idea, but Rosalie's conception seems to allow for only a limited understanding of what is involved. In this instance, Rosalie is overriding Emmy's spontaneous impulse to adjust herself in relation to her mother with pushing movements—as crucial a part of the attachment process as is coming together in yielding or flowing with another, which seem to be what the mother is aiming at achieving here. At first, Emmy's push indicated her need for physical space to continue looking around. But subsequently, her pushing took on another dimension—she appeared angry that her mother was not permitting this adjustment between them.

Emmy suddenly stops *pushing* and *pulls* her arms, legs, and head into her body. Her spine shortens (*descending vertically*), her chest narrows and hollows (retracting *sagittally*), and she sucks her hand.

Emmy has adjusted to the struggle with her mother by lowering the level of her intensity, losing the underlying push of her pelvis that would sustain her upright position and the expressive pushing signals of her arms and legs. In effect, she has just accommodated to her mother's implicit demands. This may be a useful and creative choice for the moment as it may end a frustration that is too much for Emmy to bear. If this is a momentary miscommunication and not a chronic one, there will be opportunities to work out more satisfying arrangements for Emmy. If this is chronic, however, as time goes on, the development of Emmy's overall movements and interactive patterns could very well become restricted by these repetitive experiences with the consequence of a decreasing use of push and a growing feeling of helplessness or apathy and powerlessness, at least in relationship to her mother, but also quite easily in relation to other arenas of physical, cognitive, emotional functioning, and interpersonal interaction.

In that case, her gestures, rather than being direct, strong, and determined, would lose clear purpose, energy, and vitality. Conversely, rather than becoming less energetic, Emmy might begin to feel she needs to exaggerate her "pushing" protests to get what she needs. That is, Emmy may behave with heightened demands in an attempt to be heard even when it is not necessary with other people. Her patterns of protestation may not feel enlivening to her at all but may be infused with a constant feeling of frustration and anger that she is not understood. In a more optimal direction, Emmy might eventually learn to be very assertive with her mother. In this situation, Rosalie, after some struggle, might finally understand what Emmy is after and with some instruction be able to follow her desired movements.

   With this focus, the specific aspects that are creating the dilemma move directly to the forefront, and we can thus more easily discover the meaning of the movement from the parents' *and* baby's points of view. Without closely detailed movement observation, those who meet Rosalie might capture something about her by describing her as either "a powerhouse" or as "overpowering." Close attention to movement detail reveals how she creates that impression: We note her *abruptness* and her *high intensity* when she continuously *reaches* forward to *pull* Emmy into a tight hug, as well as her proceeding without regard for Emmy's reactions. Different people might evaluate her as "unpleasantly overwhelming" or "refreshingly exuberant." These differing evaluations of Rosalie stem from sensations that emerge in interacting with her. Reflecting on our close observation of her actions with Emmy allows us to help her see herself in that context and replace general evaluations with specific observations about what she does with Emmy and what other actions might be possible. Psychotherapists might venture interpretive thoughts related to her anxiety about separateness or her need for control of the contact and discover additional possible reasons for misunderstanding or ignoring her daughter's signals. These might be useful thoughts that could facilitate dialogue, it is hoped, with the outcome that Rosalie would develop more flexible responses to her daughter. However, we find that it is always important, and sometimes even necessary, to work directly with the separate components of parents' and babies' movements. Thus, we help psychotherapists and parents to see and sense the movement roots of their own and others' reported experiences. When movement interactions do not well support the ease of communication, it is always helpful and frequently necessary to work with the separate elements of movement to discover how the emerging dissonance is created. Whether working with a parent and an infant, adult members of a couple, or a psychotherapy dyad, the same movement factors may operate with similar effects.

   When parents and psychotherapists learn to observe, identify, and "try on" their baby's or adult patient or client's movements, they learn how their emotional resonance and understanding actually arise out of their participation in specific movements and movement qualities. In parenting, these movements and their qualities can tell the parents *what movement, with what qualities,* and *in what dimensions* is needed in response. The fact is that often a parent may easily be able to decode and understand the baby's emotional expression and be willing to help but not know how to respond physically. For the psychotherapist working with an adult, kinetic resonance brings a broad range of information that can be used in a variety of ways to expand the ongoing dynamics within the therapy relationship. For example, the psychotherapist finds herself suddenly dropping her chest and notices that the patient is sitting in a similar posture. Now mirroring the patient, the psychotherapist can be more sensitive to what the patient is feeling. Further, in watching how their postures change together and separately, the psychotherapist can gain more information about the meaning of what happens between them.

NEUROSCIENTIFIC SUPPORT

Neuroscientists believe at present that the ability to understand others rests on the ability to coordinate visual information with implicit motor knowledge (Rizzolati & Sinigaglia, 2008), and that *"motor knowledge of our own acts* is a necessary and sufficient condition for an immediate understanding of the acts of others" (p. 106, italics added). That is, we use the same information to understand our own actions that we use to understand the actions of others because a cross section of the same neurons operates in doing and in seeing others doing. This immediate motor-based "empathy" with the acts of the other is a neurological given. As neuroscientists conceive it, psychotherapists come to know those they work with, and parents come to know their babies to the extent that they can draw on this "internal motor representation of what is seen" (Rizzolati & Sinigaglia, p. 97) in formulating and reflecting on their understanding.

Thus, we find in contemporary neuroscience strong support for the argument we are making for this careful and close attention to the movement details of a field of action. Reports from this area of inquiry concur that

> our mental processes are shaped by our bodies and by the types of perceptual and motor experiences that are the product of their movement through and interaction with the surrounding world. This view is generally called embodied cognition, and the version of this theory especially dedicated to language is known as embodied semantics. (Iacoboni, 2008, p. 92)

Specialized motor neurons contribute to comprehension and thought by simultaneously activating the neural infrastructure of movement even when we are seeing, hearing, or reading about action, not only when we take action (Iacoboni, p. 94).

Specifically, contemporary neuroscience demonstrates that innate and learned sequences of movement (such as reaching, grasping, pulling, etc.) become activated in situations that hold the prospect of involving them. These specific, embodied, but unformulated possibilities for action— action potentials—in themselves participate in forming perceptions and thoughts throughout life (Hurley & Chater, 2005; Iacoboni, 2008; Libet, 2004; Rizzolati & Sinigaglia, 2008; Solms & Turnbull, 2000). These action potentials allow sensory information to be discriminated according to "action affordances," that is, according to what one can do with what is seen (Rizzolati & Sinigaglia, p. 79). These neurons, known as *canonical neurons*, fire when a person grasps and holds or manipulates an object, such as a cup, and they also fire when objects are merely sighted that *can* be grasped, held, and manipulated.

Canonical motor neurons associated with reaching and grasping, for example, fire as a baby reaches for the breast or a cup; they also fire when the baby simply sees the breast or cup (Iacoboni, 2008; Rizzolati & Sinigaglia, 2008). The neural registration of the possible actions that can take place in connection with that object already participate in the baby's (or adult's) perception of it and in primary, prereflective action-based definitions such as "a breast *is* the sort of thing that it is good to grasp and suck with the mouth," "a cup *is* the sort of thing that is good to hold in the hand and mouth." These are preconceptual and prelinguistic forms of understanding that continue to be at the base of all later, so-called higher-order cognitive abilities. Sensorimotor experience with objects, gained through doing and through learning about usage via imitation (observing and repeating others' actions), extends the action programs a child and adult have available for perceiving and thinking. Put another way, movement is not only where the action is but also where the objects of the baby's world are coming into being along with the baby's interactions. This includes those special self-animated objects—people.

Thus, in focusing on the movement dimension of the earliest relationships, we are focusing on movement interactions that can foster the increasingly complex actions needed for thought or that can foreclose and cut off such development. For example, a baby needs to be able to control the focus of his eyes and then later control his eye–hand coordination to reach, grasp, and pull an object into his mouth.

As a baby handles an object in increasingly complex ways, he further explores the possibilities for its use. With every exploration, the baby's dexterity increases, as does his understanding of the object and his actions. All the while, the parent's necessary involvement with the baby can either support or sometimes interfere with the baby's explorations. This is in part because other action-involved neurons, *mirror neurons*, are involved in the recognition and understanding of the action of others, including their intentions. [The importance of mutual nonverbal mirroring—that is, imitating each other's movements—has been an area of neuroscientific study since the 1970s (Meltzoff & Moore, 1977, 1995, 2005).] Mirror neurons become active both when an individual performs an action and when that individual observes another person performing the same action (Rizzolati & Sinigaglia, 2008, p. 79). Thus, they fire as a baby witnesses another's action, and that firing simultaneously inscribes the action in the baby's internal motor system as if she performed the action herself (Iacoboni, 2008). Parents' actions *do* speak louder than words, as from the start baby and parents are interacting through mutual mirroring and internalizing each other's movements.

In the course of acting with objects, including acting with other people, a baby establishes emotion-infused sensorimotor records of how the actions and interactions take place, and these records also accompany and influence patterns that emerge later in development. Sensorimotor records and procedural memory allow a baby to repeat ways of being and acting with another. In this repetition, the baby anticipates what has been a regular occurrence (Solms & Turnbull, 2000); procedural memory is constituted in action itself and is "resistant to decay with time" (p. 157). In present situations, procedural memory is integral to the process of organizing movements, sensations, and affects. This organizing process draws on previously constructed action patterns that are constituted by the flow, shape, and effort involved in every interaction. For example, these processes are involved as babies (and adults) take actions ranging from taking baths, eating, and playing with a ball to holding a parent's hand. Just as cups are defined by what we can do with them, "mom" and "dad" are initially defined by the actions we engage in with them. The feelings that accompany those actions become part of that definition, as do anticipations regarding what will happen in the interaction.

Through practice and elaboration in many contexts, action sequences can become the basis for a sense of differentiation and autonomy. Alternatively, they can become the basis for ongoing confusion between one person and another. For example, if Rosalie begins to change her behavior and responds to Emmy's pushing initiatives with support for Emmy's aims, Emmy will be better able to develop actions that reflect her own desires. If, however, Rosalie persistently ignores Emmy's pushing protests, Emmy's reactions could become entrenched in action patterns of "giving up" or "giving in" to another's stronger pulls or pushes. We do not imagine that Emmy can think in terms like, "When I protest, I expect you to overpower me." But, we can infer her expectation by looking at the routine interactions of mother and baby. Rosalie's routinely unresponsive actions could interfere with Emmy's ability to retain and develop her own aims as well as affect her developing cognitive and emotional experience. This kind of problem remains and shapes adult behavior when, for example, action patterns are inhibiting.

Babies' procedural memory processes reflect how people in their lives have received their actions and how the babies, in turn, have responded to them. When interactions have gone well and have facilitated the baby's development, procedural remembering operates to keep adaptive capacities expanding over the life span. But, if interactions have been fraught with difficulties and misunderstandings, procedural remembering tends to foreclose exploration and development by narrowing movement options. Thus, parents' movements have an extremely important role to play in either enhancing or inhibiting their baby's movement range, impulses, and early sensorimotor skills.

In the next two chapters, we see these processes at work with babies and their parents through case studies that also demonstrate our application of this understanding to clinical work with the same population. In further chapters, we elaborate the application of an understanding of movement in work with adults in individual treatment as we examine how meanings are generated by movement interaction and how these meanings may be recognized and integrated into the treatment.

Chapter 3

Six Fundamental Movements

INTRODUCTION

Using a sequence of yielding, pushing, reaching, grasping, pulling, and releasing movements, a baby communicates what he wants and needs from his parents and expresses how he reacts to what his parents want and need from him. Through these macro- and micromovement fundamentals, baby and parents coconstruct and convey desires, feelings, and intentions. From the first adjustments of a baby yielding and pushing while on his belly in the first weeks of life to aid his digestion to the greater complexity of the older infant walking toward a parent to receive comfort, these movements become part of the baby's efforts to self-regulate and regulate interpersonal relationships. They are essential to character development in that they become the preferred and routine ways we dynamically adjust, making them simultaneously psychological and physical by nature.

Imagine, for example, a 4-month-old baby yielding in the arms of her father and ready to nurse from a bottle. Inadvertently, her father does not curl his baby inward enough so that she stays close to his chest, nor does he hold her firmly enough so that the baby senses the stability necessary for fluid yielding to emerge. To find and make stability for herself, the baby must tighten the muscles of her neck, abdomen, and buttocks, creating a "false floor" as her gripped muscles attempt to do the work of securing her. With such tension, the yielding experience is so compromised that the pushing of buttock bones against the father's arms does not have sufficient leverage to emerge clearly. Without the background clarity of pushing, the reaching, grasping, and pulling of the mouth toward and onto the nipple now find less support, making it difficult for the action sequence to complete itself. The coordination of fluid sucking actions and the affective connection between parent and baby, part and parcel of the emerging movement, is affected. How does the baby now gaze up at the parent, reaching and grasping onto him with her eyes and hands, when she is struggling to make herself comfortable?

In this chapter, we describe the sequence of basic movements that emerge in the first year and are essential in all human interactions throughout life. Further, we demonstrate how our understanding of their ongoing role in forming relationships can be used to recognize and treat interactive difficulties that arise in infancy. The fundamental movements—*yielding, pushing, reaching, grasping, pulling,* and *releasing*—are integral aspects of experience.[1] That is, they enable and support the varied ways in which we connect with ourselves and within our world. Although fundamental movements are explicated here in a linear fashion for the sake of clarity, in experience one category of movement does not occur in isolation from the others. Rather, the movements are interdependent, one interpenetrating or participating with others, and together provide the basics necessary for action.

Fundamental movements always arise in relation to the surrounding environment and, particularly in the first year, in relation to the parents. In other words, when a fundamental movement pattern emerges, it is a function of relationship and cannot be separated out as if the movement were *of* the baby or *of* the environment. That is, fundamental movements are a dynamic part of the whole of relationship. Interactive by nature, these movements develop as the baby regularly adjusts to the parents and the parents adjust to the baby. When certain movement patterns are no longer useful in the changing relational field, others take their place. Sucking is no longer the dominant mode of eating when teeth are there to present another alternative. And, when it becomes possible for the baby to stand and walk toward another, crawling becomes less preferable.

But as development progresses, the earlier movement patterns do not disappear. Instead, they become part of increasingly complex patterns as babies, children, adolescents, and adults continually organize and reorganize their actions and reactions within the changing environment (Frank, 2001, 2004, 2005). That is, every fundamental movement pattern contains both the roots of the prior movement experience and the seeds for the next to develop. For example, the basic coordination of lips, tongue, and jaw that enable reaching toward the nipple with the mouth will be present and develop further in the actions of forming words as well as in more complex speech patterns. All the earlier fundamental movements employed for the baby to sit on his own, hands free to manipulate a toy or play with a parent, will form the underlying coordination necessary for crawling to emerge, which then underlies and supports standing, toddling, and walking. Later in development, these movements are essential for mastering

---

[1] These movement categories are explained in detail in this chapter. Two movement sequences—yield/push, reach/pull—were recognized and placed within the larger developmental motor system delineated by Bonnie Bainbridge-Cohen (1993). Ruella Frank added grasp and release to this system and augmented these "basic neurological patterns" to include their psychological attributes and to show how they participate in the infant's developing system of gestures (Frank, 2001, 2004, 2005).

the more complex actions of jumping, running, playing sports, and so on. It is through these evolving movements that babies learn about themselves and their world. All other learning emerges as an outgrowth or elaboration of these early organizing experiences.

Further complexity arises because the fundamental movements are also a crucial part of the infant's first nonverbal language. Although a baby has a number of cries and various sounds to tell his parents what he needs, the baby also uses yielding, pushing, reaching, grasping, pulling, and releasing movements to define and communicate needs, interests, and spatial boundaries and to express curiosity, relate to objects (human and otherwise), move about independently, and give voice to feelings. These basic movements are expressed and experienced on both physical and vocal levels as it is movement that produces and supports the emergence of sound. For example, the 6-month-old girl signals her desire to be picked up as she reaches out with her eyes, mouth, and arms to her father while "pushing against" him with her voice, saying "Ah-Ah-Ah." In response, the father looks toward her and says, "Ohhhh-kaaay," with a vocal quality that yields to his daughter's request as he reaches down, pulls his baby onto his lap, grasps and holds her close, and coos lovingly. In this case, physical and vocal signals are clearly sent and well received.

Every healthy baby develops and uses these basic movements, but babies do not execute them in the same way or at the same developmental moment. In fact, there are as many different variations of fundamental movements as there are diverse relational fields. Within each distinct relational field, every baby organizes a personal movement vocabulary—individual variations of the fundamental movements—that includes movements of all parts of the body: head and tailbone, arms and hands, legs and feet. With this personal movement vocabulary, the baby expresses himself and negotiates others' responses to that expression.

Parents' actions become entwined with their baby's actions such that babies and parents conduct their continual nonverbal dialogue—a language of bodies—as each one influences and is influenced by the other. That is, as the movement of one person modulates those of the other, movement patterns emerge within the relationship that are mutual, reciprocal, and cocreated. The process of this coregulation of movement in the crucial first year means that *how* movement emerges and is engaged has far-reaching consequences for every aspect of life. The optimal development of these fundamental movements in relationship with parents is key to fostering the full range of movements that support the baby's flexibility and creativity in all realms of development. This is expressed not only in expanding physical exploration but also in increasingly complex communication and sensorimotor thinking.

Parents express their own intentions, attitudes, perceptions, and feelings through their own movements, and all of these dimensions of experience are directly relayed to their baby through this moving dialogue. This means that the way parents respond to and shape their baby's efforts at movement not only influences the development of each fundamental pattern but also affects the emotional and cognitive dimensions of experience. For example, parents' physical support for a baby's motor development, along with their gentle encouragement, has an impact on a baby's walking as a motor activity. But in addition, the parents' physical and emotional support also have an immediate and long-term impact on other dimensions that are part of the experience of walking and that we often capture in metaphors such as "standing on my own two feet," "putting my foot down," "standing tall," and so on. While most parents want to believe that they support their babies in both dimensions, they are not necessarily able to see how their own emotional and physical expressivity become intricately entwined with their baby's and, in practice, how various elements of their actions sometimes can get in the way of just what they wish to support. For example, a 9-month-old baby boy pulls himself to standing and is delighted with his newly accomplished mastery over gravity. His parents, believing that early standing signifies an important and "special" achievement, begin encouraging him to walk before he has mastered standing. Here, the problem is that the parents have taken over the baby's initiative and are now pushing their own agenda in their eagerness to be supportive.

Identifying how fundamental movements are emerging allows psychotherapists and parents to see the complexity and intricacy of movement transactions that both support and interfere with a baby's needs. When psychotherapists observe how parents relate to the baby's uses of their fundamental movements, they see essentials of the family's psychological world, including when and how particular interactive patterns serve the ongoing dialogue to enrich the parent-and-baby relationship and expand exploration and when and how patterns develop that stifle communication and growth. Because this dialogue is based on movements that contribute to a sequence of actions at the same time a baby is developing and using these fundamentals as the basis for sensorimotor learning, she is also forming the basic processes and transactions of interactivity—what we call the *dynamics of engaging*. These are the motoric expressions that shape our interactions, when a "push comes to shove," that is, when the baby is not only pushing against the parent to make more space for herself but also is expressing annoyance at the same time. In "hugging," for example, we can see that on one level it is an action involving the smaller movements of reaching for, grasping onto, and pulling another close. On another level, hugging involves emotion and conveys a range of nuanced meanings that includes both parents' and babies' abilities and readiness to embrace or withhold. In the hugging example, the meaning of the movement is cocreated through a coordination of fundamental movements organized in relation to another—and it is this vocabulary that grows with amazing rapidity accompanied by a syntax that is ever more complicated.

Although the fundamental movements themselves appear basic and straightforward, it can be difficult for parents to observe and understand the complexity in how an infant uses them. As our case studies at the chapter's end illustrate in detail, if parents do not understand the complex role these movements play in their baby's self-expression, relational difficulties can ensue.

SIX FUNDAMENTAL MOVEMENTS AND THEIR ROLE IN DEVELOPING EXPERIENCE

Yield

Gravity draws the baby's body toward the surface of the earth. When the newborn lies belly down, he *yields to* the earth as the weight of his body is released to gravity. The baby lies on various surfaces: a mattress, the floor, and of course, the parent's body. Each surface meets and differently resists the weight of the baby's body in opposition to the downward force of gravity. The baby experiences a heightened pressure on those parts of the body that are in touch with a surface, so the muscles of each dimension of the body (front, back, and sides) are stimulated when the baby rests that part against a supporting surface. This slight increase in pressure leads to a slight countervailing muscular tone that gives the baby a *sensation of weight*, which flows from center (the spine) to periphery (head, tailbone, arms, and legs). Experiencing weight allows the baby to orient in space.

In addition, moving from one position to another allows the baby to differentiate the front of his body from the back and from each side. Yielding in each position not only brings with it a different postural organization with its varied sensations but also generates a *sense of volume*, or fullness of being, for the baby. With each postural shift, a different perception of, and therefore relationship to, the environment emerges. Yielding forms the ground on which the baby rests and organizes *how* the baby rests. For yielding to emerge fluidly, the parent–child relationship must be secure enough that the baby can sense the parent's underlying support, which allows him to yield his weight *to* that support. Yielding provides the stable background from which all other movements up and away from the earth emerge.

Acts of yielding are the basis for experiences of receptivity at every level of functioning for both the baby and the adult. In a yielding moment, we are giving ourselves over to the other (person or object) and simultaneously receiving support and stability and a basic sense of orientation. The experience of yielding is not simple passivity (or the state of "no resistance"); rather, the degree and way of yielding are dependent on that to which we adjust. To sit in an easy chair is one thing, to lie on a floor is quite another.

To yield with someone receptive and inclusive is different from yielding with someone who is not. Thus, we learn something important about ourselves and ourselves in relation to others through our continual process of adjusting. The stability that the baby experiences, in the absence of neurological impairment, then forms the platform on and from which the baby can discover and make support in a variety of relationships throughout his life.

Push

Each time a 2-week-old baby squirms to adjust to internal or external tensions, there is a subtle and ongoing process of *pushing against*. In yielding, the environment provides stability; in pushing, the environment provides leverage, including the leverage needed to further investigate the environment, thus enhancing perception. For example, one part of the baby's body pushes against a surface to stabilize, enabling another part to be free to mobilize. This is most obvious when a 3- to 4-month-old pushes his hands downward to lift his head and upper torso up and away from the underlying support.

As the baby pushes, the experience of weight condenses at the origin of the push, whether at head or tailbone, arms and hands, or legs and feet, as the act of pushing compresses tissues of the body. Mass gathers at these places and forms an *experience of density*, which then flows in particular channels through the body. For example, pushing against the floor with forearms and hands creates condensation of mass and energetic flow that moves from the hands and arms, through to the body's center (spinal column), then outward through the legs and feet. Sensing one's mass, or experiencing density and energetic flow, brings about an experience of *cohesion* and *integration* as the body's periphery is experienced in relation to its center. The repeated experience of cohesion and integration in turn fosters movements that are clear and well coordinated. When the baby cannot easily push, movements appear as clumsy and ungrounded. The experiences of pushing, then, have consequences for a baby's mobility. By 3 to 4 months old, pushing his hands downward moves the baby out of a prone, horizontal position to one in which the upper body is more upright and vertical. This is a developmental step to a new perspective. Later in development, pushing against while in a prone position enables the baby to shift his weight from one side of the body to another, which becomes an important aspect of locomotion.

The earliest development of pushing and its vicissitudes not only are important to all later movement but also are crucial to the baby's developing interpersonal relationships. Babies are always moving in relation to whatever stimulates them. A baby pushes against a surface to get a better look at something or someone or to hear where an interesting sound is coming from, or even to follow an interesting odor. For instance, the baby can set a body boundary as he or she pushes hands against a parent to gain greater distance, or the baby can say "no" by pushing away a spoonful of applesauce. We cannot push without something to push against. As a baby pushes against, she is simultaneously able to experience *separating from while including the other*. In essence, pushing is a primary way of gaining information about the contours of the world of objects and people and the boundaries of the baby's body: "Here you are, and here am I." As the baby is adjusting to the surface tensions of that which she pushes against, in some fashion, the surface also adjusts to the baby and is sensed as "pushing back." There is adjustment on both sides of the boundary since even a wood floor has a certain amount of bounce to it. And accordingly, the way the baby adjusts to the "other" varies considerably—a wood floor is altogether less flexible than the body of either parent.

Since the baby is continuously establishing procedural memories of whole interactions, *how* she pushes herself upward will anticipate the parent's usual body tone and emotional tone through generalized memory processes of how they have already moved together. The anticipation of parental response often suffuses the baby's routine movement repertoire in other situations or with other people besides her parents so that her actions show a generalized anticipation of, for example, cheerful enlivening or saddened dampening. In this process, what is being perceived comes to affect the movement itself as particular emotional colorations develop with the whole experience. For example, the movements of a baby who pushes herself up to meet the eyes of a smiling receptive parent will appear quite different from those of a baby who pushes up to meet a depressed and unresponsive parent. In the first experience, the parent has provided a solid enough response against which the baby can push—"I am here *with* you." On the other hand, the depressed, unresponsive parent fails to give the baby the sense of pushing back, so the baby does not appear as sure and energetic as she might be meeting a parent eager to greet her.

Whereas how one *yields with* allows one to join another, how one *pushes against* allows one to differentiate from another. Experienced as an almost simultaneous shuttling back and forth between one and another, yield/push and push/yield are essential to and necessary for interpersonal meeting throughout the life span.

Reach

The earliest reaches of the baby involve the face and are seen as the baby searches actively with his nose and mouth for the breast or bottle. This first reaching with nose and mouth is rapidly followed by a baby reaching with her eyes and hands toward faces of her parents and toward a variety of objects that are to be mouthed and chewed. A similar reaching movement can often be observed as the baby's fingers subtly open and begin a reach, as if to accompany the movement of his reaching mouth. Carving a pathway through space, reaching with his mouth toward the nipple, is the baby's contribution to the accomplishment of a basic and necessary task: In the reaching lies the baby's search for pleasure, comfort, and nourishment. This movement is the live embodiment of wanting, needing, desiring, and longing.

Thus, how parents meet a baby's reach is clearly important in the growth of the baby's emotional and physical well-being. Both baby and adult reach in the hope of finding, touching, meeting, and discovering. When the dyad is functioning optimally, the baby's reaching gestures—"I want this" or "I want you"—and the parents' intercessions and responses organize the elaboration of a personal movement vocabulary and syntax of desire in action. A parent who consistently holds his baby in a way that facilitates easy reaching for the bottle or a parent whose holding action requires the baby to strain are only two of many possible variations with far-reaching consequences.

We call the reach space around the body, and the imaginary boundary of it, the *kinesphere* (Bartenieff & Lewis, 1980). The body has three dimensions, which are experienced by extending the limbs to the farthest reaches of its length, width, and depth of the body while in an upright position. Exploring her reach space or kinesphere through reaching enhances the baby's sense of the three-dimensional space of and surrounding her body. With every reach of the eyes, nose, mouth, and limbs, a baby expands through space and takes herself away from center, at a risk to equilibrium. Moving farther into the environment, the baby is able to explore her world and grasp hold of it.

In the earliest weeks and months, the responsive parent offsets the risk of reaching beyond center by adjusting her body to the baby's shifts until, with experience and growing strength, the baby is able to adjust his body to recover balance. The baby's reaching movements are shaped in relation to an object, very often the parent, that can offer assistance. In other words, that which is reached for (the stimulus) shapes the reach (the response). For reaching to emerge with fluidity and grace, the longed-for object, in the end, must be available. Here again, what is real for the baby is also true for the adult.

Grasp

Just as the first reaching is with the mouth toward the nipple, the first grasping occurs at birth as the baby reaches out and takes firm hold of the nipple with her mouth. The baby's earliest grasping movements of the mouth also are echoed in subtle grasping-like movements of fingers and toes. Only slightly later can the baby more fully reach and grasp with her hands.[2] Grasping movements, like others, grow more complex with development and come to include grasping onto a loved one with both arms. Again, parents play a part in the baby's movement repertoire, either facilitating or discouraging the baby's grasp with their responses.

While grasping onto and holding an object (person or thing) with their mouths and hands, babies develop an understanding of the three dimensions of these objects and their weight and textures and learn the possibilities for action that each object offers. When a baby does grasp an object, what was only seen now can be explored through many senses and becomes more precisely known. This exploration is true for the eyes as well as they reach out and "touch" objects. In other words, a baby's explorations with mouth, hands, and eyes are mutually reinforcing and integrative.

Grasping emerges from and coordinates with reaching. Whereas reaching brings with it the risk of moving to the edge of and beyond one's kinesphere, extending into what is not yet known, grasping can reestablish stability by creating balance through holding onto what is grasped. Parental support begins with firmly *being there*, which reestablishes the baby's stability and comes to include an understanding of the greater meaning that underlies the baby's reach and grasp.

What was called out for in the expression of reaching—the wanting—is satisfied in the action of grasping. Simply said, in grasping, we sense in a more immediate way what we have reached for. This relationship is expressed in metaphors about grasping a situation or grasping a difficult idea. Further, the adult's metaphor holds a background of prior experiences of grasping and the assistance or interference he has routinely encountered. In such cases, we can see in his present movement patterns the results of early interactive patterns that fostered or interfered with the security of his present capacity to grasp. These patterns could be summarized by the phrase "getting a grip." Clearly, what is metaphor for the adult in some situations is immediate and concrete for the baby in all situations.

Pull

Pulling movements are also available from birth in nursing actions. Having reached for and grasped onto the nipple, the baby uses the suction of her mouth to pull the nipple into her mouth. In the process, the baby's body reorganizes and lengthens in support. The nipple provides enough resistance that the baby can feel her own body, primarily her mouth, as well as the nipple and the milk that flows from it and into her. Thus, this first

---

[2] Due to the Palmer reaction, an action pattern that organizes in the womb, the baby is ready at birth to grasp his hands around an offered finger, but this is distinct from a reach and grasp with the hands that is far more deliberate.

experience of pulling entails an act of drawing what is other toward the baby and incorporating it.

In further elaboration, the 3-month-old baby uses his hands to grasp and pull objects into his mouth with great enthusiasm. In these pulling experiences, the baby draws something toward himself, discovering what the object (person or thing) has to offer him. Through this process, the baby can differentiate qualities of attraction, resistance, and degree of flexibility in response to his actions.

As the baby pulls the nipple into his mouth, he simultaneously pulls the mother into his gaze. Later in development, he pulls on the mother's hands for support as he pushes his feet down to stand up. The coaction that organizes here, the distinctness of one and another sensed through pulling, contributes to the growing clarity of experiencing "me with you." This is crucial to the ongoing development of self because, just as with all the other fundamental movements, these kinds of interactions serve as the basis for healthy autonomy: the capacity to differentiate from another as well as the capacity to relinquish separateness and merge. In adult life, we frequently say, "I feel myself pulled toward you," or "It's hard for me to pull away from you." These expressions are not just metaphors—they express the measure to which we draw on one another. In reaching, grasping, and pulling, both babies and adults are involved in a complex experience of "me" and "you" and in discovering the degree to which me and you can become "we."

Release

Pulling movements begin another action, and when it is complete, release can follow. In the neonate's behavioral repertoire, the action of releasing an object can be accomplished only passively. For example, releasing the nipple after nursing is a consequence of the baby's entire body yielding in relaxation. In other words, it is only when the baby yields with another (object or person) that the object held—in this case the nipple—can be given up.

During this early period in development, the baby will similarly keep a steady gaze on whatever becomes most fascinating, whether a dark ceiling fan that moves against a white background or a bright ray of sunshine on a gray wall. The baby's attention often appears "captured" in this action. The release of an evenly held gaze, necessary for allowing another object to come into view, occurs only when the baby is ready to fall asleep, when the baby squirms in rising discomfort to adjust position, or because the parent shifts the baby. In just a few weeks, however, the baby can release his gaze more deliberately and thus easily shift his eyes to move around the room.

By about the fifth month, the baby is able to grasp, pull, and actively release the grasp of her hands on an object. Babies become quite delighted by releasing objects, flinging and dropping them, all in celebration of their

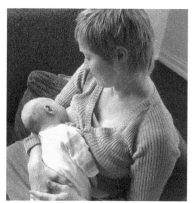

Figure 3.1 Finding stability within her mother's embrace, the baby yields and nurses. The mother also yields as she shapes her body around her baby.

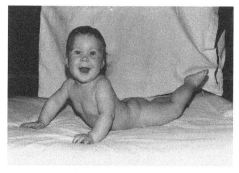

Figure 3.2 From the firm downward push of her arms, this baby is able to reach up and out with her head, eyes, mouth, and legs. That which attracts her is expressed in the excitement of her response.

Figure 3.3 Yielding on the earth, the baby first reaches with his eyes, then reaches with his right arm across his body and pushes down with his left foot, then the right to roll. Here, we see how fundamental movements emerge in concert—one underlying and supporting the other.

Figure 3.4 The energetic and downward push of this baby's lower limbs sequences upward through his spine to culminate in the reach of his head and arms. Now, he has support to grasp the drawer and pull himself to stand.

The Six Fundamental Movements

Every fundamental movement, emerging within context, holds a
psychological meaning as well as serves a particular function for the
baby and the adult. Each movement in combination with every other
offers essential support in finding and creating changing definitions
of self. All six fundamental movements operate throughout every

Yielding In yielding, we give over to and thereby take from the other.	Yielding with the other, we find and make support for ourselves.	We give our weight over to a chair as we take its support.
Receptivity. How do I receive from and give to you in any given moment?	The quality of yielding depends upon that which we adjust to and that which adjusts to us.	We lean on a friend, giving ourselves over and taking support.
Pushing In pushing, we separate from while including the other in experience; discovering and making difference.	Pushing against, we sense the " push-back" or resistance of the other. In doing so, we experience qualities and subtleties of this other and learn that there is " me" and " not me."	Sitting at the table, we push our feet onto the floor and the base of our pelvis onto the chair to keep ourselves upright and erect.
Differing. How do I make and sustain my differences in relation to you?		When we get up, we push our hands against the table and feet onto the floor in order to stand.
		During a moment of protest, we push our hand forward as if to say, " Stop!"
		Putting our hand on top of another's shoulder in assurance, we gently push against them as if to say, " I am here with you."
Reaching The act of seeking; extending beyond oneself and into the environment.	Sensing the fruitfulness of our environment, we feel invited to reach out.	We reach for a sparkling glass of water in the hopes it will quench our thirst.
How do I open to and invite you to meet me?	Our reach is an investigation into the possibility of what may be there for us. We reach toward the other in the hope of meeting and being met.	We reach toward an appealing other to comfort us.

sequence of action; however, some are more foreground than others as action proceeds. This chart defines and exemplifies each movement at a moment when they are foreground in experience. In the context of relationships,these movements become the basis of interactive dynamics.

Grasping The act of enclosing and containing what one has reached out for. How am I holding what I have attained?	In our grasping of the other, we sense in a more immediate way what we have reached. In the grasping moment, perception of the contained object expands.	We grasp onto an object and discover its utility. We grasp onto the hand of another and discover how in the holding we are held.
Pulling The act of drawing what is other toward oneself with the possibility of incorporating it into oneself. How do I draw you toward me and make you mine?	From the act of reaching, grasping and pulling arises an experience of "me" and "you" and the degree to which "me" and "you" are becoming "we." We experience the other's qualities of attraction, resistance and flexibility.	We pull the delicious looking apple toward our mouths to satisfy our hunger. We pull the longed for other toward us and discover the possibility of satisfaction.
Releasing Letting go of the held object allows the whole body to reorganize. As we release the other, the action comes to completion and yielding moves foreground once more. How do I let go in order to move onward?	The act of relinquishing what was enables one to move toward what is now becoming or what soon will be.	When we finish writing the final paragraph, we release the pen from our hand. Sensing the completion of our embrace, we let go of each other.

Figure 3.5 Simple yet powerful movements define the relationship between one and another.

Figure 3.6 Holding on to what she has just grasped, this woman clarifies her idea. Now, she can pull it toward her and incorporate it into experience.

Figure 3.7 The language of movement underlies this verbal exchange. The two women reach toward each other with head, eyes, mouth, and hands in lively conversation.

Figure 3.8 "I am here with you." Yield/push, push/yield: These are the essentials for interpersonal meeting.

new ability to "let go." Releasing is now a chosen action rather than a passive response that accompanies relaxing. Over time, releasing patterns continue to grow and elaborate with every new situation. By the end of the first year, babies enjoy handing objects to other people. At first, they expect them to be given back immediately, but soon after they seem satisfied to fully relinquish an object to another.

Releasing a held object allows the baby's whole body to disorganize and reorganize to move onward to new engagement. The act of relinquishing what was enables one to move toward what is now becoming or what soon will be. Parents must often help babies and young children release a present pleasure or safe occupation to move on to an activity that is barely understood. The way they work with their baby shapes the baby's experience and sense of mastery over this phase of action. This history can appear in adult life, in physical and emotional disorganizing and reorganizing when one "lets go" or "relinquishes" what is finished or alternately feels "torn away from" present interests in order to plan the next activity.

MOVEMENT FUNDAMENTALS IN CONCERT: YIELD/PUSH, REACH/GRASP, AND PULL/RELEASE

Combined fundamental movements are present in all action sequences, from the simple adjusting of one's gaze to bring an object into focus to the more complex action sequences that require greater adjustments.

In the following developmental and maturational progression, we show how one fundamental movement coordinates with another and in relation to the environment as the baby moves up and off the earth, with gravity and through space. Although the movement sequence unfolds in relation to these universal forces of the field, the baby is also moving toward an object that excites and stimulates interest. In this example, it will become clear how the prior sequence of fundamental movements forms the underlying support for the next sequence to unfold as the action completes itself.

A 6-month-old baby in prone position, and yielding onto the floor, pushes her hands down so that her head reaches upward. Next, she begins to wiggle and bend at each knee to alternately raise and then lower her legs. In the process, she discovers the undersides of her toes as they make contact with the floor. Every engagement of her foot touching the floor enhances the baby's awareness of that part of her body, and she begins to push with more effort. Now, the baby discovers how to push both feet simultaneously onto the floor, and the weight of her body shifts forward and onto her hands. Pushing from her toes elongates her spine, and the reach of her head is also augmented. The increased pressure on her hands sensitizes and sharpens her awareness here, and she pushes them downward, which then moves her body backward. As this coordination of upper and lower limbs is practiced, in time the baby can rock back and forth. Should she see something interesting in front of her, she might try to move toward it by shifting her weight to one side of her body, alternately reaching her free arm and hand toward the object while the other grasps the floor and pulls back.

By the age of about 7 months, however, a baby's coordination of upper and lower body is more developed. Still on the belly, when the baby sees something interesting that is just out of reach, he hikes the knee of one leg and moves it headward, while the toes of that same flexed leg push onto the floor. The push gives the baby enough leverage to propel him forward. This energetic thrust moves upward from the baby's foot through this flexed leg and thigh and into his hip socket, eventually extending that leg and the same side of the spine. This enables the baby to reach his head and arm (of that same side) beyond the boundaries of his kinesphere. Pushing at one end thus supports the emergence of reaching at the other and enables the baby to move toward the desired object or person.

The reaching action, in its turn, will culminate in a grasp onto the floor as the palm of the baby's hand meets it, pulls backward, and then releases its grip. In the experience of grasping and pulling, the center of the palm creates a subtle suction action on the floor, as if for a moment the floor is contained within the palm. Pulling the floor backward moves the baby forward and simultaneously facilitates hiking the leg on the opposite side, an action that results in a "C-curve" shape on the same side. Now, the baby can yield and push the toes of her hiked leg against the floor, initiating a similar reaching, grasping, pulling, and then releasing on that same side. It is the coordination of yielding, pushing, reaching, grasping, pulling, and releasing that allows the baby to advance. The baby crawls on the belly along the floor with first one side initiating the movement and then the other.

These fundamental movements—yield, push, reach, grasp, pull, and release—are all present as the baby moves from lying to sitting, kneeling, crawling on all fours, standing, and finally walking. Yielding flows into pushing, and pushing flows into reaching, grasping, pulling, and releasing, and these movements flow into yielding once more as the sequence begins again. Thus, movement fundamentals remain with us throughout the life span and constitute the ways we connect with ourselves and within our world.

THREE CASE STUDIES

In the following cases, we demonstrate how we work in short-term psychotherapy to solve particular problems the parent has brought to us. Here, we show how the fundamental movements constitute the *dynamics of engaging* between parents and babies, how nonverbal signals are cocreated, and the degree to which they are well sent and received. We also show how a change in movement patterns can open an interactive process that appears to be closed. This creates better mutual understanding and offers further options for the family. In addition, every example shows how much information can be gained from the observation of movement.

SUSAN, 29 YEARS, AND ABBY, 4 MONTHS

Susan, a first-time mother, comes to see F.L. because she has noticed that Abby does not enjoy being on her tummy for long and becomes quickly frustrated and cries if she is not picked up. Susan is concerned that this could limit Abby's development because she has read that babies who do not spend enough time on their tummies might have a problem with crawling, which could lead to later cognitive difficulties.[3] Susan has begun to avoid placing Abby on her tummy altogether because Abby finds it difficult and uncomfortable.

Susan sits cross-legged on the floor while Abby sits on her lap. Susan draws Abby's attention to the toys in front of them. "Oh Abby, see all those toys! Would you like to play with them?" She gently places Abby on her tummy within easy reach of the toys. Abby immediately pushes herself upward with both arms so she can get a better look. Then, quickly she fusses, and Susan moves to pick her up immediately.

It is often tricky for a parent to encourage a new pattern that is not an infant's favorite. The needed parenting skill is to provide time for practice with enough playful entertainment so that the baby stays engaged but not to overemphasize the activity so that the baby develops an aversion to the movement.

Noticing Abby's difficulty and Susan's impulse to rescue Abby, F.L. invites Susan to get down on her belly with Abby and make face-to-face contact to encourage her baby's interest. Susan talks to Abby and places a toy directly in front of her. Abby is quite able to hold onto the toy with one hand while supporting the weight of her torso on the other. Abby looks at her mother intermittently but quickly begins to fuss. As she vocalizes, she

---

[3] Some developmental thinkers believe that physical and brain experiences involved in crawling are crucial for certain cognitive tasks, specifically the ability to read. There is some evidence that when there are reading difficulties, contralateral movements (left leg moves with right arm and right leg with left arm) like crawling help alleviate these problems (Hannaford, 2005). But, there is as yet no research that definitively connects the absence of crawling with later cognitive problems. Also, there is strong cross-cultural evidence to suggest that crawling is not necessary to the development of locomotion itself (Hopkins & Westra, 1988). Nevertheless, crawling gives infants the stability of being on four limbs before they must stand on two. It also provides the satisfaction of moving from one place to another before they are ready to stand. Given all these considerations, it is important in working with children to rule out neurological difficulties when a motor pattern like crawling is significantly delayed and to encourage it if possible.

brings her head down and up again and then looks off to the side, suggesting her desire to change her position. She cannot yet roll over, so her fussing continues and increases.

Susan responds by whisking Abby off the floor and begins to soothe her by making cooing sounds and rocking her gently, "Oh my sweet baby, shhhhh, shhhh," and presses Abby close to her body. Now, Abby pushes her hands onto her mommy's chest several times, making space between them. Following her baby's signal, Susan turns her baby outward, saying, "I'm not sure what she wants. She doesn't always soothe easily when she gets so frustrated." Susan jiggles Abby and continues to make cooing sounds for her daughter. Abby continues to fuss, making deep, guttural, and "grrrrrring" noises in her throat. She pushes her head backward into Susan's chest, and the more Abby pushes and growls, the more Susan gently yields and coos.

The dynamic engagement at this moment is a mismatch between mother and baby incorporating both movement and emotion. Susan imagines that Abby needs and wants to be soothed, even though her ministrations are clearly not working. The more Susan tries to "soothe" and change Abby's angry feelings, the more Abby's frustration grows. This is expressed by the strong sustained pushing of her vocalizing along with the pushing of her head and arms against her mother.

F.L. suggests to Susan that she might try another way to relate to Abby's vocal expressions. She demonstrates this by speaking to Abby in pushing, guttural tones similar to the ones that Abby makes that express recognition of her angry feelings. F.L. growls with an intensity and rhythm similar to Abby's as she says, "Oh, you really don't *like* lying on your tummy, *do* you? You don't *like* that at all, do you? *That* made you angry! You wanted to *get* that toy, and you *didn't* feel good doing it." Abby immediately stops her own vocalizing and turns her attention directly to F.L. When F.L. pauses, Abby immediately begins to growl again. F.L. continues this back and forth and then adds some yielding moments to her vocal tones, some lighter more oozing moments that stretch her words out: "I knoooow you didn't liiike being on your belly. Soooo, we need to try just a liiiiittle bit. Let's see, maaaaybe we can practice just a little bit at a time," she says. Abby responds to the changed tone of F.L.'s voice by shifting the tone of her own vocalizations, which grow lighter too and begins yielding, pushing, and reaching as she adjusts in her mother's arms. The conversational turn-taking continues as Abby and F.L. smile at each other.

F.L.'s actions, their energy, and the abruptness of her vocal tone all at first matched Abby's push and supported her emotional expression. Then, F.L.'s gradual yielding and more sustained words and vocal tone "explained" Abby's dilemma to her. Even though Abby does not understand the content, she can mirror the quality of F.L.'s increasing yield and, in doing so, take something of F.L.'s experience inside her. Abby finds her own ability to yield fluidly. This mirroring capacity is the ground from which babies learn to self-regulate and even think.

Susan says, "I thought she needed soothing, but I can see that you let her stay upset." F.L. replies, "You're right, she did need soothing, but it seems that she couldn't let go of her frustration until she could share it with someone. Abby really 'talks' to you and has a lot of feelings to express." Susan agrees and says she realizes now that Abby's strong feelings have been scaring her a little—she wonders how such a little one can have so much going on. As F.L. and Susan talk, Susan recognizes that she has not really wanted to think about the strength of Abby's feelings.

Susan can be happily engaged with her daughter most of the time; however, if she is uncomfortable with Abby's expressions of frustration, she needs to explore her discomfort so that she can tolerate Abby's discomfort.

Susan says, "I would never have thought to talk that way with her—it seems so strong." F.L. asks, "Did you ever talk to your mother with that kind of strength?" Susan immediately responds, "My mother was always depressed and seemed disengaged and vague most of the time. And even when she was there and doing things for me, I never felt satisfied with our relationship. It's as if she wasn't really there."

F.L. says, "If I think about what you've said, I get the image that there was no one for you to push against." Susan replies with enthusiasm, "Yes, that's exactly right. If I pushed into her, it would be like pushing into thin air." F.L. holds her hand up and invites Susan to push against it, and when she does, F.L. gives her no resistance. Susan says, "Yup, that's familiar. My mother's not there and I'm ... alone." F.L. adds, "You were there when Abby pushed against you with her hands. You understood what she needed. But it seemed harder for you when she also pushed with her angry and frustrated voice." Susan says, "Yes, I'm kind of afraid when she's angry with me."

F.L. invites Susan to push onto the floor with both hands in front of her crossed legs, much like Abby was doing while on her belly, to sense how she experiences that movement. Susan executes the experiment and says that she enjoys it. "Well, I feel strong and well-met right in the palms of my hands," she says. F.L. encourages her to continue pushing and also make some of those guttural noises that Abby beautifully demonstrated.

Susan now makes intense and guttural sounds as she pushes her hands onto the floor. "Wow, I feel those sounds all the way down to my belly. It feels terrific," she says. Susan pauses for several moments and then says, "I think I have a better feel for how Abby feels when she's frustrated. It's amazing to think I need to push with her more, and she needs to push against me—it's really foreign to me because my mother was really a 'pushover' and I had to be very gentle with her." "Well now," F.L. says, "you can join her in that 'terrific feeling.'"

Discussion

It was clear that Abby had difficulty pushing with her hands while on her abdomen, but interestingly enough, she had no trouble finding her push vocally. Susan, however, had difficulty meeting Abby's vocal push and instead cooed softly and invited her daughter to yield with her as a way of soothing her. But, Abby needs the experience of her feelings being mirrored and met. Without Susan's "push back" and the recognition of her feelings, she might experience herself as "pushing into thin air" against a mother who feels like a "pushover." For Susan to match her daughter, she needs to discover the strength of her own push and what it offers. As explicated, pushing patterns give the developing baby a sense of cohesion and integration, all parts coming together, that enables the clear experience of me and you—or in this case, "*I* am here with *you*." From this more secure relational configuration, Abby finds and makes the strength necessary to push solidly against the floor.

SARAH, 35 YEARS, AND LUCIA, 5 MONTHS

Sarah brings her first-born baby, Lucia, to see R.F. because she is concerned that the back of the baby's head, which was perfectly fine at birth, has grown quite flat. The pediatrician has told her not to be concerned because when her hair grows, it will not even be noticed. But, Sarah is not convinced and worries that the flatness of Lucia's head has something to do with her baby lying on her back too much.

Wheeling a bright red carriage, Sarah enters the office. After R.F. greets her, she peers into the hooded carriage to greet Lucia and notices the baby's furrowed eyebrows and pursed lips. When R.F. begins talking to Lucia, the baby looks directly at her and for a moment smiles brightly. Quickly, however, Lucia's eyes wander in an unfocused way, and she no longer smiles. Even when Sarah extends her hands toward her baby to take her out of the carriage, Lucia does not look directly at her mother or vocalize to her. Once picked up, Lucia briefly gazes at her mother, and again her eyes float without appearing to reach toward anything in particular.

Sarah removes Lucia's cap and points to the back of the baby's head, which is rather flat and bald, making it look slightly misshapen. On her doctor's advice and as prevention against SIDS Lucia is put to sleep only on her back.[4] "She has not begun to roll over by herself," Sarah adds, "and when she is awake I think the nanny is not helping her to spend much time

---

[4] Sudden infant death syndrome (SIDS) is thought to occur when young infants, lying belly down, attempt to move their heads from one side to the other and suffocate in the process. Although the syndrome is not well understood, much of the medical community advises that placing infants on their backs while sleeping is the best prevention against SIDS.

on her belly. I ask her to put Lucia on her belly more of the time, but I can't be certain if she does this. Anyway, when I try to put Lucia on her belly, she cries pretty quickly, so I think the nanny probably doesn't try."

R.F. asks Sarah to put Lucia belly down to see what happens. Once there, Lucia pushes two fisted hands down onto the floor to straighten her elbows. The downward push manages to lift her head and upper body off the floor. But, while Lucia does have a strong initial push, she does not sustain the push to maintain this upright position for long. She does not seem to look at the toys or people around her from her upright vantage, and soon her head droops slowly downward; eventually, her forehead touches the floor, while her arms and upper torso continue to strain in keeping her upright. Her head, shoulders, and arms appear poorly coordinated. With great determination, Lucia valiantly works to right her head into a vertical position once more, but it wobbles and droops downward, as if her head is just too heavy to be supported. Finally, Lucia gives up. She lowers her upper torso to the floor and lies completely prone, fussing quietly.

Lucia appears unable to sustain the lift of her head to match the position of her upper torso. It is possible that the muscles of Lucia's neck, back, and shoulders are not yet strong enough to support her head and also are not in balance with the muscles along the front of her body. When the muscles of the front and back body are balanced, they permit proper control of the head, and that coordination enhances the baby's vision. Conversely, as visual control develops, it reciprocally influences control of the head and neck. Lucia wants to lift her head up, but she is having trouble mastering the move.

R.F. suggests that Sarah join Lucia on the floor so that she can meet Lucia's eyes. R.F. also lies on her belly and places several toys close to Lucia. Rather than notice the toys, Lucia lifts her head up just a little, skims the horizon with her eyes, and seems to find nothing much to hold on to. Her eyes appear somewhat vacant and unfocused, as if she is lost. At the same time, her hands grasp into tight little fists.

Sarah quickly picks up a toy bear from the floor and shakes it in front of Lucia to get her attention. As she stimulates her baby, Sarah's eyes appear to be on the toy rather than on Lucia. Lucia looks at the bear briefly and then looks away. Sarah brings the bear closer to Lucia's face but gets no response. Lucia drops her head and Sarah looks down. R.F. takes another small soft stuffed animal and begins gently stroking one of Lucia's fisted hands from wrist to fingers. In an instant, Lucia reaches up with her head again, gradually opens her fingers so that her palms are on the floor, and then, with some difficulty, but also with determination, she reaches and grasps onto the toy and pulls it toward her. Sarah and R.F. watch as Lucia now uses both hands to center the toy directly in front of her just under her face. She then begins to press her hands onto the soft animal and soon brings her head down to mouth the toy gently. Next, Lucia pushes her now-open palms against the floor. At the same time, her head reaches up and away from the toy and then down several times in succession as she tries to get a better grasp on the toy with her mouth. Her eyes, hands, and mouth are clearly focused, and the movement is motivated and well directed.

When R.F. stimulates Lucia's hands to open, her eyes, attention, and interest open with them. Once her attention is on manipulating the toy with her mouth and hands, Lucia immediately has more control of her head and neck. Her interest in doing something new gives her the persistence needed to work through the difficult physical effort of holding up her head. Lucia pushes down with her forearms and subtly pulls her arms toward each other. The pushing and pulling movements contract and condense the muscles of her upper torso, giving her enough support to lengthen her spine and reach her head upward. What was needed was more physical stimulation of her hands to bring out her grasping impulse and all the curiosity that is part and parcel of it. Once Lucia can grab onto the toy with her hands, the coordination of her eye, hand, and mouth; head and neck; and upper torso follow. Lucia now moves with more coherence and seemingly greater purpose.

Abruptly, Sarah takes a set of brightly colored plastic links, shakes them in front of Lucia's face, and places them near her hands. As she does this, Sarah bends her head down and looks directly at her baby. Lucia immediately releases the stuffed animal, grasps onto the links, and pulls them toward her. She already appears more confident in mastering this new task of bringing her head downward to mouth them and back up again. Her movements have greater intensity and directness. And although Sarah's timing is sometimes quick as she connects with her baby, she continues to catch Lucia's attention. As they play together, Lucia appears even more energetic, engaged, and determined, as does Sarah. Lucia remains on her belly for what Sarah says is an unprecedented 15 minutes. R.F. tells Sarah that as Lucia spends more time on her belly rather than her back, her flattened head will fill out, and her hair will grow back.

In the next few sessions, Sarah learns how to give Lucia the needed visual, vocal, and tactile stimulation that will encourage her curiosity and desire to explore. Sarah and R.F. decide together that inviting Lucia's nanny to their sessions would be useful so that they can coordinate their efforts. Both need to support Lucia's motor development, which in turn will fuel her curiosity, persistence, and yearning. Sarah also learns that following Lucia's timing more closely, in particular, will strengthen her daughter's ability to sense her own energy and excitement as they build up and diminish within her.

Discussion

Lucia's inability to reach out for, grasp onto, and pull an object or person toward her—to say with her body, "I want this, I have this, I am making this part of me"—is clearly seen here. A similar restriction in fundamental movements and their psychological function is echoed in her mother's movements as well. Perhaps Sarah does not psychically grasp onto and pull her baby toward her to more fully take her in, actions that would help Sarah better understand Lucia's experience and vice versa. In the dynamic of this situation, both mother and baby appear lost in relation to each other.

While it appears that Lucia cannot push, in fact she is having more difficulty with developing the *reasons* to push because her eyes, hands, and mouth do not fully reach, grasp, and pull. The inhibition in all these fundamentals creates negative feedback that diminishes the strength of her push, and the less-available push now feeds forward to influence and diminish her reach, grasp, pull, and so forth. R.F. first observes the baby's inhibition in these movements when she notices her lack of eye focus while in her carriage and then while on her belly. In those moments, Lucia's eyes do not distinctly and energetically reach out, grasp onto an object of interest, and pull it toward her. This pattern repeats itself with her fingers and hands, which remain fisted and unmoving when the toys are presented. Inviting Sarah to focus on and attend more closely to Lucia and then watching Lucia's response to her mother's more directed attention creates a stronger pull in the relationship and a stronger experience of cohesion between them.

GRANDMA JEAN, 66 YEARS, AND BEN, 10 MONTHS

Jean, Ben's grandmother and daytime caregiver, came to see R.F. at her office with a specific concern about Ben's inability to creep on his belly or crawl on his hands and knees. In fact, Jean said, "Overall Ben's developing very slowly—even at 10 months, when he is sitting up, he just doesn't go after a toy that's out of his reach. He just had a checkup, and the doctor says that he's just fine, but I don't know why he's not doing more." When Jean placed Ben belly down on the floor, his struggle became obvious. Ben could not coordinate the reach of his arm and hand toward the toy placed just in front of him with the push of his foot or leg that would allow him to crawl forward on his belly. Instead, his lower limbs were waving in the air and made little contact with the floor. Ben looked toward the toy for a few seconds, looked toward his grandmother, and then back toward the toy.

Not all babies creep or crawl by 10 months as each has an individual timetable of development. Observing Ben and Jean, however, it did seem to R.F. as if there were some greater difficulty here. Sometimes, an emerging dynamic is more clearly seen during a home visit, so R.F. suggested that their next meeting be at Jean's apartment to see what a typical playtime would look like, and Jean agreed. This would better inform R.F. about the relationship between Jean and Ben and how that relationship was shaping Ben's mobility.

During a home visit, R.F. is seated on the couch a short distance away from Ben, who sits on the floor, alongside his grandmother. There are many playthings around Ben. He is holding a small toy in one hand, and he looks at another on the floor in front of him just out of his reach. Ben does not move. He looks at the toy, then looks toward Grandma, and then looks back at the toy again. Grandma abruptly reaches out and grabs onto the toy and hands it to Ben. Ben smiles and begins banging the two toys together. But soon, he lowers his hands, opens his grasp, and lets the toys fall to the floor. He now stares straight ahead, and Grandma quickly reaches out to grab another toy and offers it to Ben.

Most babies at Ben's age, even if they were not crawling, would change position, perhaps lower to their bellies or lean forward to reach for the toy, but Ben lacks the push to mobilize and support his reaching, grasping, and pulling.

Seeing that Ben has nothing to occupy him, Grandma swoops him up, pulls him closer to her side, and puts him on his belly next to some of his other toys. Ben pushes himself up with both hands and then rests comfortably on his elbows. He takes some time to look at the toys and then reaches for and grabs a brightly colored ball. He pulls the ball closer to him, lowers himself down onto the toy, and chews on it. After a few moments, Ben stops what he is doing, and the ball rolls to the side. Without missing a beat, Grandma moves the discarded toy away and now offers Ben two more objects, a block and a small teddy bear, saying to R.F., "I'm trying to get him to move more on his own," and saying to Ben, "Here is something else, Ben. Ben, look ... look here ... here's a block and a teddy bear!" Instead of handing the toys directly to Ben, she puts them at a little distance, out of reach, and says, "Here, go get the toys. You can do it." Ben looks up at the toys, bends his legs at the knees, lightly waves his feet in the air, and at the same time makes small pushing movements with his arms, lightly bobbing his head up and down. But, Ben just gazes at them and appears unable to make any effective push or pull that might bring him closer to the toys.

Ben's waving feet and small pushing movements indicate some interest. But, we see here that Ben does not effectively push with his feet onto the floor, and he does not reach out with his arms and hands to follow through on his interest. R.F. suspects that a particular dynamic is taking place, and it is unclear how it began: Grandma seems to be overdoing and could even be described as "pushy." Her push is not moderated by an accompanying yield, which would allow her take Ben in, and Ben seems not to express much push at all, a necessity for his sense of separateness to develop.

Ben furrows his brow and sticks out his bottom lip as he quietly whines. Turning his head to face Grandma, who is next to him, Ben twists his neck and shoulders in her direction, pulling back with one arm while pushing down on the floor with the other in what looks like an attempt to sit up. Then, Ben stops moving and appears somewhat frozen, his face tightly squeezed to the center, probably in frustration. Jean's face mirrors Ben's worried expression. But rather than express her concern with evident emotion, she speaks to Ben in a playful, high-pitched voice, "Okay, you want up, we'll go up." She grabs onto both of his arms and pulls Ben to sitting and then brings some toys closer to him.

Jean jumps in and distracts Ben from fully feeling his own desires to push, reach, grasp, and pull himself in lots of directions to satisfy his needs. These actions would stabilize his body and provide support for his emotional experience and expression: "I see something interesting, I feel my eyes open, my mouth water, my body lengthen, and my wanting to reach." But now, Ben waits for his grandmother to complete and even start actions for him. In fact, his grandmother's takeover of action, if we can call it that, may have been going on from such a young age that Ben now has trouble feeling and showing much desire at all. We see that when he drops his toys, loses steam, and gives up. Ben needs to be increasingly self-activating, but Grandma Jean's "helping" tends to derail his own actions and the growth of his sense of autonomy.

Jean's cell phone rings, and she answers it and excuses herself for a moment to take the call. Left to his own devices and still sitting, Ben tries to reach for a ball in front of him. He pushes downward with his legs and pelvis, lengthens his spine, and reaches with his arms but does not change position. He does this several times, but then he stops, makes soft protests, and gives up on his own efforts. Ben shifts his eyes and head away from what he wants and scans the environment. He does not appear to focus on anything in particular and looks as if he is drifting through space, his face expressionless. R.F. says, "Ben do you want that ball? It's right there. Try again."

For a moment, Ben seems to know what he wants but cannot act to satisfy his desire. Then, it appears that his very sense of desire quickly vanishes. He appears to go blank as soon as he feels any discomfort instead of continuing to experience what he wants, to reach for what he wants, or even to fuss and protest with some passion. Ben fully expects that his grandmother will come and rescue him, so he waits. But in his waiting, Ben loses touch with his wanting.

After a few moments, Jean is finished with her phone call and comes back to Ben. "Okay, do you want to do some walking? Come, we'll stretch our legs." She reaches to Ben, and he reaches back with a big grin as Jean pulls him to standing. Now standing behind him, Grandma stretches Ben's arms up above his head, and he steps along in a lively way, all the while smiling and now vocalizing with some energy. Grandma also smiles and chatters to Ben, "You can really walk, huh! Soon you'll be walking by yourself, like a big boy."

Seeing Ben's enthusiasm for walking and knowing that Jean lives in an apartment building with clean and carpeted stairs in the hallway just outside her door, R.F. suggests that climbing up the stairs might be enjoyable and useful for Ben. Once they move into the hallway, R.F. asks Jean to stand Ben at the base of the stairs and place his hands onto the step just in front of him.

R.F. thought that Ben's expressed desire and pleasure in his ability to stand and walk with Jean's help would be enhanced in the task of climbing the stairs. In addition, the later patterns to develop—standing and walking, which are elements of the climbing pattern—could be used to stimulate and strengthen crucial muscles that generally develop during the prior pattern, crawling. With continued climbing practice, when Ben eventually did walk on his own, he would have greater support from these underlying muscular structures. In addition, in this moving exploration, Ben's desire and Jean's useful assistance could be united.

R.F. shows Jean how to hold her hands lightly around Ben's waist to give him as much support as necessary and no more. Immediately, Ben knows what he wants to do. To "walk" upstairs, Ben shifts his weight onto his right leg and then reaches the same-side arm onto the step above, grasps onto it, and pulls down. The downward pulling movement frees his left leg to lift off the floor, and he moves it up and onto the stair and pushes it downward so that now his left arm reaches out, grasps onto a higher step, and pulls downward. Now, his right leg is free to lift off the floor to reach another step and so on, and in this way Ben begins climbing in a homolateral style, giggling and squealing with enjoyment.

After some time and much shared delight, R.F. tells Jean that just as she had her hands lightly around Ben's waist as he climbed the stairs, she could do the same when he is learning to walk along on the floor. Although it is more difficult to follow him around, she can give Ben enough support so that he can more securely balance as he walks. As R.F. gathers herself to go, Ben and Jean continue practicing on the stairs and appear thoroughly engrossed in their play.

Discussion

There can be many reasons why a baby does or does not crawl on belly or hands and knees at particular times in development; in some cases, babies do not crawl at all and still manage to hop, skip, and jump a few years later. Although it is unclear at this moment why Ben is unable to crawl, there is an obvious dynamic emerging between him and his grandmother that contributes to this dilemma. Ben's low-key style of being and behaving is a powerful call to his overly active grandmother. And the more that his grandmother responds to Ben in her involved way, the more passive he becomes.

The fundamental movements work in concert, all supporting the achievement of connecting with oneself and another. But here, Ben's movement sequences are interrupted: There is no stable ground of yield/push from which to reach or the firm ground of grasp, enabling the clarity of pull and then release. Ben's capacity to connect is without requisite support. This inhibition in movement dampens Ben's desire; reciprocally, his dampened desire inhibits his movements.

The task of climbing stairs stimulated Ben's fundamental movements into activity and, at the same time, repositioned the dyad so that Jean was, literally, following Ben's lead and was now less intrusive. For his part, Ben was able to take the lead and enjoy doing so. As Ben strengthens his own desires and allows them to move through him, Jean can, it is hoped, become an advocate for Ben's autonomy. As Ben practices crawling up and even backing down the stairs and practices supported walking, a new phase of his life opens for him. Exploring these new and different relational configurations, Ben has a new opportunity to experience his desires and to follow them.

Chapter 4

Kinetic Temperament

INTRODUCTION

When thinking about temperament, people generally have in mind characteristics of personality and descriptors such as shy, aggressive, sociable, active, emotional, distractible, dour, and cheerful. These characterizations recognize that people demonstrate persistent trends in the way they initiate and respond to situations and other people. There have been many studies of temperament. For example, one showed that each individual's need for interaction itself emerges in a particular rhythm. This means that not everyone needs the same amount of interaction at the same time (Chapple, 1970). Another, a longitudinal study in the 1950s, identified nine unchanging temperamental factors: activity level, rhythmicity or regularity, approach or withdrawal, adaptability, sensory threshold, quality of mood, intensity of reactions, distractibility, and persistence or attention span (Chess & Thomas, 1996). In the 1980s, the reactivity (ranging from high to low) of infants was linked with a number of other physiological markers and to behavioral inhibition in 2-year-old children (Kagan, 2006).

It is not, however, conventionally understood that in all of these characterizations there is an underlying movement component recognizable in the early months of life. In this chapter, we develop this idea and show the usefulness of movement studies revealing the links between cognitive and personality functions and the favored use from birth of certain dimensions and qualities of movement that we describe (Kestenberg & Sossin, 1979; Lamb, 1965). This basic movement repertoire constitutes the kinetic temperament (La Barre, 2008), which is manifested through a set of movement inclinations that are innate and enduring. These inclinations to move in distinctive ways help make each of us recognizably and uniquely ourselves.[1]

Our distinctive movement inclinations that comprise our kinetic temperament are intrinsic foundational physical modes of operating beginning

---

[1] See Birdwhistell (1970); Kestenberg-Amighi et al. (1999); Kestenberg and Sossin (1979); Lamb (1965); Lamb and Watson (1979); Piontelli (1992).

in utero and present at birth that initially shape a baby's actions and affect and thus contribute heavily to patterns of behavior that are mutually created by baby and parents. These endogenous settings influence what kinds of early experiences are welcome or, in contrast, cause anxiety and stress; they also specify how each baby viscerally and physically copes with anxiety and stress and how adaptable each may be to different ways of being handled by parents and other caretakers (La Barre, 2008).

For example, one baby may lengthen her limbs soon after birth, while another might stay in his fetal curl much longer. Also, some babies, whose movements are generally *high intensity*, react powerfully to lights, sounds, or hunger, while others, whose movements are generally more *low intensity*, appear to maintain an unchanging demeanor despite a great deal of upheaval around them and cry less often than others. These are a few of the distinguishing features that movement differences underlie.

Movement inclinations are part of the infant's first movement patterns, and because they are active early, they become the most practiced as well. These characteristics of movement make up a baby's gauge or baseline for judging when experiences demand a response that veers too much or too suddenly from the preferred range or individual comfort zone. For instance, some babies enjoy being thrown up in the air, while others react with fear to such antics. Differences like this are the reason that we can call the early movement inclinations "the baby's first point of view": On the basis of the baby's inclinations, she determines what feels good, comfortable, safe, and pleasant when parents or other caregivers are holding, rocking, feeding, touching, looking at, playing with, and speaking to her. This means that movement inclinations are immediately significant; the physical differences in how babies like to move affect how they relate to others and how they perceive and evaluate their relationships. It is important, therefore, for parents and psychotherapists to understand these characteristics of themselves and their babies and how these movement characteristics interrelate.

Each person's movement inclinations derive from variations of body structure. While our earliest movement preferences are innate, our environments—human and physical—shape the way that movement inclinations develop and organize into movement repertoires and what they mean in the contexts in which they function. Ideally, our movement repertoires expand through development, interaction, imitation, and other kinds of learning as we continue adapting to new situations over the course of development. In addition, the environment both provides opportunities to expand beyond the range of movement with which we are born and also creates situations that promote rigidity and restriction.

In this chapter, we show the significance of the earliest movement inclinations both as they emerge and develop in the first year and as they are maintained in adults. We illustrate how extreme or entrenched differences between particular aspects of babies' and parents' individual movement repertoires (fundamental movements and inclinations) can be problematic: When parents cannot extend themselves to meet, match, and gradually expand their infant's preferred range of movement well enough, difficulties follow. Understanding this, psychotherapists can help parents see the movement differences between themselves and their child and support needed changes by recognizing and working with movement inclinations to resolve the difficulties.

MOVEMENT INCLINATIONS

Movement inclinations are not movements or actions in themselves. Rather, they refer to how (with what *quality*) and where (in what *dimensions*) a person performs any movement. In Chapter 3, we discussed the fundamental movements: push, yield, reach, grasp, pull, and release. In this chapter, we show that we may perform these actions in different ways. For example, one can push someone or something away *abruptly* or *gradually* or dismiss someone with either a *freeing* fling or a *binding,* pressing quality. These differences might reflect different individual movement inclinations or participate in constituting and conveying different emotions and intentions with respect to another person. Differences in *dimensional inclinations* define *where* in the body's immediate space action is taking place or in what dimensions the body is primarily organized. For example, one can yield one's upper torso to recline on the couch in a *horizontal* organization of the spine and limbs to feel into one's own experience merging with another. One can push feet downward to create an upward reaching into a *vertical* body organization to support the coalescence and expression of a personal intention. One can bend the knees and fold at the hips to descend in vertical to avoid conflict. Also, one can pull the chin, chest, or belly backward in *sagittal*[2] to retreat from asserting a desire or thrust the body forward in *sagittal* to reach for what one wants.

With respect to the *qualities of movement,* we differentiate the variations in the oscillations of muscle contraction and release that move our bones in all actions. We can learn to see differences in muscle contraction and release patterns in four categories of tension change: Muscle contracting and releasing is (a) *binding* or *freeing,* (b) *evenly held* or *fluctuating,* (c) *gradual* or *abrupt,* and (d) of *high* or *low intensity.*[3] We describe these movement qualities in much greater detail in this chapter. With respect to

---

[2] *Sagittal* refers to the plane that cuts through the body from front to back. It is also called the *wheel* plane. The horizontal plane cuts through the body from side to side and is also called the *table* plane. The vertical plane cuts through the body from top to bottom, called the *door* plane (Kestenberg-Amighi et al., 1999; Lamb, 1965; Lamb & Watson, 1979).

[3] These technical terms, explained in detail in this chapter, are called *tension flow attributes* in the Kestenberg Movement Profile (KMP) (Kestenberg & Sossin, 1979).

the dimensions of movement, each body prefers most often to move into and shape itself in one or two of the three possible dimensions—horizontal, vertical, or sagittal—rather than to use all three with equal frequency.

Taken together, the four sets of *movement qualities* and the three *dimensions* of movement are visible in all human actions, and their varying frequencies of occurrence give our actions their distinctive characteristics.

MOVEMENT QUALITIES: THE *HOW* OF MOVEMENT

Movement qualities are the result of the particular ways a baby or adult changes muscle tension, which refers to the way the muscles contract and release. A simple way to see this is to observe one's own upper arm as it bends at the elbow. The biceps muscle increases in tension and bulges and shortens to pull the lower arm in toward the upper arm. If the movement toward the body is opposed and restrained by a weight on the lower arm or by the pull of an opposing muscle group in the opposite direction (as in "isometric" exercises), the movement is held tight, and the tension is defined as *binding* or in *bound flow*. When the arm is straightened and not opposed by the action of another muscle group, that movement tension is defined as *freeing* or in free flow. Thus, binding and freeing are the basic muscle changes involved in all movements.

Some babies tend to use their muscles more in a *free-flowing* way and others more in a *bound-flowing* way immediately following birth. For example, some babies frequently fling out their arms and legs (in freeing movements), while others hold their limbs bent tightly against their bodies (in binding movements). The free-flowing baby who tends to fling his limbs needs more holding and swaddling to settle down, while the baby who uses bound flow may need some gentle play to loosen up and stretch her limbs. Parents might find that the free-flowing baby enjoys similarly free-flowing interactions with them—for example, to be swooped in the air. But, this same baby might also need more bound physical and emotional support because the baby cannot supply that for himself. For example, if such a baby is crying, he might not be able to bind himself sufficiently to stop. On the other hand, parents would find that a baby who prefers bound flow does not like to be tossed up into the air. Instead, this baby prefers more gradual change from bound to free flow, such as squeezes and slowly rocking hugs. In addition, this baby might not need as much binding support to hold her body and generate emotional control. This tendency difference will remain constant even when the babies develop greater control over their own movements. There are additional variations in the movement qualities used and seen in patterns of muscle tension. To identify them, three other questions must be answered.

During alert, active periods, does the baby's level of tension change *frequently, or does it remain even or the same?* Some babies seem to be always moving, wriggling or more slowly but regularly stretching out a limb, twisting, or making a face. These babies demonstrate a preponderance of *tension flow change* or *flow fluctuation*. Still others maintain one level of *even* tension for long stretches, so they seem not to move much. They are using their muscles just as much as the first type, but they are using them to hold still rather than to change tension and therefore position. These differences provoke different responses in sensitive parents. For instance, a parent might feel safe leaving an even-flowing 3-month-old baby on the bed for a moment but not a baby whose moving involves a lot of changes in flow. The latter baby cannot be left for a minute, even before he knows how to roll over, since through general wiggling he could accidentally wobble off the edge. The evenly flowing baby might move but not move much, while the baby with more frequently changing tension wiggles, flings, or stretches all the time. While in the bath, the baby whose movement flow is more even remains calmly in her bath seat, while the baby whose flow changes more rapidly wriggles or kicks and needs more support. Parents may sometimes wonder what their very even baby is thinking because he may appear somewhat contemplative, and they may marvel at such an even temper. The parents of a wiggler or flinger might be concerned that their baby demands a lot of attention or wonder about her ability to settle down. Their concerns arise out of their perception of their baby's movement qualities, understood in terms of their own previous experiences, ideals, and the present context.

Is the movement done with high or low intensity? *Intensity* describes the energy that is going into an action rather than the action itself. Perhaps you have recognized this while watching a group of people exercising: They are all performing the same actions, but some participants just put more "oomph" into it. At the same time, some actions require more intensity than others: Jumping up and down requires high intensity, while gently waving a scarf needs only low intensity. In adult experience, throwing a baseball is a high-intensity movement. But a defensive nose tackle holding his ground against multiple blockers in a football game is also showing high intensity even though, by choice, he is not moving at all.

We see both kinds of intensity in a baby's movements. Think of three babies crying for attention. Crying is usually associated with high intensity and, of course, a baby's crying will be at the higher intensity end of her vocal and motoric range. In fact, many babies cry more delicately and less loudly than others because overall they are less intense than others. Each may experience the same hunger or other urgency, but each expresses it differently. A third baby, holding in or holding back with high-intensity binding, squeezes out some low cries before bursting into high-intensity free flow with tears and flailing. Not surprisingly, the overall high-intensity baby may be more interested than the low-intensity baby in activities that require

Movement Qualities of Tension Change in Muscles

Tension Change

Refers to how muscles	**contract**	or	**release the contraction**
as they	**tighten**	or	**loosen**
	shorten	and	**bulge**
	lengthen	and	**narrow**

Qualities

As muscles contract they become	**bound in tension**	or	**free from tension**
In addition to those two basic states, muscles contract and release	**abruptly**	or	**gradually**
in other words	**suddenly**	or	**taking time**
When they contract or release the tension may reach	**high intensity**	or	**low intensity**
in other words	**strong with much force**	or	**light with little force**
The tension level can be held or the level of tension can continue changing over time	**even**	or	**fluctuating**

Lifting an object and putting it down requires *gradual* changes of tension between *bound* and *free* movement. If the object is heavy, high intensity is needed. If the object is light, low intensity is needed.

Lifting a tea cup requires *gradually increasing levels of tension*, held *evenly* on the lifting with a gradual decrease in intensity as it is placed down.

Hammering a nail into wood requires alternating *abrupt bound* and *abrupt free* movements all in high intensity.

Pushing a heavy object requires *even, high intensity* movement.

Throwing a ball is a *high intensity, abrupt, bound* movement followed by *high intensity freeing* movement.

Waving a silk scarf requires *low intensity freeing* movements with *tension fluctuations*.

Figure 4.1 Both boys match in high intensity. The baby attempts to balance and secure himself using bound flow. His older brother maintains stability in his lower body also with bound flow while allowing his upper body to be in free flow.

Figure 4.2 Tuning into the facial expressions of this trio, we can see that the man on the left and the baby match each other in low-to-moderate intensity, while the man on the right uses higher intensity.

Figure 4.3 In this family portrait, the father and son match in low-intensity flow. The father shows a more even flow, while his little boy uses flow fluctuating. The mother's movement is in moderate intensity, even, and bound, while her daughter's movement is high intensity, flow fluctuating, and free flow.

Figure 4.4 Attuning to this young boy's facial and bodily expression, you can sense his low intensity and even flow.

high intensity, such as banging on a drum; the low-intensity baby might be more interested in gently rubbing his fingers along a cloth.

Does the tension of the movement change suddenly and abruptly *or slowly and* gradually? In babies and adults, sudden tension change is seen in jumpy, jerking, jittery, or tapping movements, whereas gradual change is seen in a slow buildup, as in a stretch or yawn, and a slow let down, as in slowly sitting and settling down into a chair or onto a cushion. We might all use a bit of both according to the demands of a given situation. For example, when we are rushing to go somewhere, we might dash from one place to the next with abrupt starts and stops, shaking our hands in frustration as we look for our misplaced grocery list. We all yawn when we are sleepy. But, our inclinations toward these various qualities are seen in the movements we make that are *not* called forth by context. We might see one baby, inclined toward *gradual* movement, looking as if he were a slowly waving piece of seaweed or as if every movement shift is a yawn. Another baby, on the other hand, might appear to tremble with excitement during each waking moment, as his eyes dart from one object to the next, and the baby abruptly shoots his limbs out from his body. Adult movements in specific contexts also demonstrate these differences. Shooting foul shots is a well-practiced motion that is more successful if it is made with gradual, smooth tension changes in the movement. But, a good dribbler in basketball, like a good runner in football, will have anything but gradual changes in his movements; instead, this person will be described as a "jitterbug" in the use of abrupt and unpredictable tension changes to catch defenders off guard. The underlying kinetic temperament, the individual's movement preferences for each quality, may make one person more inclined to be a dribbler and another a better foul shooter despite hours of practice with both activities.

Such preferences for gradual tension changes or for more abrupt ones are likewise innate. These differences provoke and call for different physical and emotional responses from parents. Rocking a baby to sleep probably evokes an image of slow, gentle, and gradual increases and decreases of tension, as in swaying. That is the classic image. But, some abrupt babies may need to be jiggled and swayed more briskly or even bounced with sharper, more abruptly changing tension that shifts to high intensity. This kind of movement matches their own movement qualities and helps such babies feel held, safe, and comfortable.

In summary, movement qualities range

between *binding* and *freeing* flow of tension levels
that *change frequently* or remain *even*
and reach *high intensity* or *low intensity*
with *abrupt* or *gradual* transitions.

It is important to remember that these movement qualities operate together. Thus, we can consider the following simple movements in terms of aggregates of these qualities:[4] As mentioned in Table 4.1, hammering a nail into wood requires an alternation of abrupt bound and abrupt free movements done with high intensity. Throwing a baseball also entails a high-intensity, abrupt, bound movement followed by a high-intensity freeing movement. But, pushing a heavy object requires high-intensity movement that is also kept even, for if the object stops moving, if only for a moment, it takes increasing high-intensity force to get it started again. Not all actions are so strenuous, of course. Lifting a teacup requires gradually changing levels of low-intensity tension, held evenly for drinking, followed by a gradual decrease in intensity as it is placed back down. Waving a silk scarf requires low-intensity freeing movements with tension level fluctuations.

These movement qualities, important to adapting to various tasks, are equally significant when it comes to regulating affect and guiding interactions. That is, preferences for certain qualities of movement influence emotional expression and range. Evenness may appear calm or withdrawn, and high intensity can seem passionate or aggressive, while fluctuating tension can appear malleable and pliant or evasive.

DIMENSIONS OF MOVEMENT: THE *WHERE* OF MOVEMENT

Just as at birth infants show differences in the qualities of movement they use, they also show particular *dimensional inclinations* (Kestenberg-Amighi et al., 1999; Lamb, 1965; Lamb & Watson, 1979). This term refers to the dimensions in which the body most frequently shapes itself in space.

In this section, we examine in more detail each of the dimensions to enhance recognition of them in action. To start, when we observe babies, we can see right away that, as mentioned, some stretch out in length sooner after birth than others, who remain curled for a longer time. Those who stretch out in length use their *vertical* reach and push, or up–down dimension, most, while those who bring the head forward and curve the torso emphasize the *sagittal* or forward–backward dimension. Still other newborns may turn and twist a lot—the head and neck moving in one direction and the body facing another, moving and shaping their bodies in the *horizontal*.

---

[4] Some people find it helpful to visualize animals to illustrate these four categories of movement qualities: (a) A snake slithering through the grass is using mostly freeing tension except when it coils to strike—then it is binding; (b) a bird in flight is rhythmically changing levels of tension as it flaps its wings, a wriggling worm is constantly and irregularly changing tension, while a swan gliding is even in tension; (c) a monkey jumping up and down exhibits high intensity, but a butterfly slowly waving its wings as it sits on a flower exhibits low intensity; (d) a chicken walking uses abrupt changes of tension, as does a bat flying, while a bear's slower lumbering uses gradual changes in tension.

Horizontal *Spreading* and *Enclosing*

First, we note whether movement occurs as if along a flat surface such as a table, the floor, or the ground. In this dimension, the body twists, turns all the way around, or leans from side to side. This range of movement, such as, for example, when the body and head turn from side to side, can support the wide spread of attention. The opposite enclosing action also occurs in the horizontal plane, when the arms encircle and sweep inward, bringing actions and attention to the center.

A horizontal alignment of the body is seen as the body leans from one side to the other in sitting or standing. For example, a baby when nursing encloses the mother in his embrace but when distracted moves to spread his arms and turn his face by twisting and widening his body, so that his attention is opened out, making it difficult for him to nurse at the same time. Infants learn to bring their hands into their mouths through enclosing actions. When they learn to spread their arms, that spreading action helps them roll over. Twisting the torso in horizontal allows them to move from a sitting position into a crawling position. In speaking to a group, an adult spreads and widens the upper torso and gaze to take in several people at the same time. In the opposite action, the adult might enclose someone into a hug.

Vertical *Ascending* and *Descending*

In the vertical dimension, the body moves up and down as if along a door or ladder. The body lengthens and rises up to ascend or shortens and moves downward to descend.

A vertical alignment involves pushing down with the feet when standing or with the feet and pelvis when sitting and in both postures reaching upward with the head. A baby must use this alignment when learning to sit and, of course, to stand. Also, a baby reaches up with a fascinating object to share, lengthening his whole body as he reaches. Even before a baby can speak, she may make emphatic "remarks," lengthening her spine and babbling with lots of strength as she sits up or stands up straight.

Parents descend to talk to a young child face to face. A person may make a demand or disagree with descending movements such as banging a fist on the table and at the same time descending the upper body with added emphasis. We might ascend to present an object or an idea or offer approval.

Sagittal *Advancing* and *Retreating*

In the sagittal plane, the body moves along the same dimension as a wheel as it advances and retreats. For example, the midsection of the body may bulge forward or backward, affecting the organization of the whole body. That is, overall, the body alignment shapes to support the forward movement of face, chest, arm, or foot or to support the backward movement of the midsection, arm, or foot.

A baby advances into his mother's arms by reaching his arms and torso forward. When the hug is finished, the baby retreats by hollowing back. A father, by pulling himself back, retreats momentarily from his baby to better see her, then advances to swoop the child into his arms. In advancing, a baby enthusiastically reaches his arm and chest toward an enticing toy or retreats with apprehension at the advance of a stranger. As adults, we reach forward when we advance our ideas and agenda, and we pull back to allow others to offer theirs.

QUALITIES, DIMENSIONS, AND THE KINETIC TEMPERAMENT

In addition to using these specific dimensions as needed for specific tasks, bodies favor particular dimensions from the beginning of life—that is, one or two dimensions are used most often, rather than using all three equally. Thus, along with certain qualities, specific favored dimensions make up the kinetic temperament. These preferences involve different coordination of various muscle groups and results in different orientations toward action with objects and other people, as well as in different sensory, cognitive, and affective experiences.

The states of the body and the simultaneous subjective states are the basis for the prevailing characteristics of personality that we recognize and for the meanings that arise with these changing dimensions:

- In using the *horizontal* dimension, we can see that the body may relax more easily and diminish in muscle tension, spreading and yielding to gravity in horizontal. This often reduces the experience of boundaries between one person and another and between what is sensed as internal or external. Ease of flow and sensuality can follow. Spreading and enclosing in the horizontal can be the basis of giving and taking as well as accepting and refusing. In addition, movement in horizontal can assist exploration and communication, opening out to and then enclosing objects and other people. In action sequences, the horizontal dimension can be thought of as the first step, fostering the capacity to be in touch with one's body and the environment. One moves side to side to allow wide attention or turns the head to allow for sweeping interest. This body shaping works well with qualities of flow fluctuation, low-to-moderate intensity, and gradual changes of intensity that can allow sensations to more fully emerge.
- In establishing *verticality*, the body organizes around its center, cohering at midline and both pushing downward and reaching upward. Pushing and reaching in vertical require more bound muscle tension

so that the body's center and boundaries can be more distinctly felt. Ascending and descending are involved in lifting and letting down and, as such, in assessing the weight of objects. Movements of the body are both literal and metaphorical as in the following examples: lifting the chest in "rising to the occasion" or curling the head down over the chest, descending as one "looks deeply into oneself." Also, one can lift the whole body to rise above others and bend over others to either condescend or inspire and include. In action sequencing, the vertical would be the second step occurring as a focused thought or an impulse to act coalesces. This movement arises with a shift from a relative merger with the environment to a position of greater separateness, clarity, definition, and purpose. When this is happening, the body ascends or descends. The qualities that participate in this change may be an increase in intensity or a change to greater evenness that may occur abruptly or gradually. A sharper experience of "I" forms as wants, aspirations, aversions, needs, and interests coalesce into a point of view.

- To move in the *sagittal* dimension, the body organizes and shapes itself so that the torso narrows and extends the front body to move forward or the back body to move backward. As the torso shapes itself in either direction, it supports movements of the limbs in reaching or sweeping forward or backward. As the body leans away from its center of gravity, breathing and visual orientation and their subjective experience change. Advancing and retreating can be involved in initiating and doing or pulling back and assessing. We can move forward with confidence or trepidation or move back to reassess or withdraw in fear or defeat. We can plan ahead or act impulsively, step forward or hang back. This third step in the action sequencing is doing or operation—getting on with whatever was decided. A person who favors the sagittal can shape herself in readiness to advance toward or retreat away from an object or person. Here again, greater intensity in bound flow and abruptness in free flow might more frequently come into play when, for example, someone abruptly pulls back in surprise or gradually advances to initiate an activity.

Various movement qualities and dimensions are always combined. Imagine watching a baby using gradual, smooth, and frequent, irregular changes of tension as she squirms on the changing table by pushing and reaching with her head, arms, and tailbone or picture a very different baby's abrupt, sudden starts and stops, with frequently alternating tension, as she turns to get a toy by reaching, grasping, and pulling herself to one side and then twisting to the other side to sit upright again. Now, imagine another baby using gradually increasing and decreasing tension levels as she pushes and pulls to stand and then holds tightly to her parent with unchanging (even) levels of low or moderate intensity, while a different baby abruptly reaches forward and grasps a toy in spurts of high-intensity energy with binding tension and then, with freeing tension, eases back with the toy in hand.

As older infants, children, adolescents, and adults adapt to the demands of a variety of situations, they move through these sequences of action, employing all the dimensions. But at the same time, preferences show up in how we perform each action, in what parts of taking action we are most comfortable with, and in how we think about and make meaning from such actions. For example, a person's sagittal orientation may be obvious when she abruptly dives straight into intense conversation on meeting someone on the street and then just as abruptly turns to go. Another person's inclination to gradual and low-intensity tension changes in horizontal may show up when he gradually sidles up to someone and slowly engages in conversation. He may lean to one side in horizontal and in even, unchanging tension happily listen for a long time without needing to speak or change demeanor. A third person gets so excited and "heated up" (high-intensity quality) about many events during the day that he jumps up (vertical) and reaches forward (sagittal) to you and starts talking even before you have had a chance to say hello.

IMPLICATIONS FOR BABY–PARENT RELATIONSHIPS

In this chapter's cases we show both how movement inclinations emerge and develop in the first year and also how they are manifest in the adult parent. We also illustrate how extreme or entrenched differences between particular aspects of babies' and parents' individual movement repertoires can be problematic. Understanding this, psychotherapists can help parents see the movement differences between themselves and their child and support any needed changes by recognizing and working with movement inclinations to resolve the difficulties.

When psychotherapists and parents learn how to see an infant's kinetic temperament, they recognize that *how* any interaction takes place is important in and of itself to help babies remain comfortable, alert, and sociable—all states that are vital to the capacity to learn. In the context of problems that arise between parents and infants, psychotherapists using foundational movement analysis show parents how mismatches and matches in the use of a range of movement qualities and dimensions can either hamper or enhance physical attuning between baby and parent and the parent's understanding of her baby. Sometimes, differences in movement styles of parent and baby can make for helpful relationships because one party's movement inclinations can introduce new ways of behaving to the other. For example, a baby who uses high-intensity, abrupt movements in the vertical dimension can invite and encourage a low-intensity, even, and more horizontal (but fairly adaptable) parent to join a more energetic

The Three Dimensions of Space: Horizontal, Vertical, and Sagittal

Horizontal		
Physical: The body organizes in the side-to-side dimension; muscle tension reduces as one either spreads, leans, or twists and yields with gravity.	**Subjective:** There is a relative merger with the environment; boundaries between one and another and sensations of "inside" and "outside" are minimized.	**Functions:** Sensory exploration of body and surroundings; communing with others.
Vertical		
Physical: The body organizes around the midline using more bound muscle tension, cohering at the midline and lengthening up and down. In sitting and standing, the individual pushes his buttock bones and/or feet downward and reaches upward with spine and head.	**Subjective:** An impulse to act coalesces and there is greater separateness, clarity of body boundaries between one and another, and definition of purpose.	**Functions:** Arriving at, clarifying, and presenting a point of view.
Sagittal		
Physical: The body orients itself toward the front or back, and condenses in order to move in either direction. The reach toward or recoil from initiates from various parts of the body.	**Subjective:** Intentions are acted upon; awareness of goals and obstacles increases; doing is primary.	**Functions:** The individual moves towards and interacts with what he has selected or moves away from what he has rejected.

Figure 4.5 Here, we see similarities in four generations. The mother (far left) is vertical with a slight advance of her head and neck sagittally. The baby lengthens and ascends in vertical, and her grandmother, holding her, is also vertical. The great-grandmother, seated, is vertical and with a horizontal twist and slight lean of her head to the left.

Figure 4.6 Mother (right) and daughter (far left) advance with their heads sagittally to be close to the baby while retreating in their chests. The baby descends in vertical and encloses in horizontal.

Figure 4.7 The baby ascends, lengthening her spine in vertical and slightly spreading her arms in horizontal. The woman leans to the side in horizontal to make room for the baby and encloses her with her arms. The young girl retreats sagittally while leaning toward her mother in horizontal.

Figure 4.8 Both women lean toward the babies and each other in horizontal and enclose the babies. The baby, belly down, spreads horizontally through her chest. The seated baby both ascends in vertical and twists and leans in horizontal to touch her friend.

state that requires more clarity of intention (vertical). Needing to match his infant could expand the parent's repertoire of moving and feeling not only in interactions with his child but in other situations as well. And, as the baby develops, he can take in something of this parent's movement characteristics to help modulate his own. It is hoped that we can all stretch to new heights, or learn to soften our hard edges, and generally work to expand beyond our most familiar and practiced habits. When the earliest connecting to a baby's needs has been good enough, the baby, when it comes to adapting to others' movements and the needs they convey, can make that adjustment by actively participating.

Nevertheless, in helping a baby expand beyond her comfort zone, it is important to recognize that individual movement inclinations also determine how each baby copes with experiences that do not feel comfortable or quite safe but instead produce anxiety and stress. For example, one baby's movement inclinations help her to remain *even*, *moderately intense*, and *bound* in movements and emotional expression although the older children around her are raucously bouncing her on the bed. Under the same circumstances, another baby, a boy, with tendencies to be more *fluctuating* in muscle tension from *low* to *high intensity free flow*, cannot stabilize his own body in his comfort zone of *moderate intensity*, and he becomes distressed, screaming with fear. The first baby can be self-managing and self-soothing and therefore appears adaptable to the many different ways her parents and siblings may engage her. The second baby is less able at this early point to self-soothe and adapt to variations in the environment. The first baby seems to be able to handle more than the second, but she has not actually expanded her repertoire. She has just established that she can use her bound even flow to stay as calm as possible. The second baby has clearly signaled his distress, as if hoping it will create a change in how he is handled.

Focusing on movement inspires other kinds of questions, such as whether asking the first baby to cope is good for her, at what point the second baby might be helped to cope with more, and so on. Thus, expansion of repertoire—asking a baby to do what is not comfortable—must be done in measured doses with methods that are individually determined and must take account of the baby's comfort range as seen in movement qualities and dimensions in changing contexts. If the baby cannot adjust to her parents, along with problems of self-recognition and self-development, chaos and distress in the relationship may ensue. A less-adaptable parent, who is very low intensity and gradual, could find it almost impossible to match her baby's high-intensity abruptness and so, without help, be unable to provide the kind of stimulation her baby needs to feel well met enough of the time. In general, when parents cannot adjust their own movement repertoires to those of their baby, some strain on the baby's ability to trust and remain easily engaged begins to develop. If, instead of the parent, it is the baby who must make the needed movement adjustments to the parents' movement inclinations, life with baby may appear calm, but the baby's capacity to feel personal desires, and to trust and feel understood, may be undermined, leading to later difficulties in developing potential abilities and relationships.

Three cases are presented in this chapter to depict how three different families worked to understand their own and their babies' movement inclinations to the benefit of everyone in the family. In each case, it can be seen how differences in movement inclinations can become the basis for chronically uncomfortable situations. Over time, such interactions can result in problematic relational behaviors that have far-reaching impact. The first case is a detailed description drawn from videotaped interaction that was used to pinpoint the nonverbal miscommunications emerging early in this mother–baby relationship. This videotaped sequence was part of an ongoing psychotherapy. Once it is seen how to recognize movement inclinations in interaction, we move on to two case studies that depict how, as problematic movement differences and malcoordination between parent and baby are identified, the psychotherapist helps parents find more creative interactive options.

JANET, 30 YEARS, AND DANNY, 4½ MONTHS

R.F. has worked with Janet and her son, Danny, for several family sessions. "I try so hard, but I just don't get Danny's attention. Sometimes I don't think he wants to bother with me," she told R.F. in their initial meeting. Janet also thought that Danny was much more playful and responsive with his father and did not understand why he seemed less interested in her. Naturally, this was painful and confusing for her.

Early in the treatment, in an effort to get more information about the dynamics between Janet and Danny that both R.F. and Janet could see together, R.F. suggested that Janet make a videotape of their playtime.[5] What follows is a transcript of the video recording of Janet and Danny at home.

After first viewing the tape alone, R.F. then reviewed the tape with Janet in an individual session. Watching herself on tape enhanced Janet's ability to see those moments when her efforts with Danny contributed to the difficulties they were having and those moments when she could repair the disruption. With R.F.'s help, the integration of videotape into Janet's ongoing therapy allowed her to see herself with enough perspective that she was able to reflect more clearly on her actions with and reactions to Danny.

---

[5] In general, a home video is filmed with the camera operating automatically while sitting on a tripod. This is done so that there is no influence from a person behind the camera. Otherwise, the study appears more like a "home movie" rather than a more neutral document of the relationship. Usually, video recordings are taped anywhere from 5 to 15 minutes and show parent and baby playing, eating, bathing, or whatever else they want to capture on tape.

The Video Tape

Mother and baby have already been engaged for several moments as this video recording begins. Danny, 4½ months old, has awakened from his morning nap and has finished nursing. As the scene opens, Janet places Danny in his infant seat to spend some playtime with him.

Danny, thin and long limbed, sits directly facing Janet, whose body and face are round and full. Quietly resting, he gazes at her. Although he does not move his body much in his seat, his wide and bright eyes are active and seem to search Janet's face.

In contrast with Danny, who is sitting quite still, Janet is in constant motion and rapidly changes her posture. First, she lengthens her spine, stretching to her full height, then she suddenly drops her torso down, as if she were a popped balloon. Next, she shifts her weight from the right side of her pelvis to the left, creating a side-to-side rocking motion. No position is held for long as Janet makes her frequent changes.

Janet and Danny have different kinetic temperaments: Janet appears to hop about like a "bird on a wire," and Danny lounges like "a bear cub on a hot day"

"Hey, Danny, hey, Danny—what's happening?" Janet says, her speech rhythms in time with the rhythm of her moving body, upbeat and quick in tempo. She does not pause for Danny to respond but rather continues her cheery patter. Danny does not vocalize in return, but his eyes watch Janet's actions closely. The more Janet flits and abruptly shifts her position, the more Danny stills his body and maintains his even quality of movement, continuing to follow her with his eyes. Janet comes in closer, face to face, and as she does, her vocal rhythm accelerates and becomes more abruptly changing and bouncy.

Janet seems to be trying to stimulate Danny so that he will match her, rather than trying to match him. Danny is not quick to join his mother's liveliness, although Janet appears compelled to keep the action going between them.

In the video, Janet changes from her high-intensity, animated, and rapid vocalizing to a lowered, softer, gentler tone of voice, a bit slower and closer to Danny's lower intensity. "Ohhhh, I'm too speedy for you, huh?" she reflects. But suddenly, she raises her voice again, and it becomes as loud and quick paced as before. She says, "What'cha looking at? Do you want to play? Do you want to play?" As she says this, she thrusts her body forward and Danny startles, then freezes, and opens his eyes wider.[6] Janet does not seem to notice

---

[6] The startle response in a newborn is called the *Moro reaction*, present in the first 3 months of life. It is stimulated when the baby hears a loud noise or when the baby experiences a subtle shift of support of the head—back and downward in relation to the torso. The baby extends and then flexes the whole body, including arms and legs. A quick inhalation and then crying often accompany this reaction. At 3 months, the Moro reaction becomes integrated into the baby's developing nervous system, and the startle response is limited to the head and shoulder region alone. This response continues throughout our lives.

what has happened to Danny, and she repeats this question three or four times. Now, Janet has added a forward lurching movement to the frequent up-and-down and side to side shifts. Danny quickly blinks his eyes several times. He brings his hands together, and they clasp onto each other. Then, he looks down at them, gradually brings them to his mouth, and begins to suck. He looks up briefly at his mother and then resumes looking at his hands. His head remains down and his face softens, as if relaxing into the moment.

Danny seems unable to cope with Janet's abrupt forward lurching motion. He is caught off guard, and he startles. Janet does not notice his startle and repeated eye blinking.

Danny works with his own hands as a way to stay coherent and to cope with the excess stimulation. At his age, 4½ months, Danny is able to bring his hands together at his midline or the center of his body. At the same time, Danny curves his body in sagittal by flexing his neck and tucking his chin. Adults can feel soothed with this movement as their own bodies fold inward. It seems that Danny uses these movements to protect himself from his mother's high-intensity way of connecting with him. If Janet can learn from observing how Danny moves away from her, she can become better attuned to him. She is working from her own personal sense of play, but she is not tempering this with recognition of her baby's responses. Either Janet is not yet seeing Danny looking away or noticing him pulling away, or she does not understand that he is signaling, "Stop, this isn't what I want."

Janet sits farther back in her chair, but she continues her animated conversation with him. "Wanna go see daddy later? We can meet daddy for lunch later. Would'ya like that? We could go to his office. You like his office." At the same time, she abruptly reaches toward Danny, pulls his hands away from his mouth, and holds onto them.

Danny squirms in his chair, pulling his hands away from Janet and turning his head to the side. His mouth turns down, and his brows come together to create a furrow. Danny softly vocalizes his distress, "Ehhhhh!" Janet, still holding onto Danny's hands, seems not to notice the change in his face, posture, or vocal distress. She begins to play a game with him to liven him up. She moves his hands up and down and matches that rhythmic movement to her now more choppy vocal rhythm. "Here we go. Here we go," she repeats.

Growing more agitated, Danny pushes both hands with somewhat higher intensity against his mother's hands. Janet appears to think his pushing motion is part of the "game," and she pushes his hands back into his chest so that his elbows are flexed, and his arms are close to his body. Again, Danny pushes back against Janet's hands. He extends his elbows and then, once he is done, manages to pull his hands away from her. Now, Danny pops two freed and fisted hands back into his mouth and sucks them rapidly, with his head downcast.

It took Danny some time to build up to that clear expression of his need for distance. His movement inclination is to gradually build to medium or high intensity and then to slide slowly to low intensity. This shift is like a slow wave, unlike Janet's much quicker waves, with their peaks of higher intensity.

Since he has pulled away his hands, Janet now becomes interested in Danny's feet and swings his legs from side to side. Her vocal rhythm slows and gentles, and her voice echoes a feeling that matches his distress. "Ahhhhhh, what happened? What's the matter, Danny?" Danny now abruptly flexes both legs into his body and pushes them out and toward her with higher intensity than previously seen. He does this several times until Janet finally releases his feet. "Oh, I get it. You don't like mommy to hold your legs. Okay. I'm sorry. I won't do that. I got a little ahead of you." Danny looks down, and his head and torso curve forward in sagittal. Janet suddenly freezes as she looks at her son, then sits back in her chair.

Janet appears still uncertain about what to do, but she is now following Danny's signals about what not to do. Her statement, "I got a little ahead of you," indicates the shift in her understanding of Danny's inclinational preferences. His pattern of folding over and losing tone is also an emotional state, an affective evaluative sense of the situation—in this case, for Danny, "not good." As observing adults, we cannot know exactly what Danny is feeling, but we can tune in to some extent and mirror what Danny is doing. Then, we might feel similar sensations of an internalized downward pressure or sense of emptiness.

Now, Danny brings his hands to his mouth and begins sucking them. Janet slowly leans forward in her chair and says softly and with a lower-intensity cadence, "Danny, you just love to suck your hands." She pauses for a while and watches Danny, then says, "I see how interesting they are to you." Danny lifts his head and looks up at her. When she catches his eyes, Janet mirrors his movements and now also stays closer to his movement qualities. Sucking on her own two hands, she says, "Well, I understand now. They do taste soooo gooood. Yum. Yum." Danny pops his hands out of his mouth and quickly extends his arms to the side, widening his chest. He tentatively smiles. With the same soft cadence to her voice and low-intensity rhythm, Janet replies, "Oh, here's a little smile. That's a very nice one," and she smiles in return.

Janet now has let Danny take the lead, and she follows him more slowly and with less intensity. At the moments when Danny sees his mother seeing him, the rapport is repaired. At Danny's point in development, and given his personal capacity for resilience, he has been able to weather the disruption and stay close enough to his mother so that reestablishing their connection is possible and rewarding. These kinds of reparative moments will serve them well as they continue learning about each other.

Discussion

We have seen how Janet relied on her familiar and preferred movement qualities—high intensity, abrupt, and fluctuating flow—particularly when she appeared at a loss regarding what to do next. When Danny did not respond to her, she exaggerated her familiar and preferred qualities.

For his part, up against his mother's pushes and pulls, Danny at first used what was most available in his repertoire—low intensity and even tension—to help him bear what was difficult for him, but then he increased his intensity to abruptly pull away from his mother. The moment when Danny lost tone and folded his body was his effort to shut out his mother's high-intensity stimulation, but it also served as a signal to Janet. Finally, she recognized her son's signal and could reflect on the situation and then adjust herself to Danny's kinetic temperament.

With several more sessions and after this video was made and reviewed, Janet understood how to adjust her actions to better meet Danny's needs. As Danny developed, Janet also learned when her more animated, high-intensity, and abrupt qualities were useful to Danny to help him add some variation and animation to his low-intensity, more even style. In exchange, Janet found that Danny's manner was calming to her at times when she felt agitated. Every member of a family has something unique to offer one another in terms of their capacity to expand on preferred patterns and explore different options. When therapy concluded, Danny and Janet were well on their way to working out comfortable connections with one another that would foster good communication, mutual understanding, and empathy.

RUTH, 33 YEARS, ALAN, 35 YEARS, AND BETH, 8 MONTHS

Ruth and Alan bring their baby, Beth, for a consultation with F.L. They are concerned because Beth is 8 months old and not yet crawling, neither on her belly nor on her hands and knees. Ruth is afraid that her baby will skip crawling and move right to walking. She worries about this because she heard that a baby who cannot creep or crawl might have difficulties learning to read.[7]

Ruth says that she does not know what to do with Beth anymore when she needs to leave the room or just turn her attention to something else. "She sounds as if she needs something, and she sounds so upset that I come back right away." Ruth says that until recently she was carrying Beth around in a baby carrier, but this strategy is no longer working since she is getting too heavy to carry; moreover, Beth wants to be down on the floor playing. Both parents agree that Beth's favorite activity is jumping up and down on their laps while they hold her hands or support her under her arms. "We can always count on this to make her happy," they say, "so we find ourselves playing this game all the time."

---

[7] See Footnote 3 of Chapter 3 for a discussion about the importance of crawling for later development.

Although initially Alan had been skeptical of Ruth's concerns, he has come to agree with her. "Beth is so active. She sits very well, and loves to play on her tummy or on her back. She reaches for toys that she can get to, but she doesn't seem to be progressing to any sort of locomotion," he tells F.L. Both parents confess that they are also very dismayed by what they see growing in Beth's personality—they feel as if they are being "bullied" by her and do not know how to change things.

Although many babies roll over and crawl before this age, Beth's pediatrician was not concerned about her progress. Her parents, however, were puzzled. If we did not understand the movement characteristics that comprise a baby's innate preferred range, we might be tempted to think that Ruth and Alan have "spoiled" Beth by holding her upright, carrying her too often, and responding too quickly to her complaints. In fact, we will see that the picture is more complicated, starting with Beth's limited movement range, which derives from her strongly preferred and now almost exclusive use of the vertical dimension. As we shall see, not only does Beth have a point of view that she insists on but also she is, to some extent, trapped in it.

F.L. suggests that her parents place Beth on the floor on her tummy. Beth immediately grasps, examines, and chews on any toys she can reach. Then, she lifts her arms and feet off the floor and into the air and rocks back and forth on her tummy while making gleeful noises. But when she gets tired of this, she does not appear able to change her position or reach for new toys because she cannot yet turn over or crawl. Seeing this, F.L. next suggests that Ruth turn Beth to her back. When she is on her back, Beth demonstrates the same movement pattern as she stretches her body out in length and pushes her feet down against the floor. This action causes her to arch her back and raise her bottom up to create "the bridge," as this position is known in yoga. The adults all comment on how well she does this and how very active she is in each position. F.L. says, "Just as she can't move from her tummy to her side and back, she is equally unable to shift from this position on her back to her side or tummy. All of Beth's movements are in the vertical dimension. She lengthens, but she doesn't twist or curl."

Ruth says that Beth enjoys sitting up as well. As Alan takes Beth's hands to move her to sitting, she immediately plays the game she is used to and pushes her feet onto the floor to stand, using Daddy's hands for support. F.L. says, "There she is again enjoying the vertical—this time standing up." Alan must gently bend Beth's hip joints with his hands to help her into a sitting position. Once there she again stretches up—vertically—through her back and neck and widens (horizontal) by holding her arms and hands up near her shoulders. Beth notices a toy in front of her and directs her intense gaze toward it; at the same time, with the impulse to follow it, her torso abruptly moves just a little bit forward (sagittal), and her foot jabs out and knocks the toy diagonally, so it is slightly off to one side and just beyond her foot. With slow, even, careful movements, Beth slightly turns her eyes, head, and neck toward the toy (horizontal). She tracks it, but she does not engage her whole body in turning and following it. She repeats these actions several times. Her movement is like that of a clockwork toy in its regularity and even tension. "It's very clear here," F.L. says, "how much Beth relies on vertical and how little able she is to use the horizontal twisting and sagittal forward and backward dimensions at the same time."

Some babies, who move side to side (horizontal dimension) with more fluctuating tension or, alternately, reach with various parts of their bodies frontward (sagittal), in a burst of freeing flow, might go so far that they fall over in their impulse to reach for the ball. But Beth, tall and elegant, remains very long (vertical), holding (even) and binding (bound, high intensity) her body straight up as she pulls one shoulder ever so slightly back to turn in horizontal and promptly returns to her front-facing vertical position. She shows us her persistent attention (even, bound flow) to what she wants and her limited range of movement (vertical only) that inhibits her from getting it.

At this point, Beth begins to "talk" to us: With her arms bent, she shakes them vertically up and down abruptly and sits up even straighter as she makes some clear, vehement exclamatory sounds: "Eh! Eh! Eh!" Alan says they always interpret this behavior as Beth's wish "to do something different," and this is what is beginning to worry them. Both parents identify this as her "regal" quality, which makes them jump to her demands. Whenever she does this, Ruth and Alan attend to her. "On the one hand," F.L. concurs, "she's a baby and can't get it herself, and on the other hand, something is making you uneasy about her manner."

Like most parents, Ruth and Alan initially did not mind attending closely to Beth's needs. It is necessary and beneficial for parents to join a baby's pattern since the baby is completely dependent and requires the loan of their more able bodies. They helped Beth follow her pleasure as they wanted and needed to. But having drifted along with their first attunement to Beth's innate movement preferences, they have inadvertently reinforced its overemphasis.[8] *Now, they are frustrated with what feels to them like*

---

[8] Beth's example shows how procedural memory (Solms & Turnbull, 2000) has already come to incorporate her innate patterning and her interactions with her parents. This means that she has formed action patterns that include the way she interacts with her parents, their feelings about her, and her feelings about them. There are many components to memory, and procedural memory is one of the first. It is the locus of "how to's"—that is, the ways baby and parents do things together from diapering to feeding, to playing with a ball or a toy piano. This aspect of memory includes the baby's sensations and emotions and the parents' actions that arise during these activities along with the know-how that also derives from action. The baby comes to expect the same sensations and emotions when such an activity is approached. This is why a baby can quiet when the baby hears her mother's or father's voice after a nap: The baby knows to expect that they are coming and that they will play with her; the baby can imagine the sequence of actions to come by drawing on procedural memory. But, it is also why another baby might cry on hearing bathwater running, and it might take some doing to help this baby get over these fears and the early discomfort that quite quickly can become habitual.

bullying "demands" coupled with Beth's inability to master the next stage of motor development. Although Ruth and Alan are alert, attentive, and sensitive parents, they lack the knowledge they need to see what Beth's problem is and how to address it.

To help her parents help Beth expand her movement range and action programs, F.L. has them observe their own dimensional preferences. They notice that Ruth uses the horizontal as she twists and sweeps from side to side when shifting her attention from one person or object to another, while Alan moves more directly toward and away from a person as he speaks or reaches for something. Thus, although she does not use the vertical, Ruth moves most extensively in the sideways horizontal dimension, and Alan uses both up–down vertical and forward–backward sagittal directions.

Next, F.L. has Ruth and Alan imitate Beth's way of moving so that they can imagine what she might be feeling. As they discuss their differences from Beth, they realize why it has been difficult for them to understand Beth's particular struggle with her present limited physical range—they could not easily feel what it is like to be Beth. But, when they imitate her actions and feel her one dimensionality in their own bodies, they begin to get a sense of what she feels and how she became trapped by her own preference and their inadvertent reinforcement of it. F.L. says, "At this point, Beth's body does not tell her how to do the next step, for which she needs other dimensions." In addition, F.L. developed with Ruth, Alan, and Beth ways of playing that could help her expand in other dimensions.

They start by putting on music and swaying from side to side and wiggling more quickly as the tempo increases. Beth mirrors them, at first tentatively, as seeing Mommy and Daddy "dance" is a new experience. But, soon she is imitating them and adding fluctuation and horizontal movement as she does so. As her parents sing and dance with her and hold her hands to help her wiggle and twist, Beth softens her high-intensity binding. "Peek-a-boo" games in which Mom or Dad scuttles to her side and behind her to the other side help her twist in the horizontal as she follows them with her eyes and head and then with her torso. They do this while she sits up as well as when she is lying on her back, keeping the game fun and not teasing and always observing her reactions to gauge how she feels. After a short time and with this kind of play, Beth is crawling, able to move from sitting to all fours and back as well. Ruth and Alan comment that once she started twisting she easily got herself on all fours, then the rest seemed to follow without too much struggle.

Discussion

Beth has been trapped in her innate preference for the vertical dimension. Her parents could not see this because they perceived it as a problem of character rather than a physical dilemma. They could only imagine that she *liked* being bossy, and that she was becoming a "monster," as Alan said when he compared Beth to a friend's son who seemed more helpless. Beth's parents learned that she was not enjoying calling out for help—or "being bossy." Instead she was using the strongest actions from her repertoire that had so far worked to deal with her frustration. Instead of fussing, whimpering, and flopping (free-flow fluctuating, horizontal), she makes strong "statements" (vertical self-definition) of her needs that sound to her parents like demands.

In the sessions that follow, F.L. encouraged Ruth and Alan to play with Beth in ways that could help her add new movement dimensions and qualities to her repertoire.

Beth appeared to greatly enjoy the new options at her disposal, and her mother and father were relieved. Ruth and Alan expressed that they felt more confident now that they could help Beth recognize when her favorite methods of coping—sitting up straight and making demands—did not help her. Ruth observed that Beth continued to sit up straight and make demands at times, but equally important, she added, "I am not intimidated or worried by this—I get that she is frustrated, and I can engage her and encourage her to get a toy by herself."

ROBERTA, 38 YEARS, TOM, 43 YEARS, AND MARTIN, 10 MONTHS

F.L. first sees Roberta and Tom without Martin for a session because Roberta says that Martin is "too much of a handful to bring along." Roberta gradually, and with low-intensity flow fluctuation, strolls into the office, moving sideways first to put down her coat, and then strolls to the other side of the office to sit on the couch. She leans sideways to her right on the arm of the couch. As Tom enters with similar movement qualities, he reaches his head forward slightly (sagittal) using a straighter path than Roberta's. Similar to Roberta, he sits against the other arm of the couch and then also leans (horizontal) on a pillow. Roberta's and Tom's movement qualities are free flowing, with very gradual shifts and low intensity: Each moves like a cat on a warm windowsill. She moves mostly side to side (horizontal), and even her forward movements in space are done leading with her left side to maintain a sideways orientation. When she speaks, her tones and rhythms of speech change as her body does, yielding and changing tension levels smoothly. Her husband, Tom, uses more energy at times (higher intensities), exhibits more use of his muscle strength (bound flow), and more sagittal and vertical movement, but there is also a great deal of overlap between him and his wife: Both give the impression of ease, relaxation, and gradually changing tension levels.

Roberta reports that at first everything with Martin seemed to go very smoothly: "I did not mind accommodating to Martin's wishes—he needs what he needs. I fed him on demand, and it's easier for me to have him sleep with Tom and me. It seemed like everything was going fine." Tom says, "I tend to be 'the auxiliary' and leave the baby to Roberta, except now and then, I'm the entertainment." Roberta says, "That worked fine with our daughter, who was and is an easy child for me. But Martin is another story—I really need help. But so far, nothing is helping." "Every day is a new trial," Roberta explains. "Martin is 10 months old, but he's still completely unpredictable. He's not regular in any of his habits—feeding, napping, evening bedtimes, or eliminating. And now that he is mobile, he is getting into everything and needs constant attention so that he doesn't get injured." Roberta despairs that she and Martin haven't progressed from the patterns that were set in his early infancy.

F.L. decides to observe Martin and his parents at their home because both parents believe he will be too much to handle in the office.

When F.L. arrives, Martin is just finishing nursing, Roberta says, "for the fourth time in 3 hours." He pops off her nipple with a jerk and drops off his mother's lap. He does not look at F.L. He rapidly and smoothly creeps on all fours away from Roberta, never visually checking back to her, moving with a fast and even, strong pace toward a pile of toys in the middle of the floor. Roberta fumbles as she adjusts her bra, pulls her shirt down, and slowly and gently curls her upper body over her lower body. Then, she moves herself off the chair and across the floor with an octopus-like sideways rolling and sliding movement, following Martin, who is already across the room, rummaging through the toys that are strewn about.

Martin suddenly bangs both hands on a pop-up toy with high-intensity, abrupt movements of his whole arm. He misses the button that would open the pop-up figure as often as he hits it because he is not looking at what he is doing. He appears more involved with the hitting action than in anything else he might want from the toy. Roberta moves in closer to show him how to be more accurate. She uses her own low-intensity, gradual, catlike approach to touch one button, then another, but Martin does not seem to notice her. Instead Martin moves away to a toy bear and begins lifting it and bashing it to the ground repeatedly. Roberta again follows, watching him, and she remains in her soft curl, retreated in sagittal, softly talking to Martin. She says, "Pat the bear, Martin, say, 'Nice bear.'" Martin appears oblivious to her and moves from the bear to a series of other items, repeating the same up-and-down bashing movement, until he lets one toy fly, and it careens across the room. Martin appears surprised at first and then throws a plastic block and laughs. At this point, Roberta moves in, gently telling Martin, "We don't throw toys." He does not look at her or appear to hear her, but he moves again toward another toy that he picks up and bangs.

Martin offers his mother no reciprocity. He never seems to "ask" for anything or wait for her to reply. He sits up or stands and screams for what he wants, and he is always at his limit, where frustration overtakes him and he cries unless he gets what he wants. Roberta has not developed an effective movement exchange with Martin, with turn-taking, mutual respect, and recognition. This is in part because she has not been able to match Martin's strong, abrupt movement qualities or his use of the vertical dimension, both of which we have just seen. Martin uses all three dimensions as needed but has a preference for vertical. Moreover, Martin has dominated Roberta—she has given him her body and her mind, as a mother must do in early infancy, for some period of time. She thought that all she had to do was "to give Martin everything he needed," and he would outgrow his infant needs. But, he continues in his earliest infantile state and cannot learn from Roberta, and Roberta feels increasingly oppressed and ignored.

Martin finds a box with colored shapes inside it that match the square, triangular, and circular openings in the box top. Swiftly moving from crawling to sitting up straight, he bangs on the box and shakes it up and down in his characteristic way. He is frustrated because he cannot remove the top. He begins to make "growling" sounds as he struggles with the box. Roberta slides sideways over toward him and insinuates herself between him and the box as she begins to remove the lid. But, Martin "growls" with sustained, high-intensity sounds that express angry frustration and abruptly pounces and impatiently grabs the box away from her. She slowly and patiently says, "Martin, I'm trying to help." Martin ignores her and continues growling and grabbing. Roberta lets him hold the box as she squirms in between him and the box to get the lid off, so that it is not clear to Martin that she is doing anything except getting in his way. Once the lid is off, Martin again bangs the box upside-down, scattering the toys all over the room. Roberta, without a word to Martin, gathers the shapes and brings them to him. She wrestles the box top from him and puts it back on the box, now saying, "Here, Martin, let me show you how to play." She begins putting toys in the container, matching the shapes to the openings in the top. Martin gets interested and grabs a yellow square from the floor. He begins trying each of the openings, finds the right one, and pushes the shape through with a clunk. Next he grabs a triangle and finds it more difficult to match. He tries several times, using more force each time he fails. Roberta tries to show him how to turn the piece in the right direction, but he does not shift his attention to her so that he can see what she is doing. He becomes more and more agitated, throws the piece, and then throws himself face down, crying loudly. Roberta picks him up, and he grabs her breast under her shirt without looking at her. Roberta's face shows her disapproval, and she says, "Now Martin, you just got finished nursing." But, as before, he does not look at her face or appear to hear her words, but just avidly pulls at her as she positions him on her lap and surrenders to his demand.

Martin did not look at Roberta in an appeal for help or in recognition of his helplessness. It was as if he did not recognize her as separate from himself but just assumed his control over her. Roberta did not sustain her brief effort to express her frustration with what Martin was doing but found a way to let him keep doing what he wanted while she squirmed to adapt to it.

F.L. reports her observations about Roberta and Martin's movement interaction. Roberta is quick to understand the pattern and the essential differences between her and Martin.

At the next visit, Roberta brings Tom into the room so that they can work together to change what has become a difficult family situation. Martin bangs a stuffed toy on the floor, and Roberta and Tom do the same thing with other toys. F.L. suggests that they try imitating Martin's rhythm with some noises and movement. All three of them bouncing toys up and down is indeed a funny sight, and for a moment Martin smiles—something he does rarely. But, he soon loses interest and goes back to ignoring his parents as he prowls for something different to handle. They follow him, and F.L. demonstrates how they can comment on what he is doing, using their vocal tones and patterns to mirror his actions and qualities. They say, with rhythmic strong emphasis, "So, *now* you are *fin*ished with *that* gi*raffe* and you *want* something *dif*ferent!" They use high-intensity—loud, strong—sounds, emphasizing some syllables, moving in a beat that is like Martin's. At first, Martin looks down and stops what he is doing when these new sounds occur. Next, he looks up at the speaker.

After several home sessions in which we repeat these kinds of experiences, Martin is more "related" to his parents in rhythm, movement, and now, facial gaze. He looks at them much more often and appeals to them more directly for help.

During a play session with us, Martin struggles with a puzzle. His father tries to help him and shows him how to turn a piece to fit, but Martin does not attend and throws himself down on the floor in frustration. His mother moves in to hold him, he grabs for her shirt, and F.L. suggests that Tom pick him up instead.

Tom needs to become a more active participant in Martin's care. For one thing, Tom's greater involvement will allow Martin to develop a more satisfying relationship with him. In addition, Tom's active participation will help Martin and Roberta find a more distinct and much-needed separation from each other.

Martin cries and kicks when he realizes what is happening, but F.L. suggests that Tom persist and sends Roberta out of the room. Tom, in this new situation, is at a loss. He puts Martin down on the floor and gets down with him, calling his name and mirroring Martin's vocal and movement tones and intensities. "Martin, *hey*, Martin—let's *play*, look—here we *go!*" He picks up a stuffed toy and bumps it on the floor, then pokes Martin just a little with it, which brings Martin's wet face up to meet his. He bounces the toy up and down and then adds his own body bouncing to it. Martin's distress begins to ease, and Martin actually mirrors the jumping and bumping of the toy and his father's body, first with his arms and then with his upper body. This is very exciting for Tom and F.L. and a first for Martin. His father hands him the toy and grabs another so that they can bump the toys together. Martin laughs briefly and moves off to find something else with his father at his side.

Discussion

Sometimes differences in movement are so great that they become extremely difficult to bridge and demand quite a lot of work for parents. Roberta had to learn deliberately and practice how to match Martin. Tom also shared some movement and dimensional qualities with Martin, but because his range was more limited than Martin's and because he had been "out of the action" for so long, matching Martin required intentional reengagement as well.

This family went through a stormy time as they intervened to change patterns that had been overaccommodating to Martin's demands. They recognized the necessity of Roberta asserting herself as a separate person and the consequent need to help Martin cope with the sense of loss of control that is inevitable and necessary. Tom became very important in this process. Both parents had two jobs. First, they needed to learn to move more like Martin and to find their own high-intensity strength to match and surpass his. Moving in this way, they were able to help Martin pay attention to them. Then, as the second task, they helped Martin gradually learn to attune to their actions and qualities and recognize their needs as different from his own, but bridgeable.

Chapter 5

Embodied History

INTRODUCTION

In previous chapters, we showed how fundamental movements and movement inclinations are integrated within action patterns that develop in relationships from the beginning of life. In this and the next two chapters, we examine how these action patterns continue to emerge and evolve in adult life and constitute what we call *embodied history*. Here, we examine embodied history in parenting a baby; in Chapter 6, we examine in relating as a couple, and in Chapter 7, in the interactions of adult psychotherapy.

With the term *embodied history*, we emphasize each individual's movement patterns and attendant felt bodily sense within present interactive patterns as well as the enduring relational themes[1] these patterns reveal. Embodied history describes how a current interaction within a specific circumstance, dynamically similar to one in the past, elicits the emergence of action patterns that were shaped at that earlier time. All present experience involves recurrent actions since we are always using our well-practiced repertoire to operate in the present, making the past perennially part of the here and now. Action is an integral part of how we perceive, engage with, and make meaning of our world. Recall that perception itself is guided by the sensing of what one can do with an object or person (Iacoboni, 2008; Rizzolati & Sinigalia, 2008; Schore, 1994; Solms & Turnbull, 2000). Relying on embodied history, then, is part of every moment.

As we saw in Chapters 1 through 4, babies' movement patterns are cocreated with their parents and other important caregivers. First, each baby comes into the world able to move well in certain ways and not as well in others. Parents who are sensitive to their baby's movement proclivities, as well as skillful and flexible enough in their own action patterns, can both respect their baby's movement range and gradually introduce variations in new movement possibilities to meet situations that demand them. In some

---

[1] The phrase *enduring relational themes* was coined by Lynne Jacobs (2000) in relation to the historic experiences that emerge in the present in psychotherapy.

instances, however, parents are not able to access the range of movement necessary to adjust to their baby's movement needs, or they are unable to help the baby expand her movement repertoire as needed. If this is so, the outcome for the baby may be a limited and inflexible movement repertoire.

As most parents know, it is unimaginable to try to parent a child without doing something one's parents did, trying to avoid something they did, or trying to do something they neglected to do. This is not a problem in itself since we could not function at all without the frame of reference provided by the patterns we have developed in earlier relationships, including those passed down from parent to child in each new generation. From the interactions shaped by their responses to day-to-day handling, children absorb the many ways their parents carry out the tasks of childrearing. As part of that process, many children absorb their parents' embodied attitudes that convey how to be dedicated to, respect, and care for another person. Later in life, when they take care of their own children, these primary relational and embodied experiences move to the forefront, enriching their present experience.

Embodied history is manifest not only in the daily care and myriad choices parents make in handling their babies but also in less noticed, but still powerfully affecting, patterns of parents' breathing, moving, gesturing, posture, and gait. For example, a parent might explicitly recognize that he feels comforted and soothed when he rocks his baby, but the historical aspect of this experience is nevertheless implicit, sensed only in the tenderness and ease he experiences and expresses as he gently rocks and cradles his baby. He may have no clearly formulated idea about the meaning or shape of his actions, aware only of the pleasure in his felt bodily experience. His pleasure is part of what his baby experiences and in turn becomes an aspect of his baby's embodied history. Another parent might nurture her child well and at the same time feel sad, without being able to name her yearning or identify her memory of feeling inadequately nurtured. This kind of experience also might remain implicit and appear only in the way she, at times, hollows her chest, dropping it down and back, in her shallow breathing, and in her occasional difficulty shifting her body to meet and mold to the baby's body. Her baby, in reacting to her mother's variations of response, creates a repertoire of personal movement responses to meet those of her mother. As Selma Fraiberg (L. Fraiberg, 1987; S. Fraiberg, 1959/1996) first pointed out three decades ago, another parent, unmindful of his own disastrous childhood, simply does not feel the impact of his child's cries any more than he can feel his own. His child will then develop his own record of this neglect, a variation on the theme.

All of these emergent aspects of embodied history are experienced and expressed in the parents' fundamental movements and movement inclinations. Appearing now in action patterns coconstructed with their own babies, these movements are a crucial part of the story that is being told and retold in the acts of parenting that are always part of the new family scene.

Parents' action repertoires are a combination of actions that have become stable, reliable, predictable, familiar, and routine and those that support flexibility and spontaneity. The latter aspects of repertoire arise from experiences that allow improvisation, experimentation, and play. The ability to improvise is needed most when a parent's actions do not match her baby's patterns often enough. At these times, the routine ways of tending to and relating to her baby need to be questioned and modified. Without change in these instances, the safety, comfort, and pleasure of their relationship are threatened, creating escalating difficulties. But, even when parenting is going well enough, in the context of uncertainty that every birth brings, recognizing the movement dimensions of even small stumbling blocks that individual parents encounter can be an opportunity for new discovery about themselves and their relationships with each other as well as with their baby.

In engaging a parent and baby, a psychotherapist is explicitly or implicitly trying to influence the evolution of movement patterns. The earliest developing interactive patterns can and often do evolve over time to satisfactorily incorporate ways for an individual's needs to be met while attending to the needs of others. This happens through the elaboration of fundamental movements and movement inclinations as the body grows and changes, while the baby or child learns to cope with new and increasingly complex circumstances. Action patterns also evolve throughout life when, in meeting new challenges, people either rearrange routine sequences of movement in new ways or can call on movement elements outside their comfort range to develop different approaches to familiar and novel situations. Too often, however, people find themselves struggling, unable to rearrange what they do or to find a new set of actions. In these circumstances, using their routine repertoire does not allow them to engage easily with others and frequently brings only pain and insupportable suffering, such as when a parent cannot comfortably play with his baby.

In each of the case studies depicted here, we demonstrate how the embodied history emergent in the movement patterns that arise in caring for a baby leaves parents unable to respond creatively in adapting to their child. Each of the following case studies is about a parent who as baby or as a child was not well-enough met in the movement patterns of her parents, and all that they entailed, and who subsequently finds it difficult to access the creativity necessary to parent her child. Complex historical determinants are at work and cannot be addressed, as previously, simply by clarifying the baby's fundamental movements (Chapter 3) or by identifying a clash of movement inclinations (Chapter 4). These parents require more than the identification of missing movement elements and instruction to facilitate needed changes in their relationships to their babies. Although our methods—a psychoanalytic approach in the first case study and a gestalt approach in the second—are different, we each work from our understanding of how recognizing action patterns both enhances diagnosis of a problem and facilitates treatment.

HELEN, 34 YEARS, AND ROBBIE, 8 MONTHS

Helen came into treatment with F.L. because she felt increasing distress in parenting her first child, Robbie. The following vignettes are taken from different points during Helen's treatment, which lasted several years and involved parenting guidance integrated within psychoanalytic psychotherapy.

Vignette I: Helen and Robbie

"As you can see, Robbie has begun crawling and he is into everything," Helen says as she follows Robbie around F.L.'s office. Helen's knees are bent and her body is tilted forward at the hips. Her hands hang down limply toward Robbie as she hovers over him. She speaks quietly and precisely and uses only occasional small, abrupt, low-intensity gestures of her hands and head. Apart from these few gestures, and apart from when she is interacting with Robbie, Helen's movement is minimal and stays at an even, low intensity of tension; she appears still. With a similarly flattened tone, she describes her dilemma: "Now all I do all day is follow him about. I don't know if that's the right thing to do. I don't get anything else done anymore. He is napping, but only in short spells. I wonder, is this just a temporary problem, or is there something wrong with me or with him?"

F.L. senses herself leaning forward, too, as she watches Robbie's high-intensity activity. She tells Helen that parents often feel just this way when very active babies begin locomotion. She reframes Helen's question: "The question might be asked, 'What does Robbie need from you at this point and how can you address that need in a way that will help you be together as comfortably as possible?'"

F.L. sees how immobile Helen is except when following Robbie; Helen's stillness appears neither to express nor hold back any impulses of her own. F.L. feels concerned without yet knowing why. She believes that there is a problem here, but at the same time she believes it would not help Helen to think in those terms.

F.L. asks if Robbie ever stops to play with toys. Helen answers, "No, he used to, but now he goes on like this until he becomes quite exhausted. And even then he does not want to stop, and so he fusses and begins falling. As she says the words, Robbie cries and falls, but when Helen picks him up, he pushes his hands against her.

When his mother puts him down again, Robbie stands upright (pushing down to ascend in vertical) and holds the couch with one hand as he reaches one foot and then the other to draw forward (advancing in sagittal). Soon he cries again. Helen remains bent over Robbie, ready to catch him if he falters, but she frequently looks away from him and toward F.L. Helen appears increasingly flustered, unable to decide what to do next.

Robbie tends to move forward and upward only in the sagittal and vertical dimensions. He neither twists nor bends his spine sideways in the horizontal. Along with the development of the horizontal dimension can come greater flexibility, a wider approach to exploration, and openness to alternatives. In Robbie we see ceaseless high-intensity, evenly sustained movement forward that appears in this instance to be the embodiment of a determination not to be deflected. It is difficult to be sure about Helen's full range of motion, since she is always bent forward, descending in vertical, hovering over Robbie, and following him. But it is clear that at this point Helen does not attempt alternative actions with Robbie.

F.L. asks Helen what she would prefer to see happen right now. Helen, still bent over Robbie, answers with questions: "Should I try to get him interested in something so that he'll settle down for a while? Do you think he will be a problem child who stands on the furniture?" F.L. feels her own back tighten as she listens.

F.L. does not always feel reluctant to answer parents' questions or encourage them to think about problems themselves. But with Helen, she finds herself quite uncertain about whether to answer her questions or address Helen's desire for her to do so. For the moment, she counter-questions:

"What keeps you from trying to interest him in something else to see what would happen if you did?" Helen quietly responds, "I guess I feel like I don't want to interfere with what he's doing. It feels like that would be wrong. I want him to have a very good sense of himself." Helen is quiet for a moment. Looking down, she adds, "He never seems to want to do anything I want him to do." F.L. remarks that Helen seems sad about that. Helen replies, "I suppose I am. I feel I'm not doing something right, and so he is not very happy with me."

In fact, Robbie seems quite happy, even gleeful except when forced to stop moving. Helen's worry that he doesn't want to do what she wants to do seems to come from something other than the present situation. She worries all the time, and that does create a striking mismatch and emotional disconnection equally evident in their movement. The two seem lost to each other: Helen in her slavish, worried following and Robbie in the exhilaration of his actions without her as a reference point. In watching their interaction, F.L. notices herself tightening with increased bound and even intensity. Feeling fidgety and barely breathing, F.L. realizes that she is holding back from her own impulses to intervene to effect a better physical and emotional connection between mother and son. The implications of Helen's way of framing her dilemma seem to be, "If I have a say, Robbie will be over-controlled and lose all sense of himself, just as I have somehow."

Wanting more information, F.L. asks Helen, "What do you sense in your body now and how do you feel?" Helen replies, "I feel worried and bad. I'm tired, but I also feel guilty and foolish. I think I should know what to do. There is something wrong with me, I'm sure of it. That's what Phil, my husband, thinks. He thinks I'm hopeless. He thinks I'm just spoiling Robbie."

Before F.L. can respond, Robbie slides down from the couch and crawls quickly to the other side of the room, where he tries to get behind a large easy chair in a corner, where there are lamp wires and dust. Helen follows him and moves a lamp and table out of the way so that he can easily get behind the chair.

Here Helen facilitates inappropriate access, distorting the realities of safety to allow Robbie's initiative instead of teaching him that certain areas of the room are off limits especially those that could be hazardous to him.

F.L. asks Helen, as she moves in to stop Robbie, "Have you ever thought about saying, 'Hey, Robbie, that's not a good idea'?" Helen startles, looks at F.L. with surprise, and says, "I never talk to him. Well, not never, but almost never." F.L., thinking that this is a complex state of affairs, responds with information: "Even babies can understand emotional messages when we talk to them and let them know what we need."

Helen responds to only one piece of the message. The missing piece is that Helen can also direct Robbie with her actions and her body and still leave room for Robbie's point of view.

Vignette 2: Helen and Robbie, Two Weeks Later

Helen again brings Robbie to one of her sessions. As soon as Helen puts Robbie down on the floor, he is off on his own. Ignoring his mother, F.L., and a variety of toys on the floor, Robbie attempts to climb on a rocking chair. At the same time, Helen moves in to help him and says to him, just above a whisper, "Oh, I don't know if you should be getting up here." Speaking to F.L., while holding onto Robbie, Helen continues, "Phil thinks I give in too much to Robbie, but I think Phil is just jealous because I spend a lot of time with Robbie and not as much time with him."

In cautioning Robbie, Helen tentatively follows F.L.'s suggestion made in the previous session to speak to Robbie. At the same time Helen indirectly disputes F.L.'s suggestion by bringing in her disagreement with Phil. Rather than challenging F.L. directly, she dismisses Phil's view, and tacitly F.L.'s, as the expression of Robbie's jealous rival for her attention. Thus, she is using her opposition to Phil's ideas and her dismissive understanding of it not as a reference point for thinking about what she is doing, but as a fortifying rationalization for her over-accommodation to Robbie's wishes.

F.L. explains her view that she and Helen are in a double bind at this juncture: Helen needs help because she feels lost as to what to do, and, at the same time, F.L. feels in danger of occupying a position similar to that of Helen's husband. F.L. says, "This is also like the position you feel yourself in with Robbie: If I suggest you do something different with Robbie, you feel controlled and, worse, unable to find or trust your own impulses. This is what you fear will happen to Robbie." Helen says, "Yes, I don't want him to grow up the way I did—no sense of self and not even knowing what he wants."

F.L. and Helen agree to pay close attention to how they are responding to each other, especially how Helen feels about F.L.'s suggestions. But even in identifying this dilemma, F.L. worries that she has compromised Helen's initiative. Nevertheless, having recognized and talked about the difficulties involved in making suggestions to Helen, F.L. feels freer to offer her ideas, which she can see Helen needs.

Helen says, "I feel at a complete loss. Please can you recommend a game to play with Robbie?" F.L. takes up a two-and-a-half-inch bean-filled ball and suggests that she and Helen roll the ball back and forth and observe what Robbie will do. After glimpsing F.L. and Helen playing with the ball, Robbie quickly crawls over to get the ball. He grabs it, plops his bottom on the floor, and abruptly raises and flings both arms toward his mother. The ball flies through the air and lands some distance away from him. Robbie laughs and quickly crawls after the ball. He grasps onto it, sits up, eyes gleaming and mouth open, and watches his mother as he attempts to throw it to her. Helen smiles and plays at rushing over to get to the ball but lets Robbie get there first. And when he does, he screeches and laughs, grasps the ball, looks at his mother's smiling face, and shows her the ball.

The point of this game, beyond having fun, is to allow Helen to be a more alive, active, and distinct agent while engaging with Robbie. Now she is not just following his lead, but offering herself as someone who can be fun, encouraging, and intriguing, not just forbidding, controlling, or slavish. Robbie immediately engages his mother.

There is added value to the game because it requires Helen to mirror Robbie's movement characteristics and to expand her movement range. In creating this exploration for them, F.L. foresees that Helen will mirror Robbie's movement qualities and dimensions beyond her own narrower range. The game can help Helen expand her range because it requires movement characteristics like Robbie's—abrupt, flow fluctuating, free and bound flows, high intensity, and sagittal. Helen might then be more able to match and connect with Robbie emotionally and find her own emotional range. The game will help Robbie to add movement in the horizontal that he lacks at this point since his preferred movement is in the sagittal dimension. With more movement in horizontal, Robbie could grow to be more flexible in his action.

Vignette 3: Helen Alone

In her next session, Helen and F.L. talk about the game. F.L. asks, "What does the game reveal about Robbie and you, and about you and me?" Helen says, "I had fun playing this game with Robbie at home. We both laughed and crawled after the ball. But even though I had fun with Robbie, I still feel overwhelming doubt about what else to do with him." Helen says that she keeps playing the ball game at home but has not been able to create other activities that connect them. With small increases in vocal intensity, Helen says, "So now I just do that game over and over. He likes it." Immediately Helen looks down. F.L. asks her what she is feeling. "I don't know—sad, maybe angry," she replies. For a moment she seems angry, and then she begins to cry. Helen insists that she has no idea why she is angry and says, "Maybe I'm not angry, just frustrated." She and F.L. talk about how difficult it feels to Helen to be in touch with any of her own impulses. "I am always thinking, 'I don't know what to do,' when I need to have an idea."

F.L. talks with Helen about her movement range and its importance in her parenting, and in other areas of her life as well. Her low-intensity evenness, F.L. notes, is very different from Robbie's fluctuating tension, which often reaches high intensity. Helen recognizes herself and Robbie in these descriptions and agrees that their differences present a problem for her. She notices that her movements do not obviously show needs or desires, other than to keep still and follow. Helen says, "I was always seen as calm as a child and I used to feel calm. With my parents, I just followed their directions and never questioned them. They didn't have to discourage me from disagreeing or exploring on my own. I don't remember thinking that there was anything else I would want to do," she says. "But now with Robbie," she continues, "I don't feel calm, just frozen. It's as if Robbie is my parent now."

Helen realizes how easy it was, without her own bodily sense to direct and guide her, for her to let her parents lead her. She did not sense any initiating impulses of her own to instigate and guide her actions, and certainly nothing strong enough to use for rebellion. Unfortunately, this observation is a hair's breath away from self-blame.

F.L. wonders out loud: "I imagine that your parents didn't know how to watch you closely when you were a baby and small child to see and facilitate your small and gentle movements. These more subtle movements would have shown them your shifts in feeling and desire. But instead they imposed their own agenda." "So what do I do now? I don't know how to *do this*. I don't know what *you* can do." Saying this, Helen raises one hand just a little bit when she says, "do this" and "you." F.L. says, "What are you feeling now? You seem to have a little more energy there." "Just mad at myself as usual," she responds. "Not made at me for being unhelpful?" F.L. asks. "I suppose, but how do I go from here?"

F.L. imagines here that although Helen's words deny that she can do anything, there is still some energy in her gestures that belies her statement, "I don't know how to do this." F.L. observes this potential for change in

Helen's posture change, and her quietly expressed anger as she lengthens her spine to ascend in the vertical dimension.

Vignette 4: Helen Alone, One Year Later

As she enters the office without her son, Helen's upper body is tipped forward from the hips, while her back remains straight. Not fully straightening her legs as she walks, she shuffles her feet and appears to hesitate with every step. She does not push down through her feet or reach up with her head so she remains folded and descended in vertical.

F.L. notices that Helen's posture is strikingly similar to the one she uses when hovering over Robbie, even though he is not present. This way of shaping her body, as though Robbie is still there, parallels her inability to find and include her own needs and aims when adapting to various situations. Moving over to the chair, Helen puts her bags down beside it, and tucks them out of view. Then, still bent, she backs into the chair to sit down. Once sitting, she centers herself and sits up straight. Although her feet do touch the ground, it appears to F.L. that they don't because there is so little weight pressing through to them. Her posture, F.L. thinks, is like that of "a good little girl." Helen gradually places her hands in her lap. The quality of her movement remains even, low intensity, and bound.

Helen begins the session in her usual way, with doubt: "I don't know what to say today." But *un*usually today, Helen advances her head and chest forward and upward. Helen then rotates her body by inching her left side a little forward. Now her body is facing sideways with her left side toward F.L. Helen spirals her spine so that she looks over her left shoulder at F.L. In this sideways-facing posture, she tilts her head and sometimes looks away rather than directly at F.L. who notices that in response to Helen's different posture, she is also shifting positions in her chair.

This sideways posture replaces Helen's usual vertical, straightforward sitting with hands in her lap. F.L. feels enlivened; as she shifts more in her own positions, she sees further expansion in Helen's movement. Helen's movement repertoire now includes more horizontal spreading and enclosing and seems less reliant on her familiar verticality. This change indicates for F.L. the potential for greater openness to exploration.

"I think I am very angry at Phil," she says. As Helen describes bringing Robbie, now an active two-year -old, to the park, she is more animated and lifts and reaches her arms and hands up and forward. She reports that she brought all the equipment and lunch down the stairs by herself and spent the morning throwing and kicking a ball with Robbie, while Phil stayed home in bed. As Helen says this, she tilts her head, throws her weight slightly to one side, and lightly moves her feet and hands in a pantomime of what she was doing with Robbie.

Just as Helen can now talk about her angry feelings toward Robbie and Phil, she is much more animated as she speaks. This newly exercised shift in affect is the corollary to the changes in her posture and movement repertoire. Although she may be unable to express her feelings directly to Phil, or Robbie, she is now cautiously expressing a fuller range of feeling to F.L.

Catching Helen's excitement, lifting and tilting her upper body forward, F.L. says, "I see that you are angry with Phil for shirking his duties as a father and husband, and at the same time you seem quite alive and excited, and energized." Helen says that she liked playing with Robbie, but quickly adds, "It wasn't my idea, though. I was just following what Robbie likes." As Helen says this, she descends her body in vertical. F.L. notices the shift as she, too, leans back and remarks, "So I took you off your track— you were saying that you are angry with Phil, and I interrupted you and changed your focus." "Oh," Helen says, "I didn't notice." She stops talking and moving. F.L. says, "What happened? You look frozen. What are you feeling?" "Blank," Helen replies. F.L. says, "Did my comment upset you in some way?" Helen says, "I don't think so, but I don't know what to do with it." F.L. says, "When I noticed your excitement, something happened." F.L. pauses. "Can you sense in your body what happened?" Helen says, "I don't know. I don't want to know. I can't do that." She shifts her body so that she sits again with her back to the chair, and her upper torso presses down, descending in vertical. F.L. notices also that she appears sad.

This dynamic between F.L. and Helen came, for a time, to define Helen's experience in therapy. Helen despaired that she could not be helped. F.L. came to understand Helen's extreme vulnerability to any of her own movements or statements that did not align with Helen's present intention. Once F.L. moved off very close alignment with Helen, repair was impossible because Helen had such a fragile hold on her own impulses that any distraction or hint of another possible direction derailed her.

Summary of the Next Phase of Treatment

In working on this problem, Helen and F.L. went on to identify Helen's need that they both completely accept her, as she was, unable to find and develop her own impulses and aims. This meant that Helen wanted F.L. to accept that her present movement repertoire (descending in vertical, frozen in even, low-intensity, bound flow) was all that was available to her. F.L. did think that Helen's reactions to her own parents had so powerfully reinforced her kinetic temperament that she could not allow herself to move beyond this range. Helen's favored vertical dimension did not, as it does for some, reflect a position of certainty about her aims, helping her ascend to assert and reach them. Rather, she descended vertically in certainty about her self-doubt. Her feeling that she was limited was her strongest conviction. Helen could not at this point hear that there might be alternative ways to think about her present experience. In response to Helen's clarity about herself, F.L. was moved to examine and question her own ideal of striving for positive change over acceptance of what is.

As they worked out better alignment of their aims for treatment, over time Helen and F.L. came to define an aspect of Helen's embodied history in Helen's ideas about herself. When she and F.L. could accept Helen's self-described "limitations" and make a space for that experience between them, Helen was able to identify her overwhelming shame, fear of taking action, and her conviction that her parents were right—that she was just a disappointment. F.L. also recognized and discussed with her how, by encouraging Helen to expand her repertoire of behaviors, she had unwittingly participated in what Helen could only experience as the enactment of this shaming embodied history; that is, F.L. became another disappointed parent who wanted her to be different. Any slight encouragement for her to do something other than what she was doing in the way she was doing it made her feel criticized and more ashamed. This was paralyzing.

Even though it felt better to Helen that F.L. was accepting her "as-is," it sometimes seemed to both Helen and F.L. that they were in a vicious circle, or at an end. With the identification of Helen's need to be accepted with her limitations, there sometimes seemed no point in going on with the therapy. Yet Helen remained in treatment. When F.L. wondered what Helen found in it, Helen reminded F.L. that she had a hard time with change. It was a good reminder, and they laughed about it. Helen also recognized that their painstaking definition of their "state of affairs" had provided some relief for her previously unrecognized shame.

Helen's life went on as usual, with her disappointment in herself at times for her inability to socialize outside a small circle, find interests of her own, or stand up for herself against perceived insults. F.L. refrained from questioning this, and offered understanding of and sympathy for Helen's hurt feelings and difficulties. Together they were creating a new repertoire of movement and thinking that came from their acceptance of Helen "as is." This was recognizable in F.L.'s more closely mirroring Helen's posture and movement qualities. Their sessions took on a meditative character, and they laughed about how "zen" they were. Helen no longer saw in F.L. a replica of disappointed parents. In this way, they acknowledged Helen's embodied history as defining, and, without the aim or hope of doing so, began to undo it through acceptance.

In this atmosphere of greater security for both therapist and patient, Helen gradually and incrementally began to change in sessions. Her range of movement, expression of feelings, and initiation of the conversation very slowly continued to grow. In response to changes in Helen's movement range, F.L. gradually began to feel freer to gently challenge their earlier definition of the problem. There was, after all, more than one way to feel about F.L. encouraging Helen to explore possibilities.

In the context of having established a new basis of relationship, a dissociated movement range began to find its way into Helen's movement in sessions and into her life in her family.

Vignette 5: Helen alone, Two Years Later

Helen walks into the room, ascending more toward her full height than she has in the past, and moves more quickly to the chair. After leaning to put down her bags on the couch next to the chair, she ascends to straighten before sitting. Helen says, "I had some fun with Robbie—I chased him in the living room and he was laughing—but then the next day I was back to following him around, just as bad as ever."

Despite her words, which convey the same pattern of self-denigration, Helen's manner is markedly changed: She is using more flow fluctuation, higher intensity free flow. In addition, instead of hiding her bags behind the couch, as she had always done in earlier sessions, she places them out in the open. Her interactions with Robbie have also changed.

F.L. is moved to ask Helen how she played with friends when she was a kid. Helen twists her left side forward in her chair and looks over her shoulder at F.L. as she reports, "I didn't have friends. My parents didn't encourage friends. I had one playmate who lived next door for a while, but I think they did not want me to go out, except to school." Helen does not recoil from F.L.'s question but answers it frankly and stays with her own thoughts and in her own body attitude. F.L. says, "Tell me about her—what did you two do together?" Helen becomes tearful in recalling riding bikes together. She then remembers that she had loved sports and was really good at them in school.

Discussion

As F.L. and Helen began over time to discuss the implications of Helen's growing movement repertoire, and the growing revelations about her history, they realized that Helen had been unable to develop in any way beyond the Helen her parents had identified—her "limited" self. She was given very little opportunity to have experiences outside the family. Any brief friendships she began were nipped in the bud by her parents. These relationships and the entire action repertoire that emerged in them remained forbidden and dissociated, outside the identity recognized and permitted by her parents. Helen's innate kinetic temperament certainly emphasized evenness and verticality. Through treatment and in time, she grew to use the much wider range of movement options available to her that had first appeared in play with childhood friends but had remained unrecognized and undeveloped in Helen's relationship to her parents. By fulfilling her parents' expectations of her being "disappointing," it was as if the Helen who had been a playful child was lost. Despite her ability to use them, all the fundamental movements, qualities, and dimensions used in sports and games had been missing from Helen's repertoire in treatment and interactions with Robbie until recently.

Helen and F.L. hypothesized that especially after marrying and having a child, Helen could not access these less recognized elements of action. Because the dynamic similarity between her family of origin and her new situation so powerfully evoked the restrictions of her embodied history, her additional repertoire was defined as bad and remained unformulated and out of her awareness. The two worlds and the two body–mind states that inhabited those worlds had been kept apart, and only now could be imagined as one.

KAREN, 40 YEARS, AND LONNIE, 5½ MONTHS

"Something doesn't feel right between us," Karen says. "… I feel something's missing. I want to make a family life that's different from the way mine was; I want Lonnie to feel wanted in a way that I never did." At the same time, Karen also reveals to R.F. that she wants to feel wanted by her son and feels afraid that this may not be the case.

Karen had previously been in psychotherapy with R.F. for approximately 3 years, during which time Karen and Paul became engaged and married. Lonnie was born a few years later, and Karen decided to be a "stay-at-home" mom. When Lonnie was about 4 months old, Karen returned to therapy because she was worried about their lack of connection.

Karen reports that her husband Paul has no difficulty connecting with Lonnie and often takes over for his wife when she feels uncertain about how to respond to their baby. Paul's natural excitement with his son and Karen's lack of it make her feel even worse. Karen increasingly feels on the periphery of her family.

Karen and R.F. agree that she will bring Lonnie to some of their sessions and that Karen will make a video of their interactions at home to be used in a later therapy session. This gives Karen the opportunity to watch herself with Lonnie while involved in their routine patterns. By freezing frames or replaying particular sections during session, Karen can better experience herself as she views a variety of her interactions with Lonnie. This process allows her to remember what she felt at the time of the video recording and what she was thinking, as well as what she feels and thinks as she watches herself and Lonnie now. In other words, rather than being caught up in the action, a more aware Karen can see what she has done.

Descriptions of Lonnie and Karen

Lonnie is now 5½ months old. He is a big baby with a wide, round face, wide shoulders, and long legs. Overall, his body gives an impression of length and softness. Rather than actively explore and push out into the world to discover what it holds for him, Lonnie is content to lie back and watch the passing scene. He appears quietly entertained by whatever comes his way. In general, Lonnie seems peaceful, and it takes a lot to perturb him. He rarely makes a big fuss or cries with great abandon. This is seen in Lonnie's facial expressions, which often appear somewhat muted and short-lived. That is, when he is distressed, he narrows his mouth and eyes and furrows his brow, but he holds this position for mere seconds. Similarly, when he appears delighted, with eyes open and mouth widened into a smile, his response is usually fleeting.

Lonnie's actions unfold gradually and are rather light or low in intensity. He is slow to react to stimulations from "within" as well as from "without," and when he does, he seems to contain these sensations and the feelings that may accompany them. His bodily tensions change gradually, allowing him to maintain his low intensity and sense of calm, like an underwater creature in a tranquil sea. This smooth and gradual flow of movements allows Lonnie to soothe himself easily when he is distressed. But, because Lonnie is so quiet, he sometimes has trouble discovering and clearly signaling his needs and desires.

Karen is long, tall, and thin with an overall low muscle tone that lends softness to her appearance. Her face is delicately featured, and the focus of her large, deep blue eyes appears far away. Karen's upper chest hollows, rolling her upper arm bones inward, and each arm hangs loosely by her sides. As she walks, with every step Karen foreshortens the full length of her stride. In other words, the push off from the heel to the ball of her back leg is of such low intensity that it does not lend adequate support for Karen to reach fully with her forward leg. The inhibition in both push and reach lend a measured look to Karen's walk, and she appears to linger in the horizontal as she moves forward. In addition, when Karen sits, she tilts her head over to her right side, which collapses her spinal column, and she pushes that same-side hip to her right, also emphasizing her preference for the horizontal.

Karen's movement inclinations are quite similar to those of Lonnie. They develop and subside slowly like his and have an even, unchanging quality about them. Unless pushed from the outside, Karen does not move abruptly or with high intensity. When she is under stress, Karen's even quality becomes more pronounced. As she has come to realize, it helps her keep her world calm and routine, which by her own admission, she prefers to excitement.

Video Transcript

The video recording that is described next captures a typical afternoon for this mother and baby. In this transcription, R.F. brings in observations and thoughts culled from prior therapy sessions with Karen and from previous couples sessions with her husband, Paul, to fill in needed details. For this session, Karen comes alone.

In the video, lying belly down on a brightly colored quilt, Lonnie is resting quietly. Although there are several toys placed in front of him, he appears interested in a streak of sunlight shining onto the parquet floor several feet away. Seemingly to get a better look, he gradually lifts his head and pushes his elbows and hands down onto the quilt beneath him. This downward movement lifts his trunk upward as he stretches his legs outward. But rather than maintain this vertical position, Lonnie soon gently lowers himself to the floor again, as if the upright posture takes more energy than he can muster. All the while, Lonnie's attention remains fixed on the streak of light, and he smiles.

Lonnie, like any 5½-month-old, is pushing up from his belly to see the world better, but he is not able to stay upright and vertical for very long. Instead of reaching out to explore the world from this more vertical position, he descends and lies quietly. Although he can move his head and his eyes in all directions, the position of his body limits his exploration. Smiling, he appears quite fascinated by what he sees.

Karen sits in a chair in front of and close to Lonnie. She leans forward and softly calls his name several times, but when Lonnie does not respond to her, Karen picks up a stack of envelopes on the table near to her and begins to rifle though them. She sits back in her chair, her chest hollows, and her shoulders narrow and press inward. In a moment, Karen again looks up and toward Lonnie, lengthens her spine, widens her chest, and noticeably sighs. Then, she tilts her head to one side and resumes her previous hollowed and narrowed postural pattern as she returns to her stack of mail. This pattern of looking up and toward Lonnie and soon returning to look through her mail happens several times.

Karen's repeated glances toward Lonnie, although brief, appear to be forays toward connection. If Lonnie were able to grab and hold Karen's attention through more active behaviors, there might be greater possibility for engagement, but that is neither his style nor hers. So, both partners remain in their separate worlds for the moment.

Vignette I: Using Video Within Session

Observing the tape, Karen says, "I'm lucky that Lonnie is a very undemanding child. After the first month, he slept through the night, and now he very rarely fusses or cries much at all." Karen adds that she sometimes worries that Lonnie is not a "happy" baby as he is generally so quiet and does not seem to require much from her. R.F. says, "I don't sense that he's unhappy. But it does look to me as if you're waiting for Lonnie, and Lonnie appears to be waiting for you." Karen ponders this and tells R.F. that she has moments when she feels connected to her child as well as moments when she pulls away from Lonnie, usually because she thinks she is not giving Lonnie, or Lonnie is not giving her, the "right" response. Not always sure what the right response is, she still finds it difficult to relax in her daily interactions with him.

R.F. and Karen return to observing the video: Lonnie has moved his attention from the streak of sunlight to the brightly colored plastic chain links on his quilt. Slowly, he begins to run his fingers over them. Karen lifts her head to look at Lonnie once more. Her mouth noticeably narrows as her lips press together, and her eyebrows furrow, then she again returns to the envelopes. This interaction occurs in a matter of seconds. R.F. freezes the frame of the videotape. "So far, I have seen that you repeatedly look toward Lonnie, and I imagine that you want to connect with him. That's a fine impulse on your part. And here again, we can see that you look toward him and then something happens just before you return to your mail. Can you remember what you were feeling just then—just before you looked away?" Karen looks at the image on the stopped tape and replies, "He seems so content by himself. Maybe he doesn't need me?" Karen's vocal tone is somewhat flat and without intensity, and her cadence progresses without much variation. R.F. says, "That's a sad thought—a baby who doesn't need his mother. And a mother who doesn't feel needed by her child." Karen's eyes suddenly grow moist. "That is sad," she replies.

Rather than purely observing Lonnie's movement style—his way of being and behaving in the world—Karen makes an interpretation of it. She believes that his low-intensity push (which does not support a sustained vertical posture), his evenness and unchanging qualities of movement, and his slow reaction to her subtle stimulation mean that he does not need her. Lonnie's movement characteristics and Karen's response have brought a historic and embodied relational theme to the foreground: A child cannot need a mother because a mother did not need her child. Karen's mother was living with her parents when she became pregnant. Soon after Karen's birth, her mother and her boyfriend moved away, leaving Karen in her grandparents' care. Karen reported in earlier sessions that her mother came home every once in a while but not to see Karen. Generally, when her mother returned home, it was because she had been fighting with Karen's father. Sometimes, these visits would last for a couple of weeks or sometimes for several months. Karen never knew when her mother was coming or when she would leave again.

Some moments pass, and R.F. says, "Karen, your question of Lonnie's not needing you certainly makes sense to me. I remember you telling me that your mother was nineteen years old when she gave birth to you." Karen answers, "Yeah, that was a huge shame for my grandparents. They gave my mother such a hard time. So, what happened was—she moved to another state and left me—she left me with them. When mom came back, Grandpa would be really critical of her, just like he was critical of me, and Grandma would take to her bed. They did this all the time anyway: Grandpa always criticized me, and Grandma took to her bed, but it was much worse when mother came back."

Now, Karen's eyes appear soft and as if she has lost focus. At the same time, she pulls her chest back and down, shortening the verticality of her spinal column, and both her head and pelvis tilt sideways on the horizontal. Karen continues, "And if I looked like I wanted to be with mother instead of them, they'd really be angry with me and let me know it. That was awful for mother and awful for me. And then she'd just up and leave when she had enough of them or when her and my father made up again. Sometimes, he'd come to pick her up and stay for a few days. Those are the only times I remember seeing him. My grandparents were not too pleased when he showed up."

Her mother's comings and goings, along with the critical, dismissive treatment she received from her grandparents, left Karen deeply confused and ambivalent in each of these relationships. She never knew if it was right to want her mother and whether it was right to want her mother to want her. The kind of neglect and abandonment that Karen lived with throughout her growing up left her with a deep sense of longing. She generally felt on the outside, not knowing how to get in—how to belong. Now, the intensity of this feeling was sometimes heightened in her relationship with Lonnie.

Karen says, "It seems funny to say aloud, but I never felt my mother needed me, and then I pretended that I didn't need her. I hope Lonnie never has to pretend he doesn't need me." "Why did you have to pretend not to need her?" R.F. asks, and Karen responds, with a noticeable increase in intensity, "Oh, it's just too awful to show how you feel and have someone not care ... or maybe look like they just don't care. I hope Lonnie never feels that way." R.F. replies, "That would be awful for both of you." Karen and R.F. remain silent, and after some moments, R.F. takes a few obvious, deep breaths. Karen directly looks at R.F. and then takes a few deep breaths herself. Then Karen asks, "Can we see more of the video?"

R.F.'s deeper breathing not only is a response to what has just transpired—the weight of the moment—but also is a subtle, deliberate invitation for Karen to join her. The invitation, once taken, brings Karen into a shared experience, in contrast to her general feeling of isolation. As simple as it sounds, a shared breath can provide supportive ground for the therapy process.

On the video, Lonnie catches sight of Karen looking at him. He extends his legs from their flexed position and then pushes the toes of each foot onto the quilt. For a few moments, the movements of his pushing toes alternate in rapid succession. Lonnie's mouth opens, his lips purse as if to reach toward Karen, and his eyes seem to look directly at his mother. But, in the time it takes for Lonnie to lift himself off the floor and turn himself more directly to meet his mother's glance, Karen turns away and continues going through her mail. Lonnie lingers, looking in Karen's direction for a short while. He closes his mouth, his head droops downward, and his body loses muscular tone. Then, he turns away from his mother and lies down on the quilt. Grasping onto the chain of plastic colored links in front of him once more, Lonnie grabs hold of them and slowly pushes them into his mouth.

Lonnie has already made several attempts to connect with his mother, and now he again looks toward her as he reaches with pursed lips. As R.F. watches this portion of the video, she experiences sensations of emptiness in her chest, feels sad, and wonders if Lonnie is feeling discouraged at this moment.

For Lonnie's reach to complete itself, he would need his mother's receptivity. But for the moment, this does not happen. Lonnie neither cries nor vocalizes to gain his mother's attention. We might imagine that he already knows that her attention is difficult to get and that he is not willing to go through the frustration of asking for and not receiving it. If this were so, we might think that to avoid his feelings of not being met, he drifts away to some other focus. Or, perhaps he cannot sustain his desire for his mother since the momentum from wanting to having requires an incremental build from lower to higher intensity, which, given Lonnie's movement inclination range, is difficult for him to bear or sustain alone. But again, these are only imaginings. What we can see is that Lonnie moves his attention to something else and finds a creative way to adapt to his mother's lack of engagement.

Karen asks to rewind the video to the point at which a stimulated Lonnie is kicking his legs. Karen says, "Boy, look how excited he is." R.F. adds, "Yes, he seems so delighted to find you." Karen responds, "Wow, I really didn't see that at all." Karen pauses and lowers her tone, "I feel bad." R.F. asks, "What does 'bad' mean?" Karen says, "I'm not a good mom to him."

Although not being a "good mom" is the oft-felt experience of any new mother, it is a core issue for Karen: She never felt she was a "good daughter," good enough to elicit her mother's interest and care, and now she is not a good mom, good enough to care for her baby.

R.F. asks Karen, "When you believe you're not a good mom to Lonnie, what do you do?" Karen considers this and then says, "I criticize myself, and I pull away." As she says this, Karen quite abruptly shortens her torso, pulls her arms to her sides, and pushes her chest down and back.

"Can you be aware of your posture right now?" R.F. asks. "I'm sinking— my whole body feels like it's sinking," Karen says. And R.F. responds, "Stay with that sensation—that you're sinking—and maybe even exaggerate it a bit." R.F. gives Karen the time to experience her exaggerated posture fully and then asks, "What do you imagine is in front of you or around you that makes you sink so?" Karen spends some time pondering the question and then responds, "It's just empty space. That's the thing—no one is there." Karen's vocal tone is soft and tentative. After pausing for a time, R.F. says,

"When I try on your posture, I feel empty. What is it that *you* feel?" Karen replies, "Yes, you're right. I'm empty, too. I feel empty on the inside, and it's empty on the outside. I feel like somehow it's my fault that no one is there. I did or didn't do something, but I can't figure out what it is. And I'm bad ... somehow I'm bad. Boy, that's familiar. I felt like this a lot as a kid."

Knowing that prior relational experiences and their ongoing embodied themes exist as part of Karen's routine and core pattern, R.F. asks her to imagine what is around her. She hopes to elicit the projected stimulus that is part of Karen's postural response. The pattern of shrinking and diminishing her self was formed early in Karen's life and contains the childhood experiences of loss and emptiness that she sensed both "inside" and "outside." Her posture, now familiar and preferred, brings with it the expectations of an earlier relational field projected here and now—the "nothing" outside to go with the "nothing" inside. By exploring herself through movement, Karen is offered an avenue for realizing the influence of her past on her present experience.

When R.F. imitates Karen's posture, she can understand better the world in which Karen lives. She tells Karen how she feels as she assumes her posture to illicit a response from her. In turn, Karen then tells R.F. what she experiences. This serves to heighten the connection between them. Now, there is fullness to the dialogue as more relational support is offered.

Because Karen can now reflect and understand that her sensations of emptiness and the thoughts that accompany them have a historic origin, R.F. imagines that she is ready for the next step. She invites Karen to experiment with a wooden block that she can place between her thighs and squeeze. R.F. believes that in doing this, Karen might reorganize her sinking postural pattern and, in turn, the accompanying projection that "no one is there." And if her postural pattern does not reorganize, still more information will be gained in knowing how entrenched Karen's pattern is. These kinds of props were utilized during Karen's individual therapy with R.F., so she is open to exploring her movements through their use.

After a long, quiet pause, R.F. gives Karen a wooden block (5 × 5 × 9 inches) and asks her to place it between her thighs and squeeze it. As soon as she does this, Karen's spine slowly lengthens, and her chest widens. "I feel so much taller now," she remarks. "I feel longer, and I feel the floor under me. That's something. I don't think I notice the floor most of the time." R.F. waits for some time and then stands directly in front of Karen, asking, "How is it for you when I stand in front of you? What do you notice now as you look at me?" After a moment, Karen says, "Good. I feel good. I see you clearly. In fact, I see you much better than before. You look here with me." R.F. agrees, saying, "I feel here with you, and I feel you're here with me." R.F. and Karen remain together in silence for some moments. Then, R.F. suggests, "Now, take the block away, Karen, and see what that's like." Karen removes the block and continues to experience this different posture:

the length of her, the floor underneath her. Again she says to R.F., "I'm still here with me *and* with you."

The use of the block immediately disorganizes Karen's routine postural pattern and allows a more stable and upright posture to emerge. That is to say, Karen squeezes the block, which rebalances the muscles of her inner and outer thighs, and through a kinetic chain, from thigh to leg to foot, enables her to feel a more substantial push of her feet onto the earth. When this push is established, Karen's spine quite naturally lengthens and reaches upward in response. Squeezing the block also organizes Karen along the midline of her body, narrowing her pelvis and allowing sensations of cohering to emerge.

With more support in place, the historic, embodied, and relational theme loses its singular hold on her along with her "shrinking" postural pattern. Now, Karen is able to feel herself more clearly and to see R.F. more clearly. This experience of differentiation enhances the experience of connection: "I am here with you, and you are here with me." Once the block is removed, Karen feels its kinesthetic imprint and continues to feel supported in her uprightness.

R.F. rewinds the video once more so that Karen can view herself and Lonnie from this different perspective. Karen does this and then places her hand over her heart and says, "I feel so warm when I look at him. I feel so warm."

Although the exploration with the block—leading to a new postural pattern and its attendant perceptions and meanings—is over for the moment, the immediate shift in experience will be remembered well. With a new and more stable movement pattern, Karen will be better able to notice herself alone or in relation to Lonnie with greater clarity, and there will be fewer negative evaluations to skew the process of seeing and feeling just what is. And when evaluations do arise to obscure the actuality of the moment, most likely they will be accompanied by some variation of her shrinking posture. But for now, an aware Karen can more clearly distinguish the contrast between these two states of being. All the while, Karen's fascination with her process of shrinking and growing (in all dimensions) indicates her readiness to be open to new understandings.

Vignette 2: Four Weeks Later

Karen begins, "I have been thinking a lot about my similarity to Lonnie, and it's so true. Sometimes I see him as a little slug, and maybe he thinks the same of me," she laughs. "But I have been trying to do something different with him. Sometimes, we have a lot of energy between us, and then it dies. I'm not sure what happens—what I do or what he does. When I was looking at this new video, I saw the same thing happen between us, so I want to look at it with you and get some help."

In prior sessions, R.F. had reminded Karen about how similar she and Lonnie were in kinetic temperament, and that in matching him so well, there was not always enough difference between them to create sufficient interest and to sustain both their attentions. For something to change in the relationship, Karen needed to approach Lonnie more directly (sagitally instead of horizontally) and to approach him more often. For example, she was encouraged to give Lonnie greater vocal stimulation as this would heighten his muscular tone, grab his attention, and raise his level of excitement. And above all, R.F. suggested that Karen meet Lonnie's eyes as often as possible so that he could see her interest in him, and she in turn could see his interest in her.

As the video begins, Lonnie is lying on the same colored quilt and sucking on his plastic links. Karen is seated on the floor directly in front of him. She watches for a moment and then lightly and quickly touches one of Lonnie's hands and then the other, followed by his nose and the top of his head. She does this several times, as Lonnie smiles and looks directly at her. "Oh, you're looking at me with such a handsome face," Karen says, and Lonnie smiles widely and begins vocalizing. As he does this, he lifts all his limbs off the floor and makes "swimming" movements with his arms and legs. "Oh, I love when you swim. Let's both go swimming, okay?" Karen suddenly places herself belly down onto the floor in imitation of Lonnie. Lonnie's vocalizations increase and demonstrate a novel tone. They have a guttural quality coming from deep within his belly. "Wow, that's some kind of sound you're making today," she says. Now imitating him, Karen makes similar sounds. "Awwwaahh, awwwaaahhh!" they say to one another.

In Karen's excitement, she spontaneously lays belly down on the quilt to join Lonnie. Lonnie, in turn, responds to Karen's shift of position and energy with a new sound. Although Lonnie's pattern of pushing his hands onto the floor usually appears without much energy, he seems to muster all his strength now and abruptly and repeatedly condenses his spine from head to tailbone, then expands his body and expresses himself with a guttural push of his voice as well. The new vitality of Lonnie's vocal pattern stimulates Karen, and she matches his energy with her own guttural pushing sounds.

This shift from her usual gradual, even movements to more abrupt movements adds liveliness to the interaction with Lonnie and augments his ability to push. Both mother and baby seem energized in the conversation and delighted to have something to talk about. Here, the relationship has found mutuality and reciprocity. In this moment, nothing is missing.

Watching the video, they see Karen continue to echo Lonnie's sounds. In response, his face lights up—his eyes widen, he smiles broadly, and he keeps looking directly at his mother. Karen also smiles and maintains her higher level of intensity as she repeats these guttural pushing sounds and looks directly at him. Lonnie appears so absorbed with his mother that his eyes never leave her face. R.F. says, "He seems to adore your attention. You've encouraged his liveliness."

In the videotape, Karen is seen looking away from Lonnie. She unties the red scarf around her neck and places it in front of Lonnie's face, obscuring his direct view of her. "Want to play with Mommy's scarf?" she asks. With light and gradual movements, Karen gives life to the scarf, floating it between them and from side to side. As both mother and baby watch the scarf float in front of them, their vocalizing stops. For a while, Lonnie is interested in its graceful and gentle movements and swipes it with the fingers of one hand. But after several passes, the scarf's movements never vary. After a while, Lonnie grows quiet, loses intensity, and slowly looks away. Watching this section of the tape, Karen says, "This is where I feel 'off.' I knew it when I started playing with my scarf, but I didn't know what else to do. I think I got uncomfortable, and then I pulled away."

The excitement of connection creates an anxiety that Karen has trouble bearing, so she changes the dynamic by placing the scarf between her and Lonnie. To now have the connection and closeness Karen has always wanted brings up a mix of emotions—the warmth of this present moment as well as grief for the closeness she had missed and learned to live without. Karen can identify a troubling pattern—she is aware that something feels "off" with her when she disconnects from her baby—but she does not yet recognize what she brings to this moment.

R.F. rewinds the tape to play it again, and both she and Karen watch that particular section a few more times. Now, R.F. asks, "What makes you uncomfortable here?" Karen waits for some moments, and with a soft and broken cadence, she says, "I—I don't know. Lonnie—expects me to do something. And I don't—I don't know what it is, but he expects something."

Karen is surprised at this last comment and says she immediately recognizes the familiarity of this experience in relation to both Paul and her family of origin. In her family of origin, Karen could never feel safe enough to yield or give herself to the experience of being with either grandparent because she feared not meeting their expectations and then receiving their criticism.

R.F. says, "It's interesting to me that you covered Lonnie's eyes with your scarf. What does that mean to you?" Karen's eyes fill, and she spontaneously says, "I don't want to see him criticize me."

In Karen's family of origin, affective connection occurred through criticism. Neither of her grandparents had learned how to be intimate with each other, with their own daughter, or with Karen. The result for Karen is that any situation that provides the hope for intimacy leaves Karen anxious and confused. Even the action of looking into Lonnie's eyes—seeing and being seen—is fused with the expectation of disparaging remarks.

Discussion

In working with and through those moments when Karen engages with Lonnie and those moments when she pulls away in avoidance, Karen also is working with and through the historic and embodied experiences of her past. The tape is over, and the session soon ends, but the images from the video remain with both Karen and R.F. and lend significance to their ongoing sessions with Lonnie. By the time Lonnie is 10 months old, Karen is able to make and sustain greater connections with her son, and Lonnie is able to make his needs more clearly known. This is not to say that Karen does not fall into her familiar routines with Lonnie. Sometimes, she feels "stuck again," but these periods are more easily recognized. Now, she is aware of how she gets stuck, and this creates the potential for change. Both R.F. and Karen agree to conclude treatment.

Chapter 6

Working With Parent Couples

INTRODUCTION

It is rare for a baby to enter a household without causing some kind of anxious disruption along with excitement. No matter how well a couple functions before a baby arrives, the baby brings an unprecedented set of issues to deal with that can cause anxiety. One or both parents might be surprised and worried by the weight of their responsibility for the baby's survival or by feelings of jealousy when the couple's focus moves from care of each other to care for a third. In addition, many couples have unresolved relational difficulties before the arrival of a baby that, without attention, can worsen and grow to threaten the fabric of their partnership. In their anxious state, the parents often cannot create enough safety and comfort for the baby. Then, the baby's anxious state increases, and, in a vicious cycle, escalates the parents' anxieties.

Thus, couples who come for psychotherapy treatment at this time are often struggling with powerful emotions that they do not fully understand. Examining the movement patterns that underlie their emerging experience offers the opportunity to shape the new family relationships in a way that better meets the needs of all. As we discussed in Chapter 5, in this new context, elements of each parent's embodied history inevitably emerge that may never have appeared before. These bring with them both skills and challenges that neither parent may yet have encountered. Even a second baby brings about substantial changes and new challenges.

In this chapter, we look at two cases in which the parents' complaints at first focus on their disputes about how to manage their baby; as the sessions continue, however, it becomes evident that the problem is primarily centered on how the couples' interactive patterns elicit inflexible attitudes that grow from the dynamics of their unrecognized embodied histories. Instead of harmonically blending their various ways of moving and being, these parents come to disparage each other's ways of taking care of their child. In addition, rather than recognizing that each parent brings his or her own action repertoire to the task and that each has strengths as well as limitations that are particular to the new relationship, the parents compete and attempt to control each other's actions. These kinds of interactions, in time, undermine their relationship. Moreover, when communication between parents is fraught with tension because they cannot find safety and containment in their own relationship, the needs of the baby are not seen clearly and are not well attended. Parents have difficulty in making a consistent and reliable environment for their child—one in which the baby feels well held.

In each case study, the use of foundational movement analysis reveals how each parent's specific embodied history is emergent and active in the newly formed family relationships. As parents bring individual movement repertoires to parenting, they meet a new baby who, as we have seen in previous chapters, also has an individual movement repertoire. Elements of each parent's movement repertoire will emerge as both talents and limitations in the context of the specific demands of the baby's needs. All the ways in which each parent is similar to and different from the baby and from each other will play a role in how comfortable, safe, and contented each will feel in the other's company. When parents can learn to move in new ways through observing each other and their baby, each benefits by the addition of new action possibilities. Alternatively, or in addition, parents can recognize that each has talents and limitations and work as a team with their baby so that neither parent needs to be a duplicate of the other.

Foundational movement analysis is used, then, to teach parents to sense their specific movement repertoire, to understand those of their partner's and their baby's, and to learn how to coordinate themselves better as a couple and a family. From that position, their parenting efforts improve. Here, movement awareness becomes the foundation for a developing kinesthetic empathy that includes, but also goes well beyond, the idea of "acceptance" of another's differences. That is, attunement and better ease naturally develop once partners more clearly experience and understand their movement styles and see and feel how these influence other family members. In fact, it is often surprising how dramatically relational shifts can occur when movement understanding is introduced within psychotherapy treatment.

In this chapter's cases, the parents initially believed that they needed help only with childrearing problems. We found, however, that before dealing with the parents' handling of the baby, the parents' relationship needed to be addressed.

VERONICA, 30 YEARS, MARK, 32 YEARS, AND THOMAS, 5 MONTHS

Vignette 1: The Whole Family

The family settles in F.L.'s office, Veronica on a chair, Mark on the couch, and Thomas in his stroller, fast asleep. Veronica says that she fed Thomas right before they came for the session. The walk has put him to sleep, but Veronica remarks that he might wake up soon. He remains asleep through the entire session.

Veronica begins by asking for advice about how to get Thomas to sleep for longer stretches, especially at night, because he is not sleeping more than 2 hours at one time. At 5 months of age, he still has night feedings as well as feedings at 2-hour intervals during the day. Veronica and Mark both worry that they are not handling Thomas correctly because in the daytime he is very fussy unless one of his parents holds him and plays with him. The pediatrician has said that he is healthy and that they should read some books on helping infants sleep, but they are at odds about what advice to follow.

Veronica says, "I'm not breast feeding anymore—I tried for 3 months—but my milk didn't come in enough, so it was just better to bottle-feed. But I want to do most of the feedings because I'm Thomas's mother—I want to stay as close to what's natural as possible—but we agree that Mark should do one night feeding." When she speaks, Veronica runs her hand through her hair, continuously moves in her seat (fluctuating intensity), and changes the position of her whole body as she gazes and gestures in all directions, looking and reaching forward, sideways, and downward (advancing in sagittal, horizontal spreading, vertical descending as she reaches). Even when she is not speaking, Veronica continues to move a great deal and increases her quick, higher-intensity rhythms as she fidgets with her hands (abrupt changes from low to high intensity, freeing and binding). Mark looks directly at Veronica when she speaks. He sits still with his back pushed against the couch (retreating in sagittal) and rests his arms next to his sides (even intensity), his palms facing downward. But before Veronica has finished speaking, Mark slowly pushes his hands down onto the seat cushion, gradually lifting him to a more vertical posture, and then barks at her (gradual build from low to high intensity, push-reach, gradual to abrupt). Loudly and forcefully, Mark says, "*Look*, Thomas is old enough and heavy enough now to skip a feeding at night, and the pediatrician says so." Continuing with his high-intensity pitch, he reports that Veronica will not allow Thomas to awaken without feeding him. As Mark speaks, Veronica continues shifting around on the chair and only now and then glances directly at Mark or at F.L. Despite Mark's loud vehemence, Thomas remains asleep.

Veronica now rests her upper body on the arm of her chair and lifts her legs sideways onto its seat (horizontal, abrupt change to moderate intensity). Interrupting Mark, she describes how difficult it is for her to get back to sleep. Her speech tones are similar in their changing rhythm to her movement's rising and falling intensity, adding emphasis to whatever she describes. Veronica insists that Mark do what she asks because sometimes she takes medication: "Since I *don't* wake easily when Thomas cries,

Mark—I mean, we *agreed* to this—he often gets Thomas and *brings* him to me." Using his palms to push himself upward again, Mark says, "Yes, but I resent it now—after all, if I *am* getting up all the time, why shouldn't *I* try to pat Thomas to see if he will go back to sleep, or why shouldn't *I* feed him? She treats me like I am the messenger boy." Veronica angrily cries out, "I'm not breast-feeding, but *I* want to be the *mother!*" We hear Thomas making little noises as he squirms. Veronica jumps up (another abrupt increase in intensity) to look at him in his carriage, sees he is asleep and seats herself again, reclining in her chair (abrupt drop in intensity).

It becomes clear in watching this couple's interaction that Thomas's problems cannot be understood until his parents' problems are understood. Veronica and Mark talk over each other, competing for airtime. Veronica appears not to be paying attention because her focus and her movement are continuously and abruptly changing in intensity. Indeed, it is surprising when she seems to know anything about what Mark has said. It is also surprising that Mark does not remark on how little Veronica seems to acknowledge and pay attention to him.

When conversations take place in which there is a good sense of rapport and give and take, this is seen in mirrored postures, shared rhythms of postural change, and in more easily flowing turn taking (La Barre, 2001). Veronica and Mark have no rhythmic or postural harmony and appear to have no give and take (yield/push) in their verbal dialogue or in the actions they perform when they speak and listen to each other.

Mark says, "Veronica claims she can't stand to hear Thomas cry when we can help him stop. I agree with her—I think that would be bad parenting." While Mark is talking, Veronica reaches down from her position sitting sideways in her chair to search for something in her large bag. Pulling a zippered bag out of it as she talks, she unzips it and takes out lip balm, uses it, and replaces it (high intensity, abrupt, fluctuating flow), while speaking the whole time without looking at either F.L. or Mark (enclosing in horizontal). She says, "If you go in to him right away, how will he ever learn to do without us for a minute? Mark won't let me even try to let him cry for 2 minutes!"

They seem to have reversed content, but what is consistent is their lack of attention to each other. It appears that neither of them is observing what is happening between them or what Thomas is doing. In addition, neither is open to trying out the other's suggestions. The area of agreement that exists between them—that Thomas can go longer between feedings at night—is not evident in their movements or in their expressed feelings about the situation. They are at odds with each other, and this is very apparent in how they move.

This couple uses their distinctly different movement inclinations to polarize each position rather than to mirror and contain each other in movement and in their verbalizations. For example, when Veronica speaks,

Mark does not respond to her by matching her posture or her movement qualities but rather moves in his own distinctive way: He reaches upward and forward with his head and neck toward her and then alternately pulls his head backward and pushes it forward (sagittal), leaving his limbs or lower torso static with even moderate intensity. At the same time, the intensity of the movements of his head and neck increases from low to high and stays even at that level. These are his preferred patterns and as such are exaggerated in this stressful situation. Likewise, Veronica's preferred patterns in this moment also grow more exaggerated as she limits her movements to spreading and enclosing as she reclines in the horizontal plane and to increasing the fluctuations of her intensity by fidgeting and shifting from side to side. Also, while Mark focuses directly on Veronica, Veronica focuses on everything but Mark.

Vignette 2: Mark and Veronica Without Thomas

Rustling around in her bag, Veronica begins, "Mark must learn to control his temper—that is the *only* problem we have as a couple. Mark has endless patience for Thomas and loves to play with him, but he is horrible to me—he's impatient, inflexible, and always angry." Mark makes grumbling sounds that slowly build from low to high volumes (high intensity), and then, with his arms still resting next to his sides, he vigorously gestures with his head, pushing it forward and whipping it abruptly backward in time with his words, "*You know,* you *know,* you *know* what?—My *anger* is more *ob*vious than hers because I am more honest, but she is *al*so angry and short-*tem*pered with me. She makes these *snip*ing and really nasty remarks. She just doesn't show that side to you here, but you should see her at home." F.L. remarks that it seems there is a lot going on that is upsetting for both of them and wonders what their relationship was like before Thomas was born.

Mark momentarily looks down as Veronica immediately takes the lead. She leaves her reclining position, sits up, and says, "Mark tends to like to stay home together to watch TV and talk, but I like to go out to dinner, museums, movies, and see friends." Now moving only her head lightly from side to side, Veronica adds, "I guess we had sort of worked things out, you know, before Thomas—I mean, we would get into little moments of tension, but actually we always managed to sort of have fun, I think, right, Mark? We didn't ever fight like we do now. ... Life was a lot easier then, you know, but that's the way it goes, I guess." Mark, who has been nodding his head in rhythm with Veronica's movement and vocal pattern, once more gradually pushes his hands down onto the couch to lengthen his spine. He clears his throat, reaches his head up and forward, and gently joins the flow of conversation: "We really worked out our differences by taking turns doing what each of us liked. I admit that when I first met Veronica I liked that she pushed me to get out. I thought it was good for me." As he speaks, he gestures with his hands and arms, now for the first time in session spreading them forward and sideways, mirroring the side-to-side movement of Veronica's head. Veronica now holds still, looks directly at Mark and says, "Staying home with Mark was good for me because I can exhaust myself with activity and can't always stop. I like that he helps me stop."

F.L. now describes to them her observations of their movement interaction as they were talking about their earlier relationship, and she discusses how very different it appears from their movement interaction when they fight about Thomas. As she describes these patterns, she imitates their movements to clarify the observations. They nod in recognition and, at F.L.'s suggestion, begin to explore their different patterns themselves. Now with awareness, they each repeat the way that they ordinarily move and try to imitate the movement patterns of the other. In purposefully executing their own patterns and those of their spouse, they discover how their rhythms and orientations become more or less well coordinated.

Here, Veronica and Mark are a good example of the kind of kinetic and emotional regulation that couples can supply to each other. Mark's slower rhythm of both movement and breathing is comforting and soothing to Veronica and establishes phrasing; that is, a beginning, middle, and end. In other words, Mark's movements grow more intense and then less intense gradually, and each wave of increase and decrease forms a "phrase" that can contain the smaller movement changes that Veronica typically uses. Veronica's quicker pace, her small and abrupt movement jitters, provide excitement as they prod and enliven Mark. A greater awareness of their individual movement repertoires and how they affect each other will offer an expanded range of interactive options to improve their collaboration.

Veronica adds, "I always liked to lie on Mark's lap when we watched TV. But then I would feel fidgety and want to get up and do something. I don't know why." Mark says, "Yeah, I miss your lying on my lap." He now remarks that he has been feeling abandoned and angry since Thomas arrived. And Veronica admits that she also misses her time alone with Mark. F.L. asks, "How else is Thomas coming between you—are you having sex—has your sex life changed with the birth of Thomas?" They both quickly report that they haven't had sex "forever—actually, since Thomas was conceived." Although they both find the issue embarrassing, Mark wants to talk about it and says that they never had an easy time with sex. Veronica quickly makes the excuse that Thomas is not sleeping at night and presses the point: "It's so hard to have sex when we're both so tired." But she does come to agree with Mark—they never had an easy time with sex. Veronica says, "We can't talk about this; it's too embarrassing." Mark is quiet. After some discussion about how to proceed with this issue, they decide to meet with F.L. in individual sessions to feel freer to discuss their separate issues.

When couples spend time together or work toward a common purpose—such as mutual understanding or sexual pleasure—they tend to develop a shared rhythm that is composed of elements that each brings to the connection. Even with different movement repertoires, partners can learn to adjust to each other's rhythms and intensities sufficiently to create a good sexual experience. But, it seems that something is hampering Veronica and Mark's ability or willingness to work toward such collaboration in sexual engagement.

Vignette 3: Veronica's Individual Work

Veronica looks with unusual directness at F.L. and blithely says she does not like sex and never has. She again sits leaning sideways onto the arm of the chair, but with much less fidgeting and change of position than in previous sessions. She goes on: "Mark's not the problem—I've never had pleasure with anyone or even on my own. It just doesn't interest me." She says her parents were formal with each other and removed from their children—not at all "touchy-feely." So, she did not observe any easy, warm physical connections between adults. "I know it's unusual—I can't remember any early sexual feelings, and all through my adolescence I felt unattractive because I was extremely skinny. I did not menstruate or fully develop breasts until I was a junior in high school, far later than my friends. I just couldn't compete—I was always so behind them."

As she and F.L. continue talking about her history, Veronica realizes that she has falsely built up the idea that sex with Mark was just recently disrupted by his unreasonable angry outbursts, as if the outbursts have pushed her away. But, the discussion makes it clear that her reluctance to engage physically with Mark predates his angry outbursts and, in fact, predates him. "Really, I 'put up with sex' for Mark in the beginning of the relationship, and I guess I was feeling relieved that he seemed to stop wanting it."

F.L. asks if her "disinterest" in sex relates to feeling behind and different from her peers. Veronica responds that it makes sense, but the idea does not open any doors. She recalls that a cousin used to talk about masturbating, but all that felt like another world. She could see in her aunt and uncle their physical attraction to each other, but it made her shudder, and she felt sure her own parents did not approve. F.L. remarks that Veronica was not always just "not interested" but found the idea of sex quite repulsive. Veronica agrees but says she does not feel that strongly about it in any direction any more. F.L. asks how Veronica presently feels about her body. She says that she feels much better and had begun to feel better about it in college, when she felt it "caught up" to the other girls. F.L. wonders if Veronica feels attractive to Mark. Veronica says that she does but then, laughing, says that she does not want him to feel too attracted. But, she also says that she would really like to be more in touch with her sexual feelings. Then, F.L. asks, "What's going on in your body as we speak about all this?" Veronica laughs and says, "What body?"

Veronica affirms that her statement is not just a joke and that she really does not know what the question means. So, F.L. suggests that Veronica now simply pay attention to her body and stay with *any* sensation that she notices. She guides Veronica by telling her to sense the pressure of the couch under her pelvic bones and behind her back. After a few moments, Veronica says that she feels both. F.L. then directs Veronica's attention to the air moving in and out of her nose and the movement of her chest as she breathes. Veronica finds this difficult and becomes aware that she is beginning to move around a lot, "which," she notes and says, "makes it impossible to sense anything." For a moment, Veronica attempts to still herself. She lengthens her spine, places her feet on the ground and her hands in her lap, and closes her eyes. But then, she says, "This is too hard."

F.L. suggests a different exploration: "How about trying to pay attention to your experience of moving rather than trying to hold still, which may feel like you're stifling yourself. You can even 'talk' your movement, give it a voice—just say what you are doing and feeling as you do it and feel it." Now speaking from her movement flow, Veronica says: "I don't settle down, I don't know what I feel; well, I just feel restless; I am looking for a comfortable position, but I don't know what I'm looking for; I feel agitated, like I'm worrying about this, like it's a test; oh, this position sideways on the couch is better than sitting up; I'm tired [yawning, stretching]; that's better, but I am still kind of squirmy, actually I want to stretch and press against something." Veronica stretches again as she lies on the couch, hands overhead, legs and feet reaching away from her center. She yawns several times. "Wow, this is starting to feel better, I can feel my body sort of oozing around—it feels kind of good, rather than just a fidgety feeling."

In the succeeding individual sessions, Veronica discovers more about her feelings by exploring what she identifies as her "fidgeting" movement.

F.L., watching Veronica, is reminded of a baby squirming to find a comfortable position as she moves in and out of a parent's embrace. F.L. shares that image with Veronica, who recalls seeing Thomas do that sort of thing and then Veronica talks about her mother. Veronica recalls that her parents found her "annoying," especially her mother. Her mother always told her to stop fidgeting. For years, Veronica tried to stop, but to no avail. One of the things she loved about Mark was that he did not mind her fidgeting—he used to call it "lively." She and F.L. talk about how to bring these discoveries into her relationship with Mark, adding a sensual, but not necessarily sexual, dimension at this point.

Apparently, Veronica's search for comfort and pleasure with her parents was disturbing to them. Their discomfort may have derived from the wide differences between their kinetic temperaments or critical attitudes about "fidgeting," which many adults hold. Her parents' discomfort might also have stemmed from their discomfort with their own sensuality. *Veronica could not be sure. Veronica's discovery of this complexity is important in uncovering the embodied history enacted in her fidgeting with Mark that has yet to be understood in her own terms.*

Vignette 4: Mark's Individual Work

Mark sits, as usual, with his back pressed against the couch (retreated in sagittal) and his hands slightly pushing down onto the couch on either side of his body. He says that he has given up on sex since it is clear to him that Veronica does not enjoy it. "I can't keep wanting what she doesn't respond to—I feel like she avoids me, and I stop caring." He looks down. F.L. suggests that "not caring" is sometimes an attempt to control a lot of other feelings, such as hurt, anger, frustration, and fear. F.L. asks how it would be to talk about sex with Veronica. Mark tries to imagine it and comes up against an image of her skillful evasion, which again feels daunting for him to challenge. "You know when Veronica said she would put her head on my lap and then start to fidget—she did that all the time—I didn't mind at first—when she jumped up so quickly, I would jump up after her, and we'd be off doing something. But then I grew to hate it—whenever I thought I'd have her for a minute and she'd jump up. Whatever Veronica wants, she goes after. Before Thomas, before I gave up altogether, I would lie in bed wondering why she didn't come after me." F.L. asks why he did not go after Veronica. He is surprised by the implicit observation and remarks, "I guess I've always just followed her lead, but I don't know why." As he speaks, his arms remain inanimate at his sides, while his head abruptly reaches forward and pulls back.

F.L. *notices to herself that the pattern of Mark's head reaching forward and pulling back parallels his expressed desire to engage and his speedy retreat.*

F.L. asks Mark to talk about his parents and their relationship. He reveals that he lost his father when he was 6 years old. Mark's face shifts from irritable and angry to sad when he tells how his grief has reemerged with Thomas's birth because he often thinks about how his father would have been thrilled to have a grandson. He remembers how he used to play ball with his father. After sharing this, Mark sits very still, then sinks his chin down into his body and weeps. Through his tears, Mark says his mother was "a pretty good mother" who listened to his problems, which he remembers as having been few. Recovering composure and pressing his hands down onto the couch to adjust his spine to sit up and forward again, he reports that as far as he knew she never looked for another husband or for any intimate connection with a man. She worked as a schoolteacher, took care of Mark, had quite a few men and women friends, and was on the faculty bowling team. F.L. notes that the picture he is painting seems a lot like Veronica, who also loves her friends and going out and does not seem to need an intimate, sexual relationship with a man. Mark then sits back, pushes his hands down on the couch again to lengthen his spine, and looks directly at F.L. After some moments, F.L. asks how he felt when his mother went out with her friends. As he answers, Marks frowns, his head reaches forward, his mouth opens, and he gradually reaches his hands forward, moving into high intensity, and opens his palms: "I felt lonely sometimes when she went out, but I wanted her to find me a new dad. Instead, she kept telling me what a great team we made. 'I like being your mom and dad,' she'd say. Then, I'd feel guilty because I didn't want to be a great team. She was always 'supermom'," Mark continues, "just like Veronica." F.L. says, "Looks like you're angry—and like you want to reach for something." Mark retreats in sagittal, moving back to his former position with his arms at his sides.

F.L. suggests that he notice what he just did. He recognizes his retreat immediately but not as readily the reach that preceded it. They connect this to the question of his trying to get what he wants with Veronica. Then, F.L. asks, "What just happened to your feelings when you were reaching with your hands and talking about your mother?" Mark appears to review the movement, and he says, "I dropped it—so it stops mattering." F.L. asks, "So could it be that you drop your connection to your own sensations and desires when you feel blocked—just like when Veronica moves away?" Mark lightly nods his head while the rest of his body remains motionless. Mark does not directly deal with the question but recalls that he always acquiesces to Veronica's desires when she has plans for them to go places and see friends even though he does not want to go. "I know I could say 'no,' but I just can't imagine doing it." At first, he blames Veronica for being too persistent and not giving him any room to refuse. As he says this, Mark's body changes from lifted (in vertical) to more dropped backward (in sagittal), appearing to have lost energy. F.L. remarks on this physical change to him, calling it a "downshift." Mark says this feels familiar. F.L. asks him to repeat this downshift as he moves from vertically lifted to dropped downward and backward in sagittal. Mark does the movement a few times and says that he feels "a sense of dread and disappointment." Encouraged by F.L. to repeat the movement a few more times, Mark recalls feeling this same way when his mother was unhappy after his father died. Although he remembers his determination to make her happy again, he had forgotten the accompanying feeling of dread until this moment. He remembers being able to cheer up his mother by talking to her, telling her his news from school (especially the good news), and doing chores for her. He says, "But just before I went into my cheering up routine, I had a sense of dread ... of disappointment that she was feeling bad again." "How did you know she was feeling bad?" F.L. asks. Mark replies, "She got 'fidgety' when she was upset." F.L. asks him what kind fidgeting she did. Mark recalls her loss of focus and her starting one task in the kitchen and then moving to something else, "Like I couldn't get her to be with me, you know, actually be with me."

In this description, Mark makes it clear that he disliked his mother's fidgeting and linked it with feeling devalued by his mother. When his relationship with Veronica had been fulfilling for him, her fidgeting did not consciously disturb him. With the strain of the new baby, and his increasing feeling of unimportance—of being just the messenger—he is very disturbed by it but retreats rather than raise questions or protests. We see this in his body, enacting the giving up, alternating with explosive anger at his position. He starts to accommodate to Veronica's need to be supermom by retreating from being the dad, but then he feels furious.

Discussion

Separate embodied histories were explosively enacted in Veronica and Mark's relationship. Therapy—both individual and couple sessions—allowed each set of issues to be seen individually and then to be understood in connection to the other. When Veronica and Mark could see that the roots of their problems together had elements that came from their individual embodied histories, they no longer fought about who was to blame and were each more understanding and helpful to the other in finding solutions.

The continuing work with F.L. focused on helping them become significantly more aware of their own bodily sensations and movements in their interactions with each other. Including an awareness of movement within their individual and then couple sessions, Mark and Veronica began making progress toward better affectionate and sexual relations with each other. They started by not avoiding or giving up on affectionate encounters that gradually became more sexual. Veronica worked to recognize in the moment how she fidgeted and then immediately felt the need to move away from Mark—a pattern that seemed related to her early life and current avoidance of sex. Veronica recognized more clearly her yearning for contact and learned to keep herself from moving away from Mark when he came toward her and at the same time to stay in touch with her own feelings. Mark invited Veronica's fidgeting, now not taking it as a rejection, and helped her to stay in contact while she fidgeted, getting past her fear of rejection. She came to understand that this sequence probably related to her parents' difficulties with her squirming and fidgeting. This process was directly related to their sexual difficulties since Veronica needed to be able to fidget to be in touch with herself.

Mark then worked on changing his worried feelings when Veronica began to fidget and staying with his own feelings while allowing her to stay with hers. He grew more assertive of his needs and more able to sustain his vitality and desire when he approached Veronica. He practiced ignoring Veronica's diffuse focus and holding his steady. Veronica began to understand Mark's feelings of being left out and addressed her own anxiety about not being a good enough mom if she was not "doing it all."

In one of their later sessions, Veronica and Mark reported that Thomas's "sleep problem" had diminished and disappeared without their direct attention to it. When F.L. asked how they had helped Thomas sleep through the night, they did not exactly know. What they did know and reported was that Mark was now often taking care of Thomas at night without argument from Veronica. Veronica also learned to respect and value Mark's wish for them to be home together more often.

DEBRA, 38 YEARS, ROB, 35 YEARS, AND JENNA, 3 MONTHS

Debra and Rob come to therapy with R.F. because their 3-month-old baby Jenna has been troubled by digestive difficulties since birth and cannot be easily soothed. The parents deal with their baby's difficulty in different and often conflicting ways, which creates tension between them. As a result, they are continually arguing.

Both Debra and Rob had been in individual treatment for several years prior to their baby's birth. Debra had been a client of R.F., while Rob had been in treatment with another psychotherapist. At her request, Rob would occasionally join Debra in meetings with R.F. Generally these sessions were focused on Debra's difficulty in expressing her anger toward Rob. From her perspective, when she became angry with him, his response felt overwhelming to her. Rob became more aware of the intensity of his ardent and vehement expressions and brought this information back to his own individual psychotherapist so that, over time, he was better able to listen to Debra's angry feelings and address them rather than blow up. Debra grew more adept at standing up for herself, even when Rob's expressions were emphatic. But, it now appears that with the stress of their new baby, old patterns have returned. It is Rob's idea to seek treatment with R.F., and Debra agrees.

Vignette 1: Working With the Family

Debra and Rob enter the office. He walks quickly and directly toward the sofa, while she walks more gradually and indirectly. Rob abruptly seats himself at one end of the long, deep couch. Once seated, he lengthens his spine from his navel to his collarbones (vertical), slightly bulges his chest forward (sagittal), and tilts his head slightly to one side (horizontal). Debra, seating herself at the other end of the couch, slowly takes their sleeping baby out of the sling in which she is carried and places her onto her lap. Pulling the baby closer to her, Debra gradually shortens her spine (vertical), narrows her chest, and leans sideways against the cushioned arm of the sofa (horizontal), curling herself around her child.

Taking her time, Debra begins explaining to R.F. how difficult the past 3 months have been for her. Jenna has been struggling with a constellation of digestive disorders since she was born. She has been terribly uncomfortable and complaining loudly a good deal of the day and long into the night. Debra, who says she is sleep deprived, cannot soothe her wailing child. "I feel desperate," she says, "and like a real failure."

As she describes the situation in greater detail, Debra moves the forearm of her free arm (the one not embracing her child's head) and gradually opens and glides it outward and sideward (horizontal), with very low intensity, almost as if it is moving through water, and then softly moves it inward, wrapping it around the baby once more. Debra's vocal tone is low in intensity and drawn out, and she pauses frequently when she speaks. The evenness of her tone allows for little variation. When talking, she slowly lengthens her spine (vertical), her eyebrows tightly knit together, and her forehead narrows. After she finishes speaking, Debra again slowly shortens her spine (vertical) and leans sideways against the cushioned arm of the couch (horizontal). Then, she presses her upper lip over her lower. Her eyes soften and fill.

Debra seems to do this pushing movement with her lips when a feeling is about to emerge spontaneously, and she must hold it at bay for a little while longer, as if to prepare for its expression.

Rob tells R.F. that he has a lot of difficulty when Jenna cries. Although she is only 3 months old, Rob remarks, she cries at great length and with "ferocity." Although he says he has not been around very many babies, he thinks that Jenna's cries are unusually loud and persistent. In contrast with Debra, Rob's gestures are of high intensity and are quite sharp or abrupt. When speaking, he moves his forearms up and down and in a chopping manner (vertical), which mimics his abrupt style of speech, while pressing his upper arms close to his side. Similar to his gestures, Rob's vocal tone is abrupt and choppy, and his rapid words spurt out of his mouth and then come to an abrupt halt—spurt/stop, spurt/stop, and spurt/stop. Continually moving, Rob crosses and uncrosses his legs, stretches them out in front of him, and then quickly pulls them back (abrupt, fluctuating flow). These changes are made with a bound and quickly building intensity.

Rob's abruptness and high intensity, while part of his preferred repertoire of movement inclination, become more exaggerated with his growing anxiety and with what seems like desperation to be understood.

Rob admits that he is ill-equipped to take care of Jenna when she is so upset. "She just doesn't sound normal to me," he says. "I just get so riled up that I have to leave the room. Sometimes I even have to leave the house just to find peace. The tension in our family is so high—we are on red alert all the time," he continues. "We're always worrying, 'When will she start to cry? Is she ever going to stop? Will we ever get some sleep?'" Rob also says that he worries for his marriage. He feels that Debra is always tending to Jenna's needs and has forgotten about his. This, he says, makes him feel angry and alone. "I want things between me and Deb to be the way they were," he says. "I miss my wife!"

Here Rob's understandable feelings of loss become more apparent, but he is most likely protecting himself from feeling grief by converting it into anger. Clearly, there is a danger that these feelings could lead to a triangulated family dynamic, with Jenna and Mommy on one side and Daddy left out on the other side. The angrier he becomes, the more likely Debra will feel closed off from him and protective of herself and her daughter.

Jenna, still in Debra's arms, now begins to wake up and immediately starts to fuss. Debra says this is usually a difficult time for Jenna, as she transitions from sleep to wake. "Oh, oh, she's gonna start in now, and you'll see what it's like when she screams," Rob says. "You see, here *he* goes," Debra adds, "He's not allowing Jenna to do what she has to do. He's always commenting about her behaviors." But Jenna is not yet "screaming." Instead, she fusses and squirms in Debra's arms.

Rob has become extremely anxious and concerned that Jenna is disrupting his life. Because of this, he cannot clearly see his baby at each separate moment but only his exaggerated conception of her.

Now, R.F. suggests that Rob hold his daughter. When Rob takes the baby out of Debra's hands, he changes positions frequently and then gets up and paces around the room with Jenna in his arms. Rather than focusing on Jenna, however, he looks outward, and his eyes abruptly dart from one object to another. When Jenna's fussiness grows, the intensity of her movements increases, as does her vocal tone. At the same time, Rob presses his lips together, narrows at his collarbones, and moves his shoulders upward. He picks up his pace and, at the same time, starts to abruptly and rapidly jiggle Jenna up and down. Still not looking at Jenna, Rob says, "Come on sweetie. It's time to calm down. No crying now. You have to stop that. You should be smiling. Smile now." Each phrase grows more bound and intense and rushed. Debra comments, "That's exactly what Rob always does. When Jenna cries, Rob tries soothing her, but at the same time he's telling her to 'knock it off.' He's always telling Jenna that she's doing something wrong—as if Jenna could just stop her crying—as if she had a choice in the matter."

Here, Debra begins to criticize Rob for criticizing Jenna. Taking sides is taking shape. Debra has difficulty empathizing with Rob's fear and frustration.

R.F. asks Debra what she might be sensing or feeling at this moment, and Debra answers, "My body feels tight all over, and I feel so overwhelmed. It's as if I have to take care of the two of them, and I just don't have that kind of energy." Even before Debra has finished her sentence, Rob interrupts and says, "I can't be like you. I do things different from how you would." As Rob speaks, he jiggles the baby with more gusto, and Jenna now begins to cry. The sound of her wailing builds quickly in volume and intensity as each cry is pushed out in rapid and abrupt tones. In response, Rob jiggles Jenna even faster, and the intensity of her cry only increases.

Jenna cries as a signal to Rob that something is wrong and that she needs him to do something different from what he is doing. Rob is probably growing more anxious here, but he appears unaware of it and how his anxiety influences his daughter. He cannot pay enough attention to Jenna or to what he does with her.

Unable to calm her, Rob hands the baby back to her mother. Focusing her attention on Rob, R.F. asks, "What did you notice about yourself when Jenna became distressed?" Rob answers, "I was jiggling her pretty quickly, and I think I was pretty tense when I was doing it. I was already worried that she wasn't going to stop, and that she could go on screaming forever." "Well," R.F. adds, "if you believe she might scream forever, that really is worrisome. Can you remember what you felt in your body when her fussing and crying increased in intensity? If you take a few deeper breaths, it may be easier to remember what you sensed just before you began to jiggle her."

Rob takes a deeper breath, pauses, and then reports that he felt tight in his chest and that his breathing was "really shallow—like there was not enough air in the room. I still feel that now." R.F. asks him if he notices any feeling that accompanies the tension in his chest and limited breathing. Rob quickly responds, "I feel helpless, as if there is nothing I can do that will make a difference to the way Jenna feels."

R.F. says, "It seems that you want Jenna to feel different from the way she does. People do that all the time. They want the other person to change so that they'll feel better. But it doesn't usually work that way, and it's not working with Jenna, especially since she's a young baby and does not have the option to behave differently without help. As I listened to Jenna cry just now, I imagined that she might be a lot like you. When she's uncomfortable, she wants everyone to know it. And she expresses herself with great energy." Both Rob and Debra smile on hearing this, and R.F. adds, "In fact, sometimes you two may be so much alike, it may be hard to find a different way to be with her. She may stimulate your level of anxiety so that it increases at these times, and you inadvertently may be stimulating her anxiety."

R.F. tells Rob that he can use the fact that he and his daughter are so alike in their movement inclinations to his advantage. "Rather than asking Jenna to do something different ... as in 'don't cry,' which doesn't seem to work for your baby or for her mother, maybe you could try to connect with Jenna by telling her how you feel. For example, you might say, 'Jenna, you're so uncomfortable now. I understand. I can get pretty uncomfortable myself. Right now, you're uncomfortable, and I'm uncomfortable. We're in this together!'" Hearing this, Rob's face lights up. "You're right," he says.

"She can be as dramatic as I am." Debra chimes in, "No wonder I'm so exhausted!" and we all laugh with recognition and relief.

Although both Rob and his baby may appear to express themselves in dramatic ways, it is more accurate to say that each is reactive to certain kinds of stimulation and so responds intensely.

R.F. suggests that she and Rob explore through movement as a way of enhancing his awareness of the dilemma between him and Jenna, and he agrees. R.F. moves out of her chair and stands directly in front of Rob, who is also standing. She tells Rob that he probably jiggles Jenna when she is upset because it is his attempt to alleviate her distress but that this rhythm would be better used when he is playing with Jenna and not when she is fussing or upset. "The jiggling rhythm is out of sync and mismatching Jenna at these times as she needs to be soothed rather than stimulated," R.F. adds. To demonstrate, R.F. asks if she can hold both of Rob's hands. Once given permission, she abruptly jiggles them up and down (vertical) to replicate Rob's moves with Jenna and asks, "How do you feel when I do this? Here we go up/down, up/down, up/down." R.F.'s vocal tone expresses a kind of staccato similar to the tone used by Rob when speaking to Jenna. Rob says that the movements feel familiar and "definitely not calming. In fact, I'm getting kind of annoyed—and if you continue, I could get really angry." R.F. responds, "Good to know. Maybe it's agitating for Jenna as well," and suggests that they do something else. Now, R.F. takes Rob's hands again and begins to move them gradually from side to side (horizontal). At the same time, she shifts her weight from one foot to the other (horizontal) and begins a fluid swaying rhythm that matches the movements of her arms and her vocal quality—also gradual, low intensity, and free flowing.

Demonstrating to Rob how he might talk to his baby, R.F. says, "You look so uncomfortable, Jenna. I know just what that's like. That's just an aaaaawful way to feeeel," she adds as she stretches out her words making them more gradual and low in intensity. When she is finished, R.F. lets go of Rob's hands and takes a few steps back but still faces him. Now, she asks Rob to pay attention to any sensations that are predominant in his chest or abdominal region. He answers, "I feel 'slowed down'—quieter somehow. My chest doesn't feel tight the way it did before. And I can breathe easier. And I'm not annoyed with you anymore. I feel calmer."

R.F. tells Rob that she does not expect him to replicate her exact movements or vocal sounds: "I wouldn't want you to be someone other than you, just as I wouldn't want Jenna to be other than who she is. You'll find your own way to do this—and when you do, you'll be expanding your options for moving with Jenna and moving by yourself."

R.F. suggests that Debra and Rob come to the next session without Jenna to work with the issues between them in greater depth.

Vignette 2: Working With the Couple

One Week Later

In an effort to help Debra and Rob investigate their relationship in greater detail, R.F. invites them to try a movement exploration at the beginning of the session. R.F. asks the couple to stand facing each other and a few feet apart and then gives them a soft, round, flexible ball (approximately 5 inches in diameter) to hold between them by resting the palms of their hands on either side. Because it is always easy to talk instead of experiencing any anxiety that might emerge during this exploration, she asks if Debra and Rob would remain silent. R.F. tells them simply to notice what they experience as they feel their palms on either side of the ball. In addition, she asks each partner to notice how much or how little "push" they need to successfully meet the other or feel met by them. Either person may look into the other's eyes whenever they have the interest, or they can choose not to look.

Once the movement process begins, R.F. notices that Rob's legs are placed much wider apart than his hips, while Debra's legs are placed very close together. This makes Rob's stance quite stable but less easy to adjust and Debra's stance less stable but more flexible. In addition, Rob's elbows are extended such that his arms reach well into Debra's kinesphere—the space near her body. But, Debra keeps her elbows quite flexed so that her arms remain close to her torso.

Their positions give the appearance that Rob is shoving the ball toward Debra, who appears to comply with this arrangement.

As the exploration continues, Rob's face appears wide and open during the exchange. He lengthens his spine, bulges his chest forward, and appears to grow. In contrast, Debra's face narrows, and her eyebrows draw together as she abruptly shortens her length and narrows her chest, appearing to shrink. The ball moves closer and closer to her body.

As their postures reveal, Rob seems to enjoy this exploration as he expands in all dimensions, while Debra reduces herself in all dimensions and seems uncomfortable.

In time, R.F. asks Rob and Debra whether each feels well met by the other and suggests that if not, each tell the respective partner what he or she needs. But, each must signal through movement alone. Now, Debra begins to extend her arms, allowing them to move a bit farther away from her body. To do this, she clearly increases the intensity of her push. Almost immediately, Rob pushes back with an even more intense energy and succeeds in getting Debra's arms to move closer to her torso once more. The jolt from the intensity of Rob's movement pushes Debra back on her heels. All of a sudden and in response, Debra drops her hands to her sides, and Rob is left "holding the ball."

The exploration in pushing gives Rob, Debra, and R.F. much information to process. A visibly upset Debra shares how much this experience is like her daily life with Rob, how it illustrates what she often feels with him. If she increases her "push" and stands up for herself, Rob grows more intense. Debra then says she feels overwhelmed by his needs and his expressions most of the time and cannot find a place for herself. On hearing this, Rob is completely mystified. He says that he was so happy to feel the strength of Debra's push, and that he wanted more—"I love to feel her with me," he said, "so I pushed back to encourage her to be stronger with me."

It becomes clear that Rob needs more stimulation to feel well met, and when he asks for it in his way, Debra feels overwhelmed and anxiously withdraws. Each partner can now see and feel how the mismatch in their fundamental movements and inclinations accompanies a mismatch in their styles of asking for and making connection. With an intense focus on what they are doing and how they are doing it, the existential issue underlying their methods of interacting emerges spontaneously and therefore cannot be avoided.

As our discussion continues, it becomes clear that Debra needs to find a more energetic expression with Rob—to discover and maintain the solidity of her push so that she does not lose herself to him and so that he can feel her presence more distinctly. But, Rob also needs to be more sensitive to Debra. If he is going to feel met, he also must discover how to yield with Debra and to include her in his experience.

Debra and Rob pick up the ball to try once more. As they continue their movement inquiry, Rob says he is aware of the high intensity and driving force with which he pushes against Debra. He remarks, "I want you to push me back so that I *know* you're *there*."

Rob's desire and enthusiasm to connect with Debra fuel his push, which becomes more abrupt and intense.

Debra says, "When you shove me, I freeze." Rob wants to do something different but is not sure what to do. R.F. suggests, "See if you can soften your heart, whatever that means to you, and let Debra come to you." Taking in the instruction, Rob slowly shortens his spine, which allows the bulge in the front of his chest to lessen, while the area in the back of his chest widens. Rob's elbows bend and move closer to his torso, and the ball comes into a more equidistant relationship between them. R.F. invites Rob to become aware of his breathing and to emphasize the exhaling phase.

Taking a longer and deeper exhalation will allow Rob to attend more easily to himself and Debra.

Once Rob makes this adjustment, Debra has the space and time to become aware of her own pushing movements. "It's as if I don't know where to push from," she says. R.F. suggests that to find the necessary support to shift her pattern, Debra can widen her stance slightly so that her legs are directly under her hips. Next, R.F. asks her to bend both knees and then to push the floor away with the soles of her feet to straighten her legs. Debra tries this several times and then says she can sense both feet pushing against the surface of the floor. Soon, Debra's spine lengthens, and her head, which was pressed forward (sagittal), now reaches upward (vertical). R.F. suggests that Debra widen her elbows as they are still held close to her sides. Once she does this, her chest widens, and the intensity of the pushing of her hands against the ball increases. Debra says, "Now I feel some strength."

After a few moments, and using their newly expanded movement repertoires, they begin to move the ball in all dimensions—forward/backward, side/side, up/down—and a playlike rhythm emerges between them. It is now hard to detect who is leading and who is following.

As Rob slows and softens his push, he is able to yield with Debra and so is better able to feel her as they move together. Discovering that he can include Debra as part of his pushing experience allows the familiar anxiety—that he will not be met—to recede. As Debra increases the strength of her push, she is more resilient and not as bowled over by Rob's intensity.

Several Weeks Later

Under continued care by her pediatrician, Jenna's digestive difficulties have yet to abate. Both parents are naturally anxious and distressed about this. At the same time, they have come to realize that their clashes regarding how best to handle their baby's discomfort are the symptoms of more complex relational problems. And although their difficulties are not the cause of Jenna's dilemma, Debra and Rob understand that routinely clashing with each other cannot be helping her. For this reason, they decide to continue weekly sessions with R.F.

At this point in their work together, they have become more adept at noticing their individual contributions to their ongoing struggle. That is, they have learned about their particular movement styles and how they accompany and underlie their misunderstandings. Although their relationship has improved along with their heightened awareness, difficulties remain to be worked with and through.

In the following vignette, Jenna came to the session as their baby sitter was not available.

Vignette 3

"I often feel like the 'odd man out,'" Rob says as he watches Jenna asleep in her mother's arms. "I even get jealous of how close they are," he continues.

Rob is now more in touch with his feelings and is able to share them more easily with Debra at home and here in session.

Observing Jenna, it is obvious that the baby is completely giving over to her mother, and R.F. wonders if Rob could do something similar—give over to Debra's support. But Rob is not sure he can do this with anyone. "I think that I'm always the one who's supposed to do the supporting. I don't know that I trust anyone to support me—not even Deb," he says. "Let's experiment," R.F. replies.

The movement exploration offered in the earlier session has set the ground for this next and more intimate step. R.F. creates this new exploration to discover what happens in their dynamic that does not allow Rob to feel supported enough to yield to Debra.

Debra puts the sleeping baby down and sits directly in front of Rob, who is sitting on the floor. R.F. asks Rob if he would be willing to extend his hand toward Debra, and immediately and abruptly he does so. Next, she asks Debra to respond to Rob's gesture in whatever way she wishes. Debra slowly reaches her hand toward Rob and widens her palm so that he can place his hand onto hers. Then, she firmly wraps her fingers around his hand. After a few moments, Debra reports that she hardly feels Rob's hand resting on hers. R.F. notices that Rob's shoulders are pulled up toward his ears, and the elbow of his reaching hand is extended horizontally and slightly pulled toward him. R.F. tells Rob that he appears to be holding himself up. "I'm afraid I'll be too heavy for Debra ... or really for anyone to bear," says Rob. He realizes that he is afraid that Debra does not want to hold him. Now sensitized to how he holds himself back from Debra, memories rush to the foreground. "I had to take care of them ... but there was nobody to take care of me." Rob begins to tear and Debra moves closer and begins stroking his hand with low intensity.

The memory that emerges within Rob's posture–gesture pattern is stimulated to awareness within this immediate relational experience. Rob's father was an alcoholic, and his depressed mother grew overly dependent on her only child. Early in life, Rob realized that he could not rely on either parent and so held back his own needs in service of theirs. Although this is not new information, it is now filled with affect and here experienced clearly in relation to Debra.

R.F. asks Rob to bring all his attention to his hand—as if his hand were the whole of himself—and see whether he can give himself over to Debra's stroking. Rob says, "Debra, do it harder. I mean ... I need you to really press into me—I can hardly feel you." Debra presses rather than strokes his hand, then begins rhythmically pressing and releasing. In time, Rob's shoulders slowly drop, his breathing deepens, and he is better able to release the weight of his arm and hand into Debra's. Some moments pass until both Debra and Rob begin to breathe more easily and almost in synchrony. Debra says, "When you do that ... when you let go into my hand, I feel so much closer to you." R.F. asks Rob to now take Debra's hand in his. He begins to press her hand with high intensity. Debra says, "Can you just lightly stroke me?" And he does. After a few moments, R.F. says, "If you like, you can each take turns and play with the different ways of connecting with each other. Rob can experience Debra's lighter touch and Debra can experience Rob's stronger touch."

Discussion

Through these initial family sessions, Debra and Rob became more aware of when, how, and why they held back from each other. Rob learned that his determined push was a request to be firmly met so that he could feel someone with him. But, such intense pushing only alienated Debra, leaving Rob feeling isolated and outside the family. In the movement experiment, Rob found more of a balance between his yield and his push. Carefully adjusting to Debra gave Rob the opportunity to expand his core repertoire of movements, those forged in his family of origin, and to find more flexible ways of relating within this new family.

For her part, Debra came to understand that Rob needed a clearer response from her, and that her anxious withdrawal only led him to push harder. When Debra found the support for her own strong push, an expansion of her core repertoire as well, she became more resilient in the face of Rob's forcefulness and could meet him more easily. In addition, Debra learned how to give Rob the same exquisite attention that she gave to her baby. Now, he could more easily yield with her and feel calmed.

In subsequent meetings, Rob was able to hold and comfort Jenna in ways that had seemed impossible before. Watching Rob do this, Debra felt safe and could begin to relax her anxious control over the relationship between her husband and child. Working in greater harmony, the triangulation between all three moved toward a resolution. Jenna still suffered from digestive distress, but now both parents were able to bear her discomfort. In soothing themselves, they now could soothe her.

Chapter 7

Working With Individual Adults

INTRODUCTION

Throughout this book, we have demonstrated how the basic elements of body-to-body communication, which we observed in the interactive dialogue between babies and parents, remain active in adult life. In this chapter, we focus on the details of movement occurring between an individual adult patient and psychotherapist in session. Cases here demonstrate the similarities in structure and function between the early baby–parent relational dialogue and those of the patient–psychotherapist (Frank, 2001, 2004, 2005; La Barre, 2005, 2008). From the moment an adult walks into the consulting room, then settles, sits or lies down, gestures, and shifts positions, we note the nonverbal signals between patient and psychotherapist, coorganized, sent, and received using the same movement qualities, dimensions, and fundamental movements present between babies and their parents. The psychotherapist is moving all the time as well. The contours of change in their moving bodies are mutually affecting as each modulates and adjusts in response to the other person.[1]

Our understanding of the value of including foundational movement analysis in psychotherapy with adults derives from the point of view that psychotherapy always involves bidirectional actions. This idea is captured in such conceptions[2] as "transference and countertransference" (Freud, 1905/1953, 1905/1961b, 1909/1955b, 1912/1961a, 1920/1955a, 1940/1964; Racker, 1968); the "two-person field" (Yontef, 2001, 2002); "enactment" (Ellman & Moskowitz, 1998; D. B. Stern, 2010); "implicit relational knowing" (Boston Change Process Study Group, 2002, 2005, 2008); "role responsiveness" (Sandler, 1976); "projective identification" (Bion, 1962, 1963); "unformulated experience" (D. B. Stern, 1997, 2010);

---

[1] Even patients using the couch move a great deal; in addition, words alone carry the same rhythmic patterns and movement qualities that actions do (Condon, 1982; Frank, 2004; La Barre, 2001, 2005; Mahl, 1968).

[2] Space prevents us from presenting more than a few of the many citations that refer to these concepts.

"I see you, see me" (R. Kitzler, New York Institute for Gestalt Therapy, personal communication, 1997); and the "unthought known" (Bollas, 1987). These are formulations that capture various aspects of how interactive processes evoke in each participant many states and feelings through ways and means not always easily explained or clearly understood. We find that examining movement patterns of psychotherapist and patient provides important data needed to understand this mutual influencing.

The psychotherapist and patient experience each other through their embodied histories, constructed of patterns of actions and emotions that have evolved from infancy. Fundamental movements and movement inclinations are part of every movement and action pattern that has developed from the first year to the present. Thus, in seeing the fundamental movements and movement inclinations arising in the present moment, we are seeing embodied history. Embodied history includes procedural memory as well as the way specific "procedures" or action patterns participate in structuring perception, feeling, thinking, and any narrative meaning that has been constructed over time.

In sessions, particular elements of embodied history are elicited and shape present interactive patterns. Therefore, it is imperative that psychotherapists come to understand how and when their own actions either facilitate or inhibit the ongoing verbal and kinetic dialogue. Embodied history becomes a problem only when the present engagement is not working for one or both participants and when alternatives cannot be imagined or created. This is similar to what happens when a parent cannot adjust his movement to his child's needs or when partners of a couple cannot find alternative patterns of interaction. When psychotherapists are attentive to their movement patterns in session, interactive influences can be more readily seen and felt. Further such observation can help resolve miscommunications that develop from the inflexibility of both participants as well as elucidate troubling aspects of the interaction that neither can easily understand.

Our lexicon, foundational movement analysis, helps the psychotherapist clearly identify the patient's and his or her own present movement repertoire as it unfolds within a session. Attending to ever-present interactive movement processes always enhances understanding of the developing relationship because movements and actions constitute and convey how each individual organizes experience. Often, simply providing a direct, detailed delineation of interactive movements can be more valuable to understanding than verbal exchange. Here, the recognition of movement is significant because interactive signals are not being understood or because the movement elements say more than or something quite different from what is said in the verbal communication. It might be a particular movement or pattern of movements in a session that at once alerts the psychotherapist or patient to pay attention. Then, considering it together, they might discover disavowed experiences that are nevertheless evident in action but whose presence and significance have been kept out of awareness. Furthermore, new movement patterns involving patient and psychotherapist are created that evolve over time and directly express, without words, the ongoing narrative of therapy.

Studying the involvements and entanglements of the psychotherapist and patient's movement dialogue, then, is a compelling addition to the work of gathering information. This information is gleaned neither from the patient's nor from the psychotherapist's formulated perspective but offers an additional dimension that does not automatically designate meaning and so does not simultaneously interpret or judge data as they are collected. That is, movement observation and analysis allow the psychotherapist to expand on what data are available before reflection on the meaning begins, widening the hermeneutic field.

Inquiry into movement augments understanding of dynamics that might be conceptualized in various ways. For example, a psychotherapist might think that a patient is exhibiting a tendency toward "compliance," a concept that conjures up a spectrum of corollary ideas and hypotheses about "causes" and "cures." With the aid of movement analysis, the psychotherapist can investigate in great detail which patterns of movement interaction in the session have emerged between them that might underlie the compliance hypothesis.

Integrating an awareness of movement into psychotherapy brings what has been unspoken and unacknowledged into a growing, continuously evolving kinetic and verbal narrative. Movement awareness allows the psychotherapist to stay close to his or her own and the patient's immediate experience within the coconstructed kinetic dialogue. From here, kinesthetic empathy develops; that is, sensing and including the other person in one's own experience. How the psychotherapist shapes and reshapes his body in relation to the unfolding interactive dialogue communicates to the patient, albeit often without awareness, how well the patient has been met. Sensitivity to movement interaction, then, expands and augments the psychotherapist's ability to comprehend the fullness of himself and the person with whom the psychotherapist works.

In the two cases we present in this chapter, we show how the psychotherapist notices both the overall pattern that she and the patient coconstruct and those particularly weighted, striking moments that catch her attention and invite her to observe more closely. The first case, a gestalt case with R.F., demonstrates the observation of subtle fundamental movements that do not complete themselves, thus inhibiting lively experience within the relationship. This recognition becomes an opening for novel exploration that reveals essential information about relevant existential issues. The second is a psychoanalytic treatment with F.L. that shows how the kinetic dialogue over a longer period of time elaborately communicates the patient's conflicting states of body–mind that underlie the present, ongoing painful experiences that brought the patient into psychotherapy.

KAL, 26 YEARS

Brief History

Kal first sought treatment because, he said, "I feel uncomfortable in my body." Out of touch with his own sensations and feelings, he instead experienced chronic depression that he later recognized as stemming from feelings of deprivation and resentment. Kal also reported that he drank and often "blacked out" on the weekends. Kal, however, did not at first believe that he had a problem with his drinking.

As the therapy progresses, Kal, the fifth child in a family of eight, gradually begins to discover the roots of his discomfort. It emerges that his needs often went undetected by a mother who was "always overwhelmed" and by a father who held down two jobs and so was "always overworked." His parents argued much of the time, and Kal recalls that there was constant competition among his siblings for their parents' attention, especially at mealtimes. But Kal never believed that he could compete. He reports that the others were so much quicker than he was and better able to "fight for what they wanted."

Although he has few clear memories of his early childhood, Kal does remember the time his parents took all eight children for ice cream as this was a big treat for everyone. With great excitement, they all piled into the family station wagon to go downtown. Once at the store, everyone got an ice cream cone, and then they went rushing out to the car for the drive home. Kal, generally the child with the slowest pace and often referred to as the "dreamer," gradually made his way out of the store and down the street to where their car was parked. But, when he got there, he watched as the station wagon pulled away from the curb and headed up the street. Feeling somewhat shocked, Kal dropped his ice cream onto the sidewalk and just stood there, waiting. His parents, eventually realizing that Kal was not among them, turned the car around to go back for him. On the one hand, Kal reported, "They did come back, and I know they felt bad. They were blaming themselves and each other," but on the other hand, he remarked, "I never did get my ice cream." And, Kal never asked for it. "Why ask for something when you probably won't get it?" was his regular refrain.

At 10 years of age, Kal understood that he was not like other boys and was terrified at the thought that he "might like boys the way boys are supposed to like girls." Coming from a deeply religious, Catholic background, Kal attempted to hide his sexual identity from his family, his friends, and himself. He prayed nightly that he would have a wife and children someday so that he could be "normal." This prayer continued even when Kal went away to college. Once away from home, however, Kal could allow himself to have sexual relations with men but only when he was drunk or under the influence of drugs, which became increasingly frequent and out of his control.

After much discussion in therapy, Kal attempted to stop drinking on his own. But, he would stop and then start again. Although R.F. had some concern about his drinking, she was also optimistic that through clarifying his desires and needs, both sexual and nonsexual, and through reclaiming his body and his sensate self, he would eventually stop drinking. As therapy progressed, Kal did become more aware of his feelings, recognizing that he was depressed and recognizing also that he drank to avoid his depression. He also discovered that his depression only worsened with his drinking. On that basis, he began attending daily AA meetings.

In brief, Kal's initial presentation was of a young man with little accessible inner life who was drifting without a clear sense of what he wanted for himself. He sought a therapeutic experience that would help get him in touch with his body, and implicitly with himself, but the same vague, elusive quality also entered the therapeutic relationship. Early intervention made it clear that much work would have to be done to help Kal achieve basic awareness of his sensations and feelings and to name them. This would require patience, persistence, and perseverance on the part of both psychotherapist and patient.

At the point of therapy that is represented in the following vignettes, Kal had been sober for 6 months and in treatment with R.F. for 18 months.

Description of Kal's Movements in Therapy

Kal walks into the room with a spring to his step. R.F. notices that the heels of his feet never fully contact the floor. Instead, each heel only lightly grazes the floor and then quickly lifts off. Kal transfers most of his body weight to the balls and toes of his feet, which then push down with too much effort.

When the heel does not fully land on the floor, it does not have the requisite support to push down and away from it. The lack of push from Kal's heels is compensated by the extra pushing effort from the balls of the feet and the toes. This gives Kal's walk a bounce or spring-like appearance (vertical).

At the same time, Kal's head pushes down and subtly pulls backward so that the push from below, enabling his spine to lengthen upward, is met by a push from above—his head pressing down and back, which compresses his neck. It is as if Kal bounces up and is pushed right back down at the same time.

R.F. has come to understand Kal's manner of walking as emblematic of how he connects with the world: He moves up and toward what he wants but simultaneously pushes himself down and back. This leaves Kal with chronic difficulty getting that which he most desires. As with other aspects of Kal's movement repertoire, this "bouncing" pattern of walking suggests the great inner complexity, not yet available for reflection, of what is entailed in being Kal.

Gazing steadily downward, neither looking up at R.F. nor looking around the room, Kal walks directly to the chair. He slowly takes off his suit jacket, folds it neatly, and places it on the back of the chair. Once seated, Kal gradually and lightly (low intensity) places each arm and hand on the chair's arms, his long fingers draping over their edge. Now, he lifts himself upward from his waist and compacts and narrows his torso. These adjustments emphasize the length of his body (vertical). Kal tends to prefer this vertical dimension, rarely relaxing his posture and leaning against the sides of the chair in horizontal.

The preference for the vertical dimension suggests some attempt at "sticking up" for himself, as though Kal wants to assert himself. But, his upward-moving impulse lacks the solid push of his feet on the floor and pelvis on the chair, so there is not enough support for his assertions. He also makes use of the sagittal dimension, chiefly to pull back and retreat from another.

When he is sitting, Kal's head remains pushed not only down but also back (sagittal) as he gazes off to the left. At the same time, he also pulls his torso slightly backward and away from R.F. When he is listening, Kal lifts his head to look toward her. At such moments, his eyebrows narrow, and his otherwise softly focused eyes reach out with increasing intensity.

The movements with the eyes and eyebrows are distinctive. In this moment, the display of earnestness is the extent of Kal's reach, but it has its own forcefulness.

Kal sits with even tension, rather motionless, with infrequent gestures. When he does gesture, he restricts his movements to his hands and fingers as he gradually and lightly rotates his wrists horizontally outward to open his hands in emphasizing a point. Then, he abruptly retreats from that wider and more open position, once more returning his hands to the armrests of the chair. His gestures hardly vary and are economical. His vocal pattern is more varied. His words often rush quickly from his mouth with some intensity, as if being pushed out, but then abruptly stop as he pauses before the next rush of words.

Kal's movement inclinations are part of his kinetic temperament. He is most comfortable in moderate bound intensity. That is, his tension builds to a moderate intensity that holds even and then abruptly dissipates. This also relates to how Kal experiences and expresses emotions. Kal prefers to keep himself "on even keel," and he generally appears unruffled, although when upset, he readily becomes more bound and intense. Only his vocal pattern, with spurting stops and starts, openly shows his distress.

Vignette I

Kal sits in the armchair in front of R.F., looking down and off to the left. He lifts his ribcage up and lowers it down with each truncated breath.

After a few moments, Kal reaches his left hand to his forehead and begins to lightly grasp and gradually pull his index and middle fingers across his eyelid, as if wiping something away. He does this several times. His breathing is shallow.

R.F. has observed this hand gesture in prior sessions when Kal is on the edge of sadness but has not yet felt or acknowledged his feeling. It is almost as if Kal were wiping away an as-yet-unformed tear.

Pressing her head forward and toward Kal, R.F. bends slightly at her waist. She is aware of her own shallow breathing, narrowing chest, and a vague feeling of sadness. She then gradually settles back in her chair and, with a deeper and longer inhalation, widens her chest.

R.F. monitors her own reactions in relation to Kal as a way of understanding what is happening between them. Is this her feeling of sadness alone, or is Kal also feeling sad?

Now Kal looks up, his eyes softly focused and reaching toward R.F. Soon they dart away and toward the floor as Kal reports that he had an "unusual dream" the night before. Although he remembers only a fragment of it, he thinks it is important. R.F. invites him to tell his dream in the present tense.

R.F. suggests that Kal report the dream in the present tense to heighten the immediacy of its experience, which now includes the psychotherapist in the telling.

Kal tells R.F., "I dreamed that I had been drinking the night before. And then, I run to an AA meeting. I feel out of control—and I run to the meeting—and sit down in the group. I try to speak, but I can't—I mean—no words come out of my mouth, and I just sit there. I feel out of control—tears are rolling down my cheeks. I'm in a panic." Kal tells his dream with an abrupt and choppy vocal cadence and, at the same time, hardly gestures or shifts his posture. His breathing is shallow: Not much air comes in and not much air goes out. Kal's eyes remain fixed on the floor in front of him, and he presses his shoulder bones inward and narrows his chest. After almost every sentence, he presses his lips together. Sensitive to the gradual and subtle shifts of his posture, gestures, and vocal pattern, R.F. feels a growing tightness in her abdominal area. To get more comfortable, she again widens her chest, which has narrowed, and breathes deeply.

These subtle adjustments not only allow R.F. to find support within this anxious field but also offer support to Kal. That is, R.F. makes room for Kal's anxiety by opening to it, akin to the way a parent opens and shapes her body to embrace, yield, and breathe with her child.

Kal reports, "I feel very, very uncomfortable—in my stomach. I guess I'm anxious—even now I'm anxious. Maybe—I feel panic." His words spurt out with abrupt high intensity, and he is unmoving (high-intensity bound flow).

Kal has spent much of his life distancing himself from his sensations and feelings because he has felt so alone with these kinds of experiences.

Knowing or at least suspecting that he feels anxiety or panic is a big step for him.

Kal enters his dream once more: "I can't speak, but I can feel my tears. I feel out of control. I'm in a panic." R.F. asks, "Do you want something from the others?" And Kal replies, "What could they do for me?" "I don't know," R.F. says, "but in your dream, you're drinking, and then you run to a meeting. You run there. I don't know what they could do for you." Kal slowly takes his hands off the chair's arms and places them on his thighs as he pulls his arms and shoulder bones back and up in the direction of his ears. He looks directly at R.F. His eyes appear intensely focused. In response, R.F. moves her head slightly forward and toward Kal.

Kal says nothing for several moments and then reports, "I feel a pressure inside me," but says he does not know what that is. Immediately after speaking, Kal again presses his lips together, and his eyes remain focused on R.F. while his body remains motionless.

R.F. recognizes the movement interaction between them as part of a repetitive pattern. In his movement, Kal reminds her of a baby saying "yes" and "no" simultaneously—reaching out with the eyes as a yes while pressing the mouth closed as a no. Often, movements of the mouth and eyes work in conjunction to signify how much or how little stimulation the baby wants and is ready for. In the present situation, Kal's eyes reach out and toward R.F., but his lips are held tight. The combination does more than indicate his ambivalence; it embodies it in the moment. Kal opens to the possibility of receiving support but also potentially becomes aware of his conflicts over the issue of asking for help. Yet, he cannot articulate the separate ingredients in what he may be feeling. All he can feel is an indistinct "pressure" of some kind.

Attentive to Kal's lips, which are tightly pressed together, R.F. asks if he notices them. When Kal answers, "Yes, I feel my mouth is like a vise," R.F. encourages Kal to stay with that experience. After exaggerating the pressing of his lips for a few moments, he says, "I don't know why, but I'm shut down here." As Kal says this, he glances downward, presses his hand to his mouth, and holds it there for some moments as his other hand lifts off the chair and presses into his abdomen with a loosely grasped fist. Then, he quickly places both hands onto his lap and looks downward.

R.F. imagines Kal is trying to "figure out" what he feels rather than experiencing it. She invites him to try a different movement with his lips. She thinks that in opening and exploring with his lips—the polar opposite of pressing them together—the meaning of the movement might more readily reveal itself.

"Instead of pressing your lips together, I wonder what it would be like to part them?" she asks and then suggests that he imagine himself doing it before he actually tries the movement. Quickly and uncharacteristically, Kal agrees to "give it a try" and slowly parts his lips—opening his mouth to elongate and widen and then release. He does this with some awkwardness and in an uneven rhythm.

After the first 6 months of work with R.F., Kal is more able to say what he does or does not want to do in session. In general, these explorations have become acceptable parts of the interactions between them, but the issue of compliance, or resistance to it, can never be put totally aside. R.F. is sensitive, therefore, to any bodily sign from Kal, or her reaction to him, that might indicate either state so they can explore it.

R.F. suggests, "Kal, perhaps you can be aware of the insides of your cheeks, how your tongue sits on your lower jaw and the back of your throat." Kal continues lengthening his body, while widening and releasing his mouth, and now his movements appear smooth. Narrowing her upper torso, leaning forward with her hands on her lap, R.F. joins Kal in the movement exploration.

The new movement, considerably different from Kal's routine repertoire, may feel out of character and provoke feelings of self-consciousness and discomfort, so that it becomes just something he is doing, but neither sensing nor feeling. For this reason, R.F. joins him to offer support and encourage Kal to stay with whatever experience might emerge.

The exploration draws on the observation of babies, whose mouths are primary and fundamental to early searching experiences and convey their interest in and desire for something. The earlier reaching pattern, adapted through time, still functions in adult behavior. In creating this exploration, R.F. is still informed by Kal's dream, in which the possibility of reaching out for and getting help from the AA group is clearly inhibited by having eyes that tear and a mouth that is pressed closed and says nothing. Here, she is pursuing the possibility that the observed pattern of Kal's tight lips, the motoric converse of reaching with his mouth, might be connected to his feeling "speechless" in the reporting of his dream. Reaching with his mouth might give Kal the subsequent sensorimotor support to work through the existential dilemma of asking clearly and directly for what he needs and wants, a developing theme in therapy and in his daily life.

As Kal continues his exploration, he seems absorbed by and curious about his movements. R.F. notices that his breathing has deepened—more air coming in and more air going out. Using this as confirmation of how Kal is taking her suggestions, she adds another element to the experiment: "Now begin to rotate your head very slowly from one side to the other, similar to an organism with only a mouth to take you from place to place. Let your lips reach out and guide you from one side to the other, as if you were searching for something."

R.F. has confidence that something important will be gained through Kal's exploring, although of course, she cannot know the end result. Now, she is both with him and slightly ahead of him almost simultaneously.

There is no specific or desired outcome for the exploration other than the moment-to-moment awareness of what is real and what is true for Kal. Kal's deeper breathing pattern is an indication that he is supporting himself with greater ease. As he moves, Kal begins to get in touch with a more authentic experience of self. As he reaches with his mouth, R.F. encourages him to stay with his investigation by incrementally adding elements to heighten his awareness while continuously attending to how Kal incorporates her suggestions.

Kal slowly and gradually parts and purses his lips as he moves his head from side-to-side. R.F. continues to mirror his movements with a similar light, smooth quality, staying in low intensity and freely flowing. She sees that Kal's eyes pop open and widen even more here and there, and he narrows his eyebrows. Kal also notices this and says, "Sometimes my eyes want to take over." He then closes them, releases the tension in his forehead, and continues moving his head from one side to the other, still leading with his mouth.

Kal grows more involved with his movements as he reaches with his mouth well beyond himself and into space in many directions: horizontally, vertically, sagitally. He now rises out of his chair to stand and places his feet firmly on the floor to bring the rest of his body into the action. Still initiating the movement with his mouth, and with a push of his feet, Kal reaches his head around to the right, with his chest and pelvis following as he rotates around himself. Then, using a similar reaching process, he rotates back again.

Completing his exploration, Kal stands in front of R.F., who also is now standing. His chest appears wider and slightly bulges forward, and he no longer presses his upper torso backward. Kal takes a few deeper and easier breaths. After some moments, R.F. asks him what he notices. Placing both hands along the sides of his mouth, Kal says, "I have lips. I've never felt them quite like this before. Maybe once when I was on vacation in Amsterdam."

Without pausing for a moment, Kal goes on to say that he feels easier in his neck and shoulders and even his jaw, and that "the room looks brighter and softer somehow." This time the cadence of his words is more free flowing and sinuous (flow fluctuating) and lower in intensity. R.F. senses lightness in her chest and takes a few deeper breaths.

R.F. catches the fleeting reference to Amsterdam, where homosexual behavior is accepted and supported. However, what has the greatest impact on R.F.'s experience is Kal's apparent sense of ease and perceptual openness. The remark about Amsterdam, she believes, is a nod to Kal's sexuality, which he has only discussed in fits and starts. Recognizing that the work with Kal's mouth has helped him to open up to his sensual and sexual feelings, R.F. is encouraged but does not want to get ahead of Kal's own readiness and awareness. R.F. offered the exploration of this pattern in its most basic and elemental form as it emerges early in life.

They decide to sit down again, and R.F. asks if Kal would be willing to return to his dream. "Look around at the AA group with the same eyes that were in your dream—filled with tears—with a reaching expression but this time with your more relaxed mouth."

Kal lightly brushes his hand over his lips. After pausing for some moments, he says, "Maybe I want something from them after all ... yes, I do want something from them, but I don't know what it is." Kal says this as he lifts his shoulders upward, which narrows his chest and simultaneously opens and extends his arms and hands outward and toward R.F., and then gently folds them onto his thighs.

R.F. experiences Kal's reaching gesture toward her as a signal that he is including her in his experience of "wanting something."

"Well," R.F. continues, "You might say exactly that, 'I want something from you, but I don't know what it is.'" Kal slowly nods his head in agreement and then looks down and off to one side, but says nothing. His hands return to the arms of the chair and lightly grasp its edges. R.F. suggests that he first make the statement to himself rather than aloud to try it on. A few more moments pass until Kal says the words aloud, with a soft and halting cadence to his vocal pattern. Kal then repeats the phrase several more times, still looking down. He brings his hands to his lap, clasps them together, then abruptly looks up and toward R.F. and reports, "I want to say it. But when I do, I feel anxious."

Kal may be feeling, without recognizing it, the immediacy of his need for help from R.F. Working from the premise that she may be, somehow, in Kal's dream, she decides to risk more and include herself more directly in his present experience.

After pausing for a few moments, R.F. asks Kal to make the statement directly to her: "I wonder if you would say that to me, 'Ruella, I want something from you, but I don't know what it is,'" she suggests. Kal looks down at first and then up and toward R.F., and his forehead furrows. Taking a deeper inhalation, he begins the phrase several times, but each time the words emerge with such a light, low-intensity quality that they are hardly audible.

Kal's words seem to fall out of his mouth and onto his lap, never quite reaching R.F. Here, the therapeutic task created by R.F. and offered to Kal to heighten his awareness, "Ruella, I want something from you, but I don't know what it is," is reshaped and returned to her by the lower-intensity expression of Kal's vocal quality.

"I can't sense my mouth and say the words or feel much of anything at the same time. I just can't get all that together. I don't know why it's so hard," he says. Now, Kal's voice grows louder and more abrupt, and the fingers of his right hand, remaining on the chair's arm, make a fist. "I feel stupid," he barks.

On the surface, it may appear that Kal is angry with R.F. for asking him to do something he does not want to do. However, in experiencing Kal, R.F. feels that his anger is the result of his anxiety and frustration turned inward: He wants to say the word but is having difficulty being so direct with her. Rather than have him continue being annoyed with himself, which in the past has led to a stream of self-castigation ending in shame, R.F. intervenes to help Kal turn his criticality outward.

R.F. gradually leans forward in her chair and says, "Kal, maybe my asking you to repeat that phrase was stupid?" Kal quickly pushes the base of his pelvis onto the chair, and his spine lengthens. Looking directly at R.F. and with an evenly held gaze, he says, "You're right ... that was a stupid sentence. Don't ask me to do that again." Now, his words stream out of his mouth easily and with moderate intensity. R.F. slowly nods in response and gently says, "Yes. Good. I get it."

Again, Kal transforms the therapy experiment and now, in his way, tells R.F. what he wants.

Discussion

It is not possible to know how well met Kal was or was not in his first year of life, and it is not necessary. It is useful, however, to understand how fundamental movements emerge and continue to develop when communication between parent and baby is easy enough or when it is fraught with difficulty. As R.F. observes the emergence of Kal's movements, she imagines him as a baby, one whose parents do not respond well enough to his needs and desires. Their lack of understanding left Kal unable to clarify either his needs or his desires for himself throughout his childhood, and now, in his adulthood, they remain vague. In exploring the movement patterns of early infancy, a primary and underlying support for "wanting" is exercised and made available for use.

In this vignette, attending to what Kal senses, perceives, and knows involved not only phenomenological diagnosis but also therapeutic treatment as Kal's awareness itself heightened his capacity to connect with himself and his situation. As he reached with his mouth, Kal experienced his authenticity in the moment. He identified with himself as the doer and the doing: "This is my experience." Later in the session, when asked to make a direct statement to R.F. that involved his wanting something from her, Kal moved into his routine pattern of retreat. That was to be expected. At the cutting edge of new experience, one generally moves back and forth between new and routine behaviors. But soon, and with just enough encouragement from R.F., Kal was able to make another statement that was direct and clear. As Kal becomes more attentive to and interested in how and when he clamps down on his mouth and his wanting, he will become better able to assess his reactions and choose more adaptive and creative responses to his situation.

Vignette 2: Several Weeks Later

Kal sits upright on the chair with his right leg crossed over his left and his arms and hands placed on the arms of the chair. Although he remains fairly motionless in this position, his words are pushed out with moderately intense stop-and-start spurts. "Philip is not really someone—I'm really attracted to," he says, "but he's good to me—we have a good life—I wish—I wish he'd take better care of himself though—He needs to lose weight." Kal pauses. Then he continues, "I'd probably be more attracted—if he took better care of himself. Sometimes I tell him that—but he never does anything about it—he just shrugs me off." He pauses. "The conversation ends ..." Kal pauses, holding his breath, then goes on, "but we have a good life."

There is a striking discrepancy between his motionless posture and his more mobile vocal cadences. His body pattern retains its generally even keel, but his vocal pattern conveys his anxiety. In addition, his vocal rhythm of spurting and then stopping echoes his walking pattern of springing up while he almost simultaneously pushes himself down.

Kal is silent for some time. He remains still. His head tilts downward and his eyes narrow as he gazes off to the left. R.F. senses emptiness in her chest and feels the edge of sadness. "Well," R.F. says, "I feel sad hearing you say that. I know it can be difficult to be in a relationship with someone who doesn't seem to take in what you're saying." In response, the ankle of Kal's right foot, still crossed over his left leg, abruptly and with intensity, rotates inward, flexes, and then releases, as his lips press together and hands grasp more firmly onto the ends of the chair. "I don't know," he says. More time passes. Kal neither speaks nor moves and continues gazing down and off to the left. "I wonder what it is you don't know right now," R.F. adds. Immediately, Kal again rotates and flexes the ankle of his right foot, but this time it remains held in this contracted position. Now, R.F. holds her breath and tightens her body.

The rotation and flexion of his ankle catches R.F.'s attention. R.F. imagines that Kal is saying "no" to something in the moment, and that Kal probably does not "know" about his no.

"Kal, I'm interested in what your ankle is doing right now," R.F. says. "You've done that a couple of times now." R.F. crosses one leg over the other, looks down at her ankle and does a similar flexing and releasing movement. Kal watches her for a moment, then looks down at his still contracted ankle, releases it, and contracts it several more times. "Yeah, I didn't notice. What about it?" he asks. "I'm not sure," R.F. replies.

Kal repeats the inward rotation and flexion of his foot but this time with enough intensity and effort that his right leg abruptly lifts upward and away from his left as he pulls it in the direction of his torso. Now, Kal's eyes widen, and he smiles. He then releases the movement so that his left leg rests on his right once more. Noting with Kal that he seems to enjoy the energy of that movement, R.F. invites him to do it with even more intensity and to see what happens. With a broader smile, Kal abruptly rotates the whole of his leg inward and pulls it further toward his torso and begins subtle pumping motions: pulling his leg in and pushing it out in abrupt and measured movements, as if experimenting with the feel of it. Suddenly, and with greater intensity, Kal pulls his right leg still closer to his torso and immediately pushes it diagonally across his body and into full extension.

R.F. is reminded of how Kal's pumping action looks like an early developmental pattern of flexing/withdrawing and extending/thrusting of a baby's legs when the baby is on his or her back and kicking. These patterns underlie all later pushing movements and are crucial foundational supports for kicking, crawling, and standing throughout life. Metaphors such as "standing on one's own two feet" and "standing up for oneself" rest on these key aspects of differentiation.

Kal exaggerates the gesture and, in so doing, begins to sense the next step or the completion of the act. This is indicated by his smile, a prediction of what is to come. The suggestion of further exploration is offered to Kal to enhance his awareness and is reshaped by him as he adjusts within its frame to make it his own. As Kal embellishes his movement, the underlying impulse that accompanies the gesture clarifies itself.

Kal repeats the gesture a few more times, flexing and then pushing his leg into full extension. With every pushing repetition, the movement subtly changes its trajectory and now is made directly toward R.F. Both Kal and R.F. smile, and R.F. says, "When I see the power of your push, I feel energized."

R.F. wonders aloud if Kal's kicking in her direction has anything to do with her comments regarding his remarks about his lover, Philip. It takes some time for Kal to remember what R.F. said, but eventually he recalls, "You said something about Philip not understanding what I need."

Kal reflects on this for some time, focusing his eyes and head downward and off to the left as he tells R.F., "I felt you were criticizing me—for using Philip. Staying with him for the good life and not because we're good together." After some moments, R.F. responds, "When I feel criticized, I'm generally angry. It's my first response." Kal lifts his head and looks directly at R.F. "Yes," he says forcefully, as he abruptly lifts his hands off the edges of the chair and pushes them onto his thighs with a slapping sound, "I was angry." Once more, Kal lifts his hands and pushes them onto his thighs, but this time they strike downward in coordination with his words, "I am angry." R.F. lengthens her spine, widens her chest, leans slightly forward, and says, "Yes, I see you are, and with me." Kal uncrosses his legs, clasps his hands together on his lap, and says with a firm and even tone to his voice, "Sometimes I'm angry with you."

Kal's anger is kept in check early in the session and is first noted by R.F. in the subtle expression of his ankle rotating inward and held in flexion. Its pushing impulse appears inhibited in relation to R.F., who has contributed to its emergence. With R.F.'s encouragement and equally important postural support, Kal is able to "push back" with his angry declaration. This is an accomplishment for him.

Discussion

Pushing movements enable one to separate from, while simultaneously including, another in experience. These movements are the crucial support for differentiation. But, in Kal's family of origin, his push became buried in a series of controlled expressions and deadened experiences. This chronic dissatisfaction is now, predictably enough, embodied and restated in the present. It is, in fact, the past/present. Not being able to express the truth about himself, Kal naturally and importantly felt, and still feels, resentment and often outrage. He rarely expresses this outwardly but rather turns it inward as a troubling criticism toward himself or as an unspoken criticism of others—especially his partner, Philip.

In this vignette, it can be seen how Kal inadvertently denies his right to react negatively to R.F.'s statement and, in so doing, inhibits his capacity to push. R.F.'s awareness of how movement patterns function in infancy allowed her to recognize the small gestures of Kal's foot and ankle. These subtle patterns were by no means irrelevant incidental gestures but functioned in a significant way between them. Now, with growing awareness of his movement interactions within the session, as well as his motives and feelings, Kal was able to uncover and recover his push.

As the therapy progressed, Kal became better able to expose the vulnerable and therefore more receptive parts of himself to R.F. and was able to find greater ease within the relationship. This gave ground to further risk taking on both their parts. In later sessions, Kal continued to develop the ability to stand on firm ground as he voiced his objections when he disagreed with R.F., Philip, or anyone. This was done through ongoing discourse, both nonverbal and verbal. Discovering the ability to feel and say "no," Kal also became able to say "yes." He began to notice the stunted movement impulses that accompanied those times when he diminished his experience. His awareness helped Kal to identify with a more adult part of him and allowed him to discover and support his appropriate differences, disagreements, and anger, which in turn enabled him to express his feelings of love more freely. This capacity to attend gave Kal greater bodily comfort, something he had longed for when therapy began. By the time his 6½-year therapy concluded, Kal found more pleasure in his sexual encounters, which felt like a triumph to him.

PAULA, 40 YEARS

Paula begins psychotherapy because she is worried about her recently increasing explosions of rage at her husband, Lucas. They have been married for 10 years and have two girls, who are 8 and 5 years old. She finds her daughters for the most part easy to manage and delightful, and she never rages at them or anyone else except Lucas. She has never experienced rages before. Paula feels certain that Lucas himself is not the problem but rather that his demanding and unpredictable work schedule has become more than she can bear. She loves him, and she reports that he is patient, kind, and always ready to negotiate the problems that come up between them.

Paula says that she used to be more patient about her husband's grueling work schedule. Even if she felt disappointed, she "forced herself" to make the best of things. She was busy with her own work and their two children, so she "went along," as she puts it, expecting that as the kids got older she and Lucas would recover their former intimacy. Recently, however, she feels much less willing to accommodate Lucas's schedule and finds herself raging about it. In searching with F.L. for explanations of her rages, she recognizes that she is hurt by Lucas's decreasing attention to her in general and by the declining frequency and quality of their sexual relationship. "These problems are not new—they come and go with Lucas's schedule, and so I can't see how they have anything to do with my explosions." She laughs dismissively, "I think it's early menopause—and a stupid midlife crisis."

Vignette I

Paula enters the room with a quick, firm step (she pushes sharply from her back foot through to the reaching front foot). She keeps her back lengthened as she reaches her upper body forward and down to place her coat and sweater on a chair and her bags next to it on the floor. She bends forward with ease to untie her shoes, then straightens again, and uses her toes to push one shoe off and then the other. Next, she does several things simultaneously: She pushes downward with her feet to elongate again, pulls her hair back by running her right hand through it, pivots sharply on her feet, and then takes three firm steps to the couch next to F.L. Her brow is furrowed. She sits down smoothly and adjusts herself on the couch.

Paula's body is flexible and expressive, and she is casual and relaxed in her manner. Her entrance is direct and clear, crisp. F.L. experiences her movement as if she is saying, "Here I am—let's get to work."

Paula leans sideways on a pillow at the right arm of the couch, swings her feet up and onto the couch, and takes a deep breath. Crispness melts as she yields and pushes onto the couch, adjusting her flow and her position. Paula quietly begins to weep. Next, she twists her upper body and reaches across it with her left hand to the tissue box on her right and takes a tissue.

The crisp entry and her yielding onto the pillow and couch are two of Paula's characteristic movements in sessions. She also often repeats the reach with her left hand across her body to get a tissue or water on her right.

As she dries her cheeks, she quickly swings her legs and feet down and then straightens her back again. "It happened again—I feel so ashamed," she says sharply.

Her abrupt shift of position, the third of Paula's typical movements, goes with an equally abrupt shift in her emotional state.

She leans her upper body forward, rests her elbows on her thighs, and gestures with her hands as she speaks. She opens her palms to the front and goes on: "We were talking about our plan to go all together for a walk in the park, and then Lucas said that he would have to work after all and so would not be able to make it." She lifts her hands and upper body, then drops just her hands to her lap, and says, "And I lost it!" Then, she leans forward and rests her elbows on her thighs again, and continues, "The girls were in bed—Lucas held me and calmed me down. And then I felt so sorry." She looks sideways at F.L., "What is wrong with me? It's not like he can help it that he has to work—so I need to accept that already. I used to accept it better. Poor guy works so hard all the time for all us, and instead of feeling sorry for him, I explode at him."

In this moment, Paula has pushed away from weeping and brought herself back to the crisp firmness of her entry into the room, now also reaching forward, looking for answers. In Paula's extensive movement range, she includes all three dimensions and all of the movement qualities—gradual, abrupt, high and low intensity, bound and free, even and flow fluctuating. She uses the fundamental movements of yield, push, reach, grasp, pull, and release with grace and fluidity—that is, her movements relate easily to one another and as well lend support to what she is doing and saying in each moment. Over the course of the session, she occupies three distinct positions in a short span of time and makes very abrupt transitions between them.

She and F.L. discover over time that Paula's range contributes to her having a great deal of adaptive capacity—she appears to shape herself quickly and easily to accommodate environmental situations and internal emotional shifts. This characteristic not only helps her to be comfortable in many situations but also complicates the process of developing clarity and conviction about her own needs and desires.

Vignette 2

As Paula walks to the couch, she uses her usual direct and firm step. Her face shows strain as she presses her lips flat against each other. She is frowning. As usual, she sits on the couch to F.L.'s left. She adjusts the pillow at the arm of the couch so that she can rest her head and at the same time look at F.L. She weeps. She reaches her left hand across her body for a tissue in the box to her right.

She wipes her eyes and nose and draws her knees upward toward her chest as she continues to cry. Her legs and feet rest sideways on the couch, and the intensity of her crying increases. She sobs, "I screamed at him again last night—I even threw a plate of fruit on the floor—not *at* him, at least."

F.L. says, "Mmm. Something in this is very hard for you to bear." Paula looks up at her. F.L. finds herself leaning farther forward and then gradually leaning back again; she repeats that movement several times, creating a slow rocking movement. F.L. now speaks with a rhythm similar to her rocking movement: "Something feels *too much* for you right now." F.L. takes a breath, which involves slightly lifting her torso to lengthen, and continues, "But we don't yet know what's derailing you." Paula nods and shakes her head "yes," and then "no," in agreement and in time with F.L.'s rhythm. Paula's weeping subsides a little, and she speaks about how upset she feels when Lucas disappoints her. She says, "It's beyond reason—I know he can't help it, and I know he is hurting, too."

F.L., leaning forward and then back again, says, "There *is* something 'beyond reason,' yes—there is something that needs sorting out." Once again, F.L. takes a breath, and now Paula abruptly shifts her own position so that her feet are again on the floor and then suddenly pushes up to standing and takes a step as if to wander off. "What just happened?" F.L. asks. Paula is thoughtful for a moment and replies, "I just need to stretch."

The verbal narrative continues without a break, but the "kinetic text" (La Barre, 2005) is full of sharp disjunctions. Paula first shifted into leaning, and F.L. found herself following, then Paula abruptly straightened, leaving her own grief aside and leaving F.L. wondering.

Paula sits, upright again, and continues the report on her outburst with Lucas. She next puts her elbows on her thighs and leans forward over her knees, in a position that keeps her weight on her feet. F.L. slides back against her chair and takes a deep breath. Paula takes a deep breath, looks at F.L., and says, "It's nothing new. We had a plan to go out to dinner, and again he said he couldn't manage it. And *I* couldn't manage it." She again tears up slightly, "But then I spoiled what we *could* have." Paula is silent, again looking at F.L.

F.L. begins to notice a repetitive sequence: In response to Paula's more intense weeping, at first F.L. mirrors Paula's movements and then leans closer to her and slowly rocks forward and backward. During this rocking, F.L.'s movements constitute and convey her concern for and connection to Paula. F.L. finds herself feeling motherly toward Paula. Paula physically and emotionally responds to F.L.'s movements and shifts into F.L.'s rhythm. Then, Paula appears to cut off her grief by moving into vertical, which requires more energy and strength, and her experience of this effort brings with it control over her feelings. Neither Paula nor F.L. is at first aware of this pattern of connecting and pulling away.

F.L. says, "You were crying more intensely than you have before, and I have the sense that you are grieving." Paula moves her head sharply so that she focuses more intently on F.L.'s face, frowns, and answers, "Yes, it is grief. I didn't really see that before." F.L. asks, "What just happened?" Paula tears up again briefly and wipes her eyes. As she acknowledges her grief, at the same moment she moves out of her yielding, slightly inclined position into her erect, distanced position and sits silently.

F.L. says, "It seems to me that right now you are sitting up very straight as if moving completely away from the you that was leaning toward me and grieving. Do you notice how very quickly you moved your body up and away from recognizing and being in your grief?" "No," says Paula, "it just seems sensible—why wallow in sadness?"

At this point, F.L. recognizes the extreme polarization in Paula's movement and her experience of two very distinct selves: one oriented in vertical and one in horizontal. Right now, Paula cannot allow herself to stay in the horizontal, and there is no gradual transition between the two. It is as though she is using her body's actions to cut off her feelings. F.L.'s suggestion that she stay with her grief seems to Paula like an invitation to "wallow in sadness." This at first makes some sense to F.L. because, in her grief, Paula's capacity to think about it becomes overwhelmed. But F.L. believes that there is something more to understand in the abruptness and completeness of her changes between these two states. Paula's movement permits no "graduality" at this point and no gradients of change of intensity, position, or feeling.

Vignette 3

In another session, Paula begins by sitting up again with a straight spine and with her ankles crossed and up on the couch. She starts with the conclusion, "I should get over it—I know he loves me. Really, who can ask for more?" "Well," says F.L., who moves horizontally from side to side in her chair, "I feel a little torn as I listen to you. Maybe that's how it is, but I'm also wondering where all the hurt and sorrow went." Paula immediately rearranges her body, extends both legs to her left, and leans her upper body on the pillow to her right, toward F.L., and lifts her feet up to place them on the couch. "Mmm ... maybe. ..." She yields for the moment, then pops up and sits upright again. F.L. asks her what just happened, and she says, "I don't know—it just felt like what I wanted to do." F.L. says, "I have a feeling there is more in this—what did you sense as you lay down and then popped up?" In response, Paula repeats her movement, first lying sideways on the pillow. "I start to feel sad here, and I don't want to—it's enough!"

F.L. asks, "What were you wanting when you said, 'It's enough'?" Paula considers, and says, "I want to kick and scream, yikes, not good," and she sits up. "I have to get away from that."

Paula stops abruptly, then says, "I feel like I am my father here." At this point, Paula speaks from her memory of her parents' divorce. She was 11 years old and felt devastated and furious with her father for leaving her. For years, she says, she tried to talk to him about what happened to their family, but she could not get him to do it. "He simply would not sit and talk to me about it," she recalled. "When he actually allowed me to speak to him, he told me he would leave the house if I got too emotional. He insisted that we talk it over rationally." F.L. asks Paula if she sees any similarity in this pattern with her father and her current struggle with Lucas. "If nothing else," F.L. suggests, "you are finding out that Lucas is not your father."

F.L. moves from her own upright position, leans sideways to the left, slightly closing the distance between herself and Paula, and asks, "What would happen if you did kick and scream with me?" Paula says, "But you are always so patient." F.L., puzzled, says, "You have to be just like me right now?" Paula is slow to respond, pauses, then says, "I guess I don't know which one of us is more tired of how bad I feel. I think I am going on too much with this, and I bet you think so, too." F.L. asks, "How am I giving you that impression?"

Paula shoots back, "You're not," and jumps to her feet and says, "I feel restless, and I need to stand." She stands at the side of the couch, then walks around the room, sits for a moment, gets up, and walks some more. Paula says, "This is just weird. I'm tired today, so I don't know why I would want to be walking. I'm walking and feeling so tired." F.L. says, "Like a very young, very tired child who wants to keep going—to hold on to her feeling of independence? I have the sense of a baby just learning to walk who doesn't know when to rest." "Huh," says Paula, "that makes some sense." Sitting on the edge of the couch now, Paula recalls, "My parents were very proud that I walked early, at 9 months, and that I was very independent." Paula sits down again and takes her familiar leaning position on the pillow and then reaches her left hand across her body to her right for a cup of water she left there. In this movement, which would have been accomplished more easily and readily with her right hand, she very briefly looks at F.L.'s face as she recovers the cup and abruptly looks away. She takes a sip, continuing to look away from F.L.

F.L. senses there is some significance to Paula's reaching pattern as her arm sweeps across her body so that she briefly leans toward and faces F.L. To heighten awareness of what this pattern might mean to both of them, F.L. describes it and then encourages Paula to actively lean toward her.

F.L. asks, "So, what would it be like if you leaned on the pillow toward me again and stayed for a while to see what comes up?" Paula immediately responds by reinforcing her upright position while she smiles and says playfully, "Really? You think I don't know?" Then, beginning to try what F.L. has suggested, Paula leans on the pillow, takes a deep breath, but abruptly straightens up again, with no trace now of yielding or flowing tension. "The problem is, I like being independent. Maybe I push him away," she adds. She moves in her seat and looks again at her hands. "Sometimes when he is too busy, I just go do things for myself. I like being on my own. Last night, I had a late dinner with a friend because after I put the girls to bed, he had to work at home, so I left. When I got home, he was too tired to talk much. So, we went to sleep right away." She is upright and looking down at her hands. "What are you feeling when you look down at your hands?" F.L. asks.

"I don't know," Paula says, now sitting very straight against the back of the couch with her legs crossed again. "I was thinking about another bad encounter with Lucas—not as bad as some have been but still not as good as I would like. I didn't yell, but I had to leave the room and go cry in our bedroom, but I didn't tell him—I think he already feels too bad himself." F.L. asks if right now she is "crying by herself" and can't show how she feels in the session. She tears very briefly, while still sitting up, looking away from F.L. and down at her hands. After a pause, she says that she has been told that when she was a baby, her mother would get so upset she could not comfort her daughter. Both parents joked about how her father was the only one who could comfort her, and "what a mess" her mother was if Paula cried: "So upset she could not be in the room ... I guess I'm like that here sometimes—like my mother, I mean—I upset everyone when I'm like that, like my mother." F.L. lifts her upper body and says, "Whoa, everyone? Are you all three? The baby and the upset 1-year-old, and the mother and the father upset, and do you think that I'll be upset if you're upset?" Paula remains silent, still looking at her hands.

It appears to F.L. that Paula is ashamed and fearful that the expression of her own needs will make things worse for everyone, as in her childhood experience in her family. Because of this, she abruptly retreats from them and finds her extremely controlled, vertical independence. She and F.L. now have identified these actions as part of the embodied history of her early childhood with a distraught mother who could not comfort her and in later childhood with a frightened father who, having been her solace in infancy, now would not comfort her.

F.L. asks, "Are you worried that if you are upset I'll fall apart or leave, so you control your grief to protect me and to protect yourself from being abandoned?" "It makes sense. But it's weird, isn't it?" Paula remarks. "I really don't feel any sadness right now, and in fact, I'm a little mad at you for bringing it up. Partly, I liked that my father got me away from bad feelings. He would say, 'It's not worth moaning about it—just go out and have a good time!' That was his philosophy of life, especially after he left my mother." F.L. says that it makes sense that Paula would not want to be reminded of painful feelings when she has just successfully pulled herself up and out of them. "Do you think that's involved in what you said about pushing Lucas away?" F.L. asks. She also asks Paula how she thinks Lucas would feel and act with her if she shared her sadness, rather than her anger, about his work schedule with him. Paula says, "I just don't think I can do that. Lucas looks so sad when I'm upset. I just walk out of the room until I feel better. It's better than screaming—I'm just too needy—or demanding." She begins to compare her lifestyle and marriage to others she knows and remarks on how other people put up with much worse. "I don't need to be so upset," she comments.

F.L. *feels far away from Paula, as if she is being held at a distance.*

F.L. leans closer again, her movement seeming to pull Paula's gaze to her, and she asks, "Are you keeping very separate now from me because you are worried about the impact of your feelings on me—are you dampening your feelings so that you won't overwhelm me?" Paula says, "Maybe," as she quite clearly directs her gaze at her hands.

F.L. asks, "Tell me what you mean when you say you are 'too needy and demanding.'" Paula meets her gaze and stays with it even as F.L. leans back in her chair again. Paula leans back as well and talks about her parents, who both said that she made too many demands, that life wasn't perfect, and that she would have to get used to the new situation. Paula lifts her torso up in vertical again, gives her head a little toss, and looks up to the right, just above F.L.'s head. She laughs a little, saying, "My mother said that she saw herself in me, and that I should be careful or I would be anxious like her. Mom believed that she pushed my father away with her anxiety. She used to nag a lot—always pushing him to do something she thought was urgent—it always had to happen now. I feel like that with Lucas, but I try really hard to recognize it and curb it."

F.L. asks if that is what makes Paula avoid talking to Lucas directly about how she is feeling. Paula emphasizes her upright position by pushing her feet down onto the floor and says firmly and sharply, "I think he has enough to worry about—I don't want to add another burden to him. He already has the girls to fit into his schedule, and that's enough. I can't talk to him about this any more—it just doesn't seem fair!" With the last statement, she faces F.L. directly and glares. F.L. asks her what is making her angry, and Paula drops her gaze, turns to her right, and leans again on the pillow. As she lies there, she says, "I'm sorry ... I know you want what's good for me ... I don't know why I got angry." Then, she turns to face F.L. again.

After some moments, F.L. remarks that Paula seems very sad and also worried about having been angry with her. In another abrupt shift to vertical, Paula laughs, "Well, at least *that's* progress! I'm not throwing a plate." F.L. also laughs and then says, "Yes, but at the risk of making you throw one, I want to say that maybe Lucas can't fix his schedule, but I think he can understand how you feel about it." Paula now leans onto the pillow and weeps, "Why would Lucas be any better than my parents? He's already got too much to worry about."

Still weeping, Paula says sadly, "I think that I push Lucas away. Maybe that's why he pushes me away and doesn't want anything from me." "So," says F.L., "you said a lot. Not only do you think you upset everybody, you think you push Lucas away, that you make him push you away, and that he doesn't want anything from you." "Weird, isn't it," Paula remarks, as she pops herself back to upright, "but it doesn't matter. I don't think I care anymore. I can be independent—I don't have to care so much." F.L. asks, "So in your mind, is independence not caring?" Paula says, "Perhaps, yes, I think so."

Both Paula and F.L. are aware that they are in the territory of Paula's embodied history and that knowing about it does not solve the difficulties in the moment. There is no choice for them but to live through the conflict between Paula's push for independence and her alternate yearning for closeness and dependence and the seeming contradiction between these states. F.L. feels she is in this confusion with Paula, and that both of them can only try to grasp what is happening at each turn.

Vignette 4

In the next session, Paula sits on the couch with her back rounded and slightly leaning and her feet on the floor. She is now neither using her extreme upright posture nor leaning but maintaining an intermediate position. She says, "I'm afraid I'm just not a very nice person—I guess we found that out." F.L. asks, "Why would you think that's what I think?" She responds by lengthening and leaning slightly toward F.L. and saying, "How could I not care and not be a bad person?" F.L. quickly responds, "Who says I think you don't care?" Paula recovers her intermediate position between leaning over and sitting bolt upright as she sits back against the couch and looks at F.L. She says that she asked Lucas if he could get a weekend off. "He says he is grateful that I pushed it because he gets so involved that he doesn't remember to pull himself away—he really gets sucked into his work. And, here's the thing, even with that to look forward to, I'm still upset."

Paula sits up and leans forward, her elbows resting on her knees. "I'm just endlessly weird. I'm upset now because I really don't know what I want from Lucas." F.L. questions, "Didn't you say you wanted more time with him?" Paula says, "Yes, but it's all up to me now—I have to make it happen, so I have to know what I want all the time." Paula sits up straight, leans forward again, then pushes back into the couch and leans sideways on the pillow. Paula is now moving quickly from one position to another.

F.L. says, "You seem unsettled." Paula replies, "Yes, I am. I feel really awful because I'm not sure I want this weekend away. It's crazy, but I feel like I'm losing something." F.L. asks, "What are you losing?" Paula weeps and leans on the pillow. Looking up at F.L., she says, "I don't know."

F.L. watches as Paula physically struggles between searching for comfort and finding independent strength, which feel to her essentially incompatible, not just in the same moment, but in the same person. Her confusion about the experience and meaning of independence is visible and palpable. She has used her striving for independence to cope with the limits of comfort she could have with her parents and can have now with Lucas. In asking her to take charge of making time for them, Lucas is calling on her "independence" to make her "dependence" possible.

Discussion

Until now, "independence," as she defined it, had been Paula's escape from unbearable grief, not a route to intimacy. Paula's struggle with the purposes and meanings of independence and dependence were the focus of the next phase of work. Progress in that work was increasingly marked by attention to the way Paula's movement in session embodied those two states and isolated them from each other; change, too, was embodied in her greater readiness to explore the links between her experiences of leaning toward and straightening up away from F.L. and their significance.

Foundational movement analysis and the images of infancy that Paula's movements with F.L. recalled directed F.L.'s questions and ideas about the significance of the movements that she observed between them. In the course of their explorations, Paula began to realize how her abrupt changes of movement extremes had made it possible for her to accommodate and adapt to the fears and demands of her parents. First there had been her mother's fear of her cries that had led her father to comfort her. Then both parents had reinforced her early walking and "independence." Later, her father could not bear Paula's anger at him for causing the loss of her intact family. She reacted to these experiences by erecting a sense of irresolvable polarities in her distinct body states and desires. These were embodied in the physical positions of her movement repertoire, her embodied history. As she explored their movement and coconstructed these meanings, Paula simultaneously found an easier flow between her different states and needs, both with F.L. and with Lucas. Her explosions with Lucas ceased when she understood the meaning of her struggle.

Postscript: Explorations to Enhance the Experience of Moving

As we have shown in this book, the best way for psychotherapists to understand a baby–parent relationship is through observing how they move together. We have also suggested that the same observational skills can be invaluable for understanding the relationship in adult psychotherapy because they bring to awareness the emerging movement interaction within a session. In our own practices and in training psychotherapists, we have found that awareness of one's moving body is an important step toward understanding oneself in relation to others. In light of this, we offer here two segments of movement exploration.

In the first segment, psychotherapists recapitulate several early developmental movement patterns that enhance awareness and promote greater empathy with a baby's efforts to move in the first year. Recapitulating these fundamental movements and inclinations on the belly, on the back, and in the quadruped position also allows psychotherapists to define their preferred ways of moving as well as to discover where in their bodies they move fluidly and where their movements feel fixed. In the second segment, psychotherapists again explore fundamental movements and movement inclinations in the upright stance.

Because noticing one's movement may be previously uncharted territory for both psychotherapist and patient, sometimes evaluation becomes a substitute for experiencing. If you find that this is true for you, we invite you to notice *how* you evaluate yourself and then see if you can get closer to a simpler experience of the moment; that is, to entertain the idea that whatever you are experiencing is exactly right. When one is in "baby mind," the experience is of interest in itself. As you grow more curious about your body, evaluations become less relevant, as does the desire to change your experience and make it the way it "should be."

There are eight movement explorations in the first section of this chapter. We recommend that you read through each segment carefully to become familiar with the movement suggestions within it. As you begin exploring, if you cannot remember all the suggestions within a particular section, take one at a time. You might even stay with one movement exploration for several weeks before going on to the next. Take as much time as you need to familiarize yourself with your newly developing movement vocabulary.

RECAPITULATING DEVELOPMENTAL MOVEMENTS

Movement Exploration 1: Lying on the Floor in Supine

For lying supine, find a comfortable place on the floor. You can use a towel, blanket, or yoga mat for resting. Some bodies may need a pillow or folded towel underneath the head for comfort.

Lie on your back with arms fully extended by your sides and at about a 45-degree angle from your torso. Your palms may be facing up or down. You can either close your eyes or leave them open while allowing your focus to be soft and peripheral rather than a central activity. Rest your tongue so that it touches the floor of your mouth.

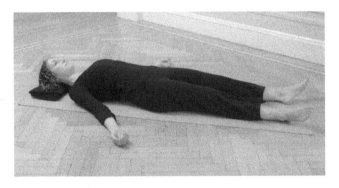

As you yield onto the floor, notice also the feeling of the floor pushing up to meet you. Here, you may feel the subtle force of gravity pressing downward as well as the equal and opposite earth force pushing upward.

Take time to notice which parts of your body are most in touch with the floor: Is it the back of your head, your shoulders and upper torso, your pelvis and legs, or your heels? Linger in these areas.

You may find that although you are lying down, some parts of your body feel ready to get right back up. These experiences vary from person to person. Some people are more inclined toward free flow and others toward bound flow, and this has an effect on the way they yield with and push against the floor.

Once you notice where your body rests downward and where it seems to lift upward, go back and forth between those areas to notice the difference between those two experiences. As you shift your awareness from one part of your body to another, see if anything changes or feels inclined to change. Notice if you most enjoy lying still (in even tension) or whether you find yourself wanting to shift your body position (in changing tension).

Move your awareness to the area of your navel. Imagine a line from the navel on the front of your body, moving downward through your abdomen, and continuing to the vertebrae just beneath your navel. Once you have located this area, attend to the movement of your breathing as you expand from front to back on inhalation and condense from front to back on exhalation.

Slowly open your mouth by reaching your lips outward and then close your mouth by retracting your lips and pressing them together. Do this several times. Begin reaching with your mouth to rotate your head to one side and then the other as if you were searching for something. To do this, purse your lips and bulge them forward and allow them to take the lead in guiding your head as it rotates. As you rotate your head, notice the areas of your jaw, tongue, back of your head, mouth, and throat. If your eyes are open during this exploration, let them be passive so that your mouth initiates the rotation rather than your eyes.

Once finished, sense your jaw, tongue, back of your head, mouth, and throat. Also notice any feelings that emerge along with your body sensations.

Movement Exploration 2: Lying on the Floor in Prone

For the prone position, lie belly downward on your towel or mat and extend your arms to either side at shoulder height and perpendicular to your torso. Bend your elbows so that your arms form a 45-degree angle. Rest one cheek against the floor and keep your hands at eye level. If you feel uncomfortable on your belly, you might try to bring one of your knees closer to the same-side elbow. This can relieve any tension in your back. If necessary, you can also place a small towel under that knee for cushioning or a rolled towel under your abdomen for additional comfort.

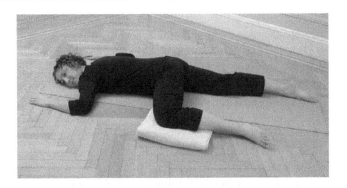

Once you sense how your body rests on the floor in this position, let your eyes wander about 8 inches in front of you without focusing on anything in particular. Let yourself be curious about the intensity of the light and the colors and shapes of the things that surround you. Try not to name the objects you are seeing but rather notice their shapes and contours and how you feel as your gaze touches them. Let your eyes freely scan near space—that which immediately surrounds you within about a foot of your body—and observe the places between objects so that the space "between" becomes as important and interesting as the objects themselves. Imagine that you are seeing everything for the first time.

Begin to move your spine and initiate that movement by "wiggling" your head, your tailbone, or the area around your navel. Notice where your spine moves most easily and where it does not. Notice which dimension you prefer as you move. Do you lengthen your spine up and down (vertical) by reaching with your head and tailbone in opposite directions? Do you prefer to move side to side (horizontal) by shortening one side of your rib cage and lengthening the other? Or, do you prefer scooping your belly or chest away from and arching back toward the floor (sagittal)?

Shift your focus and begin to gently wiggle your fingers and the tips of your toes. Imagine that it is the first time you have really moved them. Move them individually and together. Explore the floor with fingers and toes by scratching, rubbing, or tapping against it. You can experiment with the quality of these movements by changing them from light (low intensity) to more forceful or heavy (high intensity). You can also play with the rhythm by varying it from quick (abruptly changing) to slow (gradually changing). Every shift in the quality of movement or shift in rhythm gives you different feedback and a different experience. Notice if there is a particular quality of movement or rhythm that you prefer and notice if your mood changes as you change the qualities and rhythms.

Once you have examined the texture of the floor as it rubs against your fingers and toes and you have played with the different rhythms and qualities of your movement, you can place the underside of your arms, palms, and the bottoms of your toes as fully on the floor as you can. If placing the bottoms of your toes on the floor is impossible, place the tips of your toes on the floor or as close to that placement as possible.

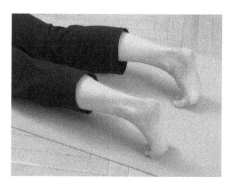

In this position and with your head slightly lifted off the floor and facing forward, push your arms down into the floor so that your body shifts backward, then push your toes down onto the floor so that it shifts forward. Alternate pushing back and forth so that your whole body rocks upward toward the head and downward toward the toes. Rocking involves the coordination of the upper and lower body and may be difficult to achieve at first, but it will feel more comfortable with practice.

Now, rest by placing your cheek back on the floor. Yielding between movements allows you to notice the effect of each exploration on your body. What did you feel throughout your body as you rocked? Does your body feel different after the movement from when you began? You might find that the rocking movement is slow and steady (with gradually changing tension) or that it is sharply changing and staccato (abrupt).

Again, facing in the forward direction, push your arms and hands onto the floor to lift your head a little higher off the floor. Stop if there is any strain in your shoulder muscles or neck. If you can push your head up with your hands without strain, do so, and then slowly lower yourself to the floor. (If you have not been able to do this without straining in your neck and shoulders, just push your forearms and hands into the floor without raising your head and neck.) Do this several times, resting completely between each movement. This is no easy task, and you may experience just how heavy your head really is.

Push down again; this time, lift your head even farther away from the floor. Once you are well supported on two arms, use your eyes to lead your head in looking to one side and then the other. Discover what catches your attention. When you tire, carefully lower yourself to the floor, rest your cheek on the mat, and yield. Did you do this action slowly or quickly, perhaps looking from side to side abruptly? Try doing it the opposite way.

This time, push yourself up once more and shift your weight to the left side of your body. With more weight on your left arm, elbow, and hand, find something in your environment that you can look at and reach toward it with your right arm. Linger in the reaching position for a while and notice what you sense and feel as you reach out. Return your reaching arm to its original position and balance your weight between two arms again. Next, shift your weight to your right side, find something to look toward, and reach your left arm toward it. Again, remain here for a while and notice your experience. Return your weight to both arms once more and lower yourself to the floor. Did you sense how the push of one arm enabled you to reach with the other?

Movement Exploration 3: The First Locomotion, Rolling

For the rolling locomotion, lie on your right side and bring your body into a fetal-like position: Your spine rounds, and your head and knees are close together. (Use a pillow or folded towel under your head if necessary for comfort.) In this position, both hands are free to meet at the midline of your body. Spend some time grasping your hands together, pulling them in toward your body, and then releasing them out and away from your body again.

When you grasp and pull your hands toward midline, you might sense concomitant sensations of cohering along the midline of your body—as if all parts are coming toward the center.

Notice how it feels to extend the fingers of your hands and then to grasp and pull them toward your midline again. Do this several times, and when you have extended them again, take your gaze beyond your hands and into the room. How does the room appear from this side-lying perspective?

While keeping your legs in this fetal-like position, place each hand on the outside of each of your knees. Your left arm and leg should now rest on top of your right arm and leg, which rest on the floor. Slowly rotate your eyes and head to your left side, as if searching for something. As you reach with your eyes, allow your left arm and leg to follow until you have rolled onto your back. Once there, continue reaching your eyes and head to the left and begin moving your right arm and leg to that same side as well. You now will find that you have rolled over onto your left side, and that your right arm is resting on your right side and your right leg is now resting on top of your left. Rest here for a minute, yield, and breathe before you repeat the movement and roll to your other side. Explore rolling from side to side several times and notice if you are rolling with free flow or bound flow. Where in the roll are you moving gradually or abruptly?

As you roll and move in space, you will begin to sense the weight of your body shifting. Sensing body weight is a significant aspect of orienting—knowing that you are here. Do you sense any difference between lying on your right or left side? Although rolling moves you through space primarily along the horizontal dimension, you can also feel the length and verticality of your spine as you roll.

Movement Exploration 4: Belly Crawling

To belly crawl, lie on your belly, rest your right cheek on the floor, and place your arms so that they are perpendicular to your shoulders and bent at the elbow. Push your arms downward so that you can lift your head off the floor and rotate it to the right. (If this movement causes pain, try doing it with your head lower or resting on the floor.) At the same time as you move your head to your right side, extend your right arm in front of you and pull your left arm behind you; simultaneously flex your left leg and bring the left knee toward the center of your body. Your right side will now be extended (lengthened) and your left side flexed (shortened). Now, again gradually turn your head to the left and slowly extend your left arm and left leg as you simultaneously flex your right arm and right leg. Moving one side and then the other completes the crawling sequence. Do this movement in a "swimming" fashion several times to make its coordination increasingly smooth. Shift the focus of your eyes from one hand to the other as you change sides. The movement may take some time to master as you are learning to coordinate alternating movements of the right and left sides of your body. Try doing these movements quickly and abruptly or slowly and gradually. Also try executing the movements with low intensity and high intensity.

Movement Exploration 5: Moving to All Fours

Still on your belly, leaving your arms and hands close to your body and on the floor, push them downward once more, and this time straighten your elbows so that your upper torso lifts off the floor. (If the process of raising the head and shoulders from prone to vertical is painful, begin instead on all fours.) Using greater effort as you push downward with your hands, reach backward with your tailbone so that the weight of your body shifts backward and onto your knees. Now, shift forward again and place your weight evenly on your hands, knees, and shins.

Here, begin to look around again. On all fours, your perspective changes once more, and you can see much farther into the distance. Keep your head erect in this quadruped position. Reaching forward with your head, push down onto the floor with your knees and shins and rock yourself forward. Next, bring your chin slightly to your chest, push your hands down, and reach backward with your tailbone as you rock yourself backward. Do both of these movements in succession so that you can sense the alternate shifting of your body weight from knees to hands to knees and back again.

Now, balanced on all four limbs, laterally shift your weight to your right side and place it evenly between your right hand and your right knee. Then, push downward with your right hand and right knee and laterally shift yourself back through center and to the left side. Continue doing this back and forth until you find a gradual and fluid movement from side to side. Make sure that you maintain your head erect as you do this.

Once you have mastered these lateral movements (through the horizontal dimension of the body), come back to a balanced position again with weight on all four limbs and try diagonal movements. To do this, push your right arm and hand down and shift your weight through the center of your body and onto your left knee and shin. Then, shift the weight from your left knee and shin through center and back to the right arm and hand. Once more, place your weight evenly on all four limbs. This time, push your left arm and hand downward and shift your weight through center and to the opposite knee and shin. Again, shift your weight from the knee and shin through center and to the opposite hand and arm. Here, you are playing with change of weight as you rock from head to tailbone and from one side to another through the diagonals of the body. Do this several times to establish the flow of movement from the periphery of your body (limbs) through the center (spine) and to the periphery once more.

Movement Exploration 6: Sitting

On all fours, sense the subtle push downward of your limbs onto the floor. Rotate your head and reach your eyes around to your left side and continue rotating so that the reaching of head and eyes initiates a spiral movement of the entire body (horizontal) with the movement traveling through the whole spine until your right and then left buttocks follow the spiral and land on the floor. Your right leg will be bent under your left leg, which will arrive with the knee bent and the foot resting on the floor. Cross both legs in front of you. Seated, reach your eyes and head around in all directions and notice the different perspective that a seated posture brings.

To return to all fours, you will spiral again. Start by bending your left knee and then place your left foot firmly on the floor in front of your right buttock. Your right hand is to the side of your right buttock. Now, reach your eyes and head over your right shoulder as your left arm also reaches across your body and around to the right side. Continue to spiral with your spine and pelvis in that same direction until you are on all four limbs again.

This is one of many possible patterns that take you from all four limbs to the seated position and back again. Try the movement several times to see where you need to push and reach to make your spiral fluid. If this method is difficult, you feel awkward, or you find yourself stuck, notice where you sense the movement does not flow easily. Try to complete the same action in your own way or break down this suggested movement sequence into smaller incremental parts and practice those until you feel more comfortable.

Movement Exploration 7: Crawling on All Fours

Balanced on all four limbs, find an object in the room that interests you and crawl toward it. Reach your right arm forward and then place your right hand on the floor. As you grasp and pull the floor toward you, allow your left knee to lift and move forward on the diagonal. Once you have placed your left knee on the floor, your left hand is free to reach, grasp, and pull your right knee forward. As you find something of interest to crawl toward, this sequence of reaching, grasping, and pulling movements should begin to feel more comfortable.

Crawling can be broken down into smaller increments. On all fours, shift your weight to one side of your body and reach outward with your freed arm. Then, return the arm to the same place. Shifting your weight to the opposite side of the body, reach the other arm outward and return it to the floor. Again, shift your weight to one side to free the opposite leg, lift it off the floor, and move the knee in the direction of your navel. Return it to the floor and do the same with the other leg.

Play with the movement qualities of your crawl. For example, you can crawl lightly and quickly (freeing, low intensity, abrupt), as if you were a squirrel, or heavily and slowly (high intensity, bound, gradual), as if you were a bear. Again, as you change the quality of your movements, notice if you change the quality of your mood.

Movement Exploration 8: Independent Standing

First, for independent standing you will move from the crawling position to squatting. Balanced on all four limbs with the bottoms of your toes on the floor, push backward with your hands, and walk your hands backward as well so that your torso moves over your feet and into a squatting position. Reach your head upward as if you were reaching toward something of interest.

Next, you will move from squatting to standing. You will need a firm push of both feet onto the floor as you reach your head up to come to standing.

An alternative method is to rise forward and up on one leg: To do this from all fours, shift your weight backward so that much of it rests over your legs. Find something that interests you to look toward. Bring your left foot in front of you and shift your body weight over to that front foot. Push that foot downward as you reach your torso over it and begin to rise off the floor. As you rise up, your left leg comes along, and you can place it alongside the right.

Pull yourself to standing with support. If both these options are somewhat difficult, you can always creep over to a chair and pull yourself to a standing position. Finally, you have arrived on two legs. Look around and see how different your world looks from this perspective.

DISCOVERING FUNDAMENTAL MOVEMENTS AND MOVEMENT INCLINATIONS IN THE UPRIGHT STANCE

As in the first movement exploration section, remember that there is no "ideal" way to move. It is useful, however, to become aware of *how* you move. Sensing where and how your movements flow or where and how the flow of movement is fixed tells you something important about yourself. Make each movement a deliberate action so that you can pay attention to all aspects of yourself—sensations, perceptions, and feelings—as you move.

Movement Exploration 1: Finding Yield/Push in the Upright Stance

Standing requires balance in all three dimensions: horizontal, vertical, and sagittal, although the vertical is most emphasized. To find the yield/push in the upright stance, standing with the weight of your body balanced equally on both legs, sense how much each foot rests on the floor and to what extent you experience the floor coming up to meet each foot. As you push down onto the floor with your feet, you simultaneously narrow and lengthen your body. If you lean your body slightly forward or backward (in sagittal), you can sense different parts of your body working to hold you in place. Now, place the weight of your body slightly in front of your ankles and evenly balance on two feet.

Once done, push more strongly with your right foot to shift your weight to the left foot, a slight movement in horizontal. When more of your weight is on the left leg and foot, push your left foot more strongly onto the ground so that you can shift your weight over to your right leg and foot. Do this several times back and forth so that you become familiar with how your push transitions the weight of your body from one side to the other. Again, balance your weight between two feet and pay attention to how you sense the soles of your feet meeting the floor. Notice now how the floor supports your weight yielding and pushing in vertical onto the floor.

Try this sequence of shifting your weight one more time, and this time shift from one foot to another using different qualities: You can shift gradually from side to side or abruptly; with bound or free flow; with a high or low intensity. Notice which qualities are most familiar and preferred and which qualities are least familiar to you. As you change qualities, what happens to your perceptions and feelings?

Once more, center yourself and balance your weight between two legs. Pay attention to the interaction between the soles of your feet and the floor once more; this time, bend your knees so that you gradually descend a few inches in vertical. Now, push your feet downward so that your knees straighten and you gradually ascend in vertical. Repeat the descending and ascending movement several times and notice if your push against the floor develops greater clarity. You can also experiment with different qualities: ascend and descend gradually or abruptly, with bound or free flow, and with a high or low intensity. Does your experience change as you change qualities?

Movement Exploration 2: Reaching in Sagittal and Horizontal

Once you have discovered how you yield with and push against the floor, begin to walk around the room and pay attention to each foot as it rolls from heel to ball, moves to the toes, and then pushes off the floor. When you walk around the room, try to notice the reaching aspect of your head and arms and notice how the push of each foot downward moves through your body to support the reaching. Notice also how the push of one foot and leg against the floor enables the forward reach of the other leg. Walk forward, advancing in sagittal and then backward retreating in sagittal. What parts of your body lead in each direction? Once you have discovered what you experience as you walk directly forward or backward, add some horizontal twisting in the hips and shoulders and allow yourself to wander a bit while moving forward or backward. What is the difference in your walking pattern between moving directly forward or backward in sagittal and moving side to side in the horizontal dimension?

You might also try advancing or retreating in sagittal while you descend in your vertical dimension or advance then retreat in sagittal while you ascend in your vertical dimension. Notice if there are changes in your experience as you shift your dimensions.

You can also add a variety of qualities to your walking pattern: advance or retreat gradually (drifting) or abruptly (jumping or leaping); in even flow (steadily pressing forward) or flow fluctuating (as if uncertain, indecisive); with high intensity (with a punch) or low intensity (a float or glide). Which qualities are most or least familiar to you? Again, notice how your perceptions and feelings shift as you move from one quality to another.

Now, stand still and allow your eyes to reach out in the horizontal dimension—from side to side—as you look around the room. At first, move only with your head and then allow your body to accompany your head by twisting to one side and around yourself and then to the other side and around yourself. Once you have explored the room through the reaching of your eyes, let them be passive and explore the room through reaching only with your mouth. To do this, purse and bulge your lips as if in search of something. Then, lead yourself around the room with your ears as you follow the sounds that catch your attention. Changing from one sensory organ to another, you will discover which of your senses are dominant and which recede to the background

Do these same movements, now with changing qualities: reach with your head and eyes, mouth, or ears gradually or abruptly; using high or low intensity; using even or flow-fluctuating qualities that are freeing or binding. With each shift of movement qualities, notice if there are shifts in your feelings or perceptions.

Movement Exploration 3: Reaching, Grasping, Pulling, and Releasing in All Dimensions

Stand with the weight of your body balanced between both legs. Make sure your weight is evenly distributed between the toe, ball and heel of the foot as well as between the two feet. Now sense the yield/push of your feet on the floor. Once you bring the underlying push of your feet into your awareness, reach your hands and arms in front of you in the sagittal dimension. Include your fingers in your reach and notice how it feels to fully extend your arms, hands, and fingers. Bend your knees to descend in vertical, and then push your feet against the floor to slowly ascend once more and notice how the push from below supports the reach of your hands outward.

Grasp or imagine grasping a pillow so that you curl the fingers of each of your hands inward. Allow your hands and arms to finish the movement as you pull the pillow toward your chest. Let your head be part of the action as you slowly push your head downward over the pillow while your arms fold inward. Repeat this curling in and out movement several times: Slowly reach your head upward and again extend your arms, hands, and fingers in sagittal. Then, grasp the pillow and pull it inward with your fingers, hands, and arms, and then curl downward and into the pillow once more.

When you have completed these actions, find the weight of your body balanced between both legs, release your hands, have your arms by your sides, and notice what you sense and feel.

You can repeat this same sequence of reaching, grasping, pulling, and releasing, but this time in the vertical dimension. Reach upward to grasp a real or imagined cup from a high shelf and be sure to include your head and face as you reach with your mouth and eyes. Now as you reach in vertical, grasp the cup and with your hands pull it to your mouth, allowing your head to curl over the cup as well.

Realigning yourself with the weight of your body placed over both legs, reach your hands and arms forward, in sagittal, once more and then extend them to either side in horizontal. Sense the width of your body as your arms now reach outward in this horizontal dimension. Try sweeping them from side to side as you twist your body to one side and then the other. Coming back to center, slowly gather your arms inward and toward your chest with grasping and pulling movements. Allow your head to curl inward and toward your chest as well. Then, uncurl by reaching your head upward again and extending your arms and hands in sagittal and then sweeping them into horizontal.

Now, reach for a real or imagined book on a table to the side of your body and allow that side to lean into the movement. Repeat this several times on each side, sensing the sweeping and reaching movements of your hands and arms as you spread into horizontal and then as you gather, grasp, and pull the book toward your chest.

After exploring these reaching, grasping, pulling, and releasing movements several times, try using a variety of qualities: gradual (glide) or abrupt (snatch); with low (gentle) or high intensity (strong); even (either careful or inattentive and floating) or with flow fluctuation (playful, teasing, or as if without control); bound (with fear, caution, or menace); or free (with abandon).

References

Ainsfield, M. (2005). No compelling evidence to dispute Piaget's timetable of the development of representational imitation in infancy. In S. Hurley & N. Chater (Eds.), *Perspectives on imitation: From neuroscience to social science: Vol. 2. Imitation, human development, and culture* (pp. 107–132). Cambridge, MA: MIT Press.

Ainsworth, H., Blehar, M., Waters, E., & Wall, S. (1978). *Patterns of attachment: A psychological study of the strange situation.* Hillsdale, NJ: Erlbaum.

Anderson, F. S. (Ed.). (2008). *Bodies in treatment: The unspoken dimension.* New York: Analytic Press.

Aposhyan, S. (2004). *Body-mind psychotherapy.* New York: Norton.

Aron, L., & Anderson, F. S. (Eds.). (1998). *Relational perspectives on the body.* Hillsdale, NJ: Analytic Press.

Bainbridge-Cohen, B. (1993). *Sensing, feeling and action.* Northhampton, MA: Contact Editions.

Baradon, T. (2005). *The practice of psychoanalytic parent-infant psychotherapy: Claiming the baby.* London: Routledge.

Bartenieff, I., & Davis, M. (1965). *Effort-shape analysis of movement: The unity of expression and function.* Unpublished monograph.

Bartenieff I., & Lewis, D. (1980). *Bodily movement: Coping with the environment.* New York: Gordon and Breach.

Beebe, B., Gerstman, L., Carson, B., Dolmus, M., Zigman, A., Rosensweig, H., ... Korman, M. (1982). Rhythmic communication in the mother-infant dyad. In M. Davis (Ed.), *Interaction rhythms: Periodicity in communicative behavior* (pp. 77–100). New York: Human Sciences Press.

Beebe, B., Knoblauch S., Rustin, J., & Sorter, D. (2005). *Forms of intersubjectivity in infant research and adult treatment.* New York: Other Press.

Beebe, B., & Lachmann, F. (1998). Co-constructing inner and relational processes: Self- and mutual-regulation in infant research and adult treatment. *Psychoanalytic Psychology, 15*, 480–516.

Beebe, B., & Lachmann, F. (2002). *Infant research and adult treatment: Co-constructing interactions.* Hillsdale, NJ: Analytic Press.

Bick, E. (1964). Notes on infant observation in psycho-analytic training. In A. Briggs (Ed.), *Surviving space: Papers on infant observation* (pp. 37–54). London: Karnac.

Bick, E. (1968). The experience of the skin in early object relations. In A. Briggs (Ed.), *Surviving space: Papers on infant observation* (pp. 55–59). London: Karnac.

Bick, E. (1986). Further considerations on the function of the skin in early object relations. In A. Briggs (Ed.), *Surviving space: Papers on infant observation* (pp. 60–74). London: Karnac.

Birdwhistell, R. (1970). *Kinesics and context.* Philadelphia: University of Pennsylvania Press.

Black, M. (2003). Enactment: Analytic musings on energy, language, and personal growth. *Psychoanalytic Dialogues, 13,* 633–655.

Bloom, K. (2006). *The embodied self: Movement and psychoanalysis.* London: Karnac.

Bollas, C. (1983). Expressive uses of countertransference. *Contemporary Psychoanalysis, 19,* 1–34.

Bollas, C. (1987). *The shadow of the object: Psychoanalysis of the unthought known.* London: Free Association.

Boston Change Process Study Group (BCPSG). (2002). Explicating the implicit: The local level and the microprocesses of change in the analytic situation. *International Journal of Psychoanalysis, 83,* 1051–1062.

Boston Change Process Study Group (BCPSG). (2005). The "something more" than interpretation revisited: Sloppiness and co-creativity in the psychoanalytic encounter. *Journal of the American Psychoanalytic Association, 53,* 693–729.

Boston Change Process Study Group (BCPSG). (2007). The foundational level of psychodynamic meaning: Implicit process in relation to conflict, defense and the dynamic unconscious. *International Journal of Psychoanalysis, 88,* 843–860.

Boston Change Process Study Group (BCPSG). (2008). Forms of relational meaning: Issues in the relations between the implicit and reflective-verbal domains. *Psychoanalytic Dialogues, 18,* 125–148.

Boulanger, G. (2007). *Wounded by reality: Understanding and treating adult onset trauma.* New York: Analytic Press.

Brazelton, T. B. (1992). *Touchpoints.* New York: Guilford Press.

Brazelton, T. B., & Cramer, B.G. (1990). *The earliest relationship: Parents, infants and the drama of early attachment.* London: Karnac.

Briggs, A. (Ed.). (2002). *Surviving space: Papers on infant observation.* London: Karnac.

Bromberg, P. (1998). *Standing in the spaces: Essays on clinical process.* Hillsdale, NJ: Analytic Press.

Bromberg, P. (2006). *Awakening the dreamer: Clinical journeys.* Hillsdale, NJ: Analytic Press.

Bucci, W. (1997). *Psychoanalysis and cognitive science: A multiple code theory.* New York: Guilford Press.

Buschell, E., & Boudreau, P. (1993). Motor development and the mind: The potential role of motor abilities as a determinant of aspects of perceptual development. *Child Development, 64*(4), 1099–1110.

Butler, J. (1993). *Bodies that matter.* London: Routledge.

Chapple, E. (1970). *Culture and biological man.* New York: Holt, Rinehart, & Winston.

Chasseguet-Smirgel, J. (2003). *The body as mirror of the world.* London: Free Association Books.

Chess, S., & Thomas, A. (1996). *Temperament in clinical practice.* New York: Guilford Press.

Clemmens, M. C. (1997). *Getting beyond sobriety.* Orleans, MA: Gestalt Press.

Condon, W. S. (1982). Cultural microrhythms. In M. Davis (Ed.), *Interaction rhythms: Periodicity in communicative behavior* (pp. 53–77). New York: Human Sciences Press.

Condon, W. S., & Ogston, W. D. (1971). Speech and body movement synchrony of the speaker-hearer. In D. L. Horton & J. J. Jenkins (Eds.), *Perception of language* (pp. 98–120). Columbus, OH: Charles Merrill.

Condon, W. S., & Sander L. W. (1974). Neonate movement is synchronized with adult speech: Interactional participation and language acquisition. *Science, 183,* 99–101.

Corboz-Warnery, A., Fivaz-Depeursinge, E., Bettens, C. G., & Favez, N. (1993). Systemic analysis of father-mother-baby interactions: The Lausanne triadic play. *Infant Mental Health Journal, 14,* 298–316.

Cornell, W. F. (2008). *Explorations in transactional analysis: The Meech Lake papers.* Pleasanton, CA: TA Press.

Damasio, A. (1990). *The feeling of what happens: Body and emotion in the making of consciousness.* London: Harcourt Brace.

Damasio, A. (2003). *Looking for Spinoza: Joy, sorrow, and the feeling brain.* New York: Harcourt.

Davies, J. M., & Frawley, M. G. (1991). Dissociative processes and transference-countertransference paradigms in the psychoanalytically oriented treatment of adult survivors of childhood sexual abuse. *Psychoanalytic Dialogues, 2,* 5–36.

Davies, J. M., & Frawley, M. G. (1994). *Treating the adult survivor of childhood sexual abuse.* New York: Basic Books.

Davoine, F., & Gaudillière. J-M. (2004). *History beyond trauma: Whereof one cannot speak, thereof one cannot stay silent.* New York: Other Press.

Dittman, A. T. (1974). The body movement-speech rhythm relationship as a cue to speech encoding. In S. Weitz (Ed.), *Nonverbal communication: Readings with commentary* (pp. 169–181). New York: Oxford University Press.

Ellman, S. J., & Moskowitz, M. (1998). *Enactment: Toward a new approach to the therapeutic relationship.* Northvale, NJ: Aronson.

Fivaz-Depeursinge, E., & Corboz-Warnery, A. (1999). *The primary triangle: A developmental systems view of mothers, fathers and infants.* New York: Basic Books.

Fogel, A. (1993). *Developing through relationships.* Chicago: Chicago University Press.

Fogel, A. (2001). *Infancy: Infant, family, and society.* Belmont, CA: Wadsworth/ Thomson Learning.

Fonagy, P. (2001). *Attachment theory and psychoanalysis.* New York: Other Press.

Fonagy, P., Gergely, G., Jurist, E., & Target, M. (2002). *Affect regulation, mentalization, and the development of the self.* New York: Other Press.

Fraiberg, L. (Ed.). (1987). *Selected writings of Selma Fraiberg.* Columbus: Ohio State University Press.

Fraiberg, S. (1996). *The magic years.* New York: Simon & Schuster. (Original work published 1959)

Frank, R. (2001). *Body of awareness: A somatic and developmental approach to psychotherapy.* Orleans, MA: Gestalt Press.

Frank, R. (2004). Embodying creativity: Developing experience. In M. Spagnuolo-Lobb & N. Amendt Lyon (Eds.), *Creative license: The art of Gestalt therapy* (pp. 181–200). New York: Springer-Verlag.

Frank, R. (2005). Developmental somatic psychotherapy: Developmental process within the clinical moment. In N. Totten (Ed.), *New dimensions in body psychotherapy* (pp. 115–127). New York: McGraw Hill Education.

Frank, R. (2009a). Interview. *British Gestalt Journal, 18*(1), 50–55.

Frank, R. (2009b). Somatic experience and emergence dysfunction: Gestalt therapists in dialogue and in response to Eugene Gendlin. *Studies in Gestalt Therapy, 2*(2), 11–39.

Freud, S. (1953). Fragment of an analysis of a case of hysteria. In J. Strachey (Ed. & Trans.), *The standard edition of the complete psychological works of Sigmund Freud* (Vol. 7, pp. 7–122). London: Hogarth Press. (Original work published 1905)

Freud, S. (1955a). Beyond the pleasure principle. In J. Strachey (Ed. & Trans.), *The standard edition of the complete psychological works of Sigmund Freud* (Vol. 18, pp. 7–64). London: Hogarth Press. (Original work published 1920)

Freud, S. (1955b). Notes upon a case of obsessional neurosis. In J. Strachey (Ed. & Trans.), *The standard edition of the complete psychological works of Sigmund Freud* (Vol. 10, pp. 155–318). London: Hogarth Press. (Original work published 1909)

Freud, S. (1961a). The dynamics of transference. In J. Strachey (Ed. & Trans.), *The standard edition of the complete psychological works of Sigmund Freud* (Vol. 12, pp. 99–109). London: Hogarth Press. (Original work published 1912)

Freud, S. (1961b). Three essays on the theory of sexuality. In J. Strachey (Ed. & Trans.), *The standard edition of the complete psychological works of Sigmund Freud* (Vol. 7, pp. 125–245). London: Hogarth Press. (Original work published 1905)

Freud, S. (1964). An outline of psychoanalysis. In J. Strachey (Ed. & Trans.), *The standard edition of the complete psychological works of Sigmund Freud* (Vol. 23, pp. 139–207). London: Hogarth Press. (Original work published 1940)

Gendlin, E. (2007/1978). *Focusing.* New York: Bantam Books.

Gianino, A., & Tronick, E. (1985). The mutual regulation model: The infant's self and interactive regulation and coping and defensive capacities. In T. Feld et al. (Eds.), *Stress and coping* (pp. 47–68). Hillsdale, NJ: Erlbaum.

Goldberg, S., Muir, R., & Kerr, J. (Eds.) (1995). *Attachment theory: Social, developmental, and clinical perspectives.* Hillsdale, NJ: Analytic Press.

Green, A., & Stern, D. N. (2001). Clinical and observational psychoanalytic research: Roots of a controversy. In J. Sandler, A.-M. Sandler, & R. Davies (Eds.), *Psychoanalytic monographs* (Vol. 5, pp. 21–91). London: Karnac.

Hannaford, C. (2005). *Smart moves: Why learning is not all in your head.* Salt Lake City, UT: Great River Books.

Harris, A. (2005). *Gender as soft assembly.* Hillsdale, NJ: Analytic Press.

Hopkins, B., & Westra, T. (1988). Maternal handling and motor development: An intracultural study. *Genetic, Social and General Psychology Monographs, 114,* 379–408.

Hurley, S., & Chater, N. (Eds.). (2005). *Perspectives on imitation* (Vols. 1 & 2). Cambridge, MA: MIT Press.

Iacoboni, M. (2008). *Mirroring people: The new science of how we connect with others.* New York: Farrar, Straus and Giroux.

Jacobs, L. (2000). Respectful dialogues. *British Gestalt Journal, 4*(2), 105–116.

Kagan, J. (2006). *An argument for mind*. New Haven, CT: Yale University Press.

Kepner, J. (1987). *Body process: A gestalt approach to working with the body in psychotherapy*. Cleveland, OH: Gestalt Institute of Cleveland Press.

Kepner, J. (1995). *Healing tasks: Psychotherapy with adult survivors of childhood abuse*. Cleveland, OH: Gestalt Institute of Cleveland Press.

Kestenberg, J. (1975). *Children and parents: Psychoanalytic studies in development*. New York: Aronson.

Kestenberg, J., & Sossin, M. (1979). *The role of movement patterns in development*. New York: Dance Notation Bureau Press.

Kestenberg-Amighi, J., Loman, S., Lewis, P., & Sossin, K. M. (1999). *The meaning of movement: Development and clinical perspectives of the Kestenberg Movement Profile*. Amsterdam: Gordon & Breach.

Knoblauch, S. (2000). *The musical edge of therapeutic dialogue*. Hillsdale, NJ: Analytic Press.

La Barre, F. (2001). *On moving and being moved: Nonverbal behavior in clinical practice*. Hillsdale, NJ: Analytic Press.

La Barre, F. (2005). The kinetic transference and countertransference. *Contemporary Psychoanalysis, 41*(2), 249–279.

La Barre, F. (2008). Stuck in vertical: The kinetic temperament in development and interaction. *Psychoanalytic Dialogues, 18*, 411–436.

La Barre, F. (2009). Movement theory and psychoanalysis: Kinetic therapeutic action. *Studies in Gestalt Therapy, 2*(2), 59–74.

Lamb, W. (1965). *Posture and gesture: An introduction to the study of physical behavior*. London: Duckworth.

Lamb, W., & Watson, E. (1979). *Body code: Meaning in movement*. Princeton, NJ: Princeton University Press.

Le Doux, J. (1996). *The emotional brain: The mysterious underpinnings of emotional life*. New York: Simon & Shuster.

Levine, P. (1997). *Waking the tiger: Healing trauma*. Berkeley, CA: North Atlantic Press.

Libet, B. (2004). *Mind time: The temporal factor in consciousness*. Cambridge, MA: Harvard University Press.

Lyons-Ruth, K. (2000). I sense that you sense that I sense … : Sander's recognition process and the specificity of relational moves in the psychotherapeutic setting. *Infant Mental Health Journal, 21*, 85–98.

Lyons-Ruth, K. (2003). Dissociation and the parent-infant dialogue. *Journal of the American Psychoanalytic Association, 51*, 883–991.

Lyons-Ruth, K., Bruschweiler-Stern, N., Harrison, A. M., Nahum, J. P., Sander, L., & Stern, D. N. (1998). Implicit relational knowing: Its role in development and psychoanalytic treatment. *Infant Mental Health Journal, 19*, 282–289.

Mahl, G. (1968). Gesture and body movement in interviews. *Research in Psychotherapy, 3*, 295–346.

Meltzoff, A., & Moore, M. (1977). Imitation of facial and manual gestures by human neonates. *Science, 198*, 75–78.

Meltzoff, A., & Moore, M. (1995). Infants' understanding of people and things: From body imitation to folk psychology. In J. Bermudez, A. Marcel, & N. Eilan (Eds.), *The body and the self* (pp. 43–69). Cambridge, MA: MIT Press.

Meltzoff, A., & Moore, M. (2000). Resolving the debate about early imitation. In A. Slater & D. Muir (Eds.), *Infant development: The essential readings* (pp. 167–181). Malden, MA: Blackwell.

Miller, L., Rustin, M., Rustin, M., & Shuttleworth, J. (Eds.). (1989). *Closely observed infants*. London: Duckworth.

Mitchell, S. (1993). *Hope and dread in psychoanalysis*. New York: Basic Books.

Mitchell, S., & Aron, L. (1999). *Relational psychoanalysis: The emergence of a tradition*. Hillsdale, NJ: Analytic Press.

Moskowitz, M., Monk, C., Kaye, C., & Ellman, S. (Eds.). (1997). *The neurobiological and developmental basis for psychotherapeutic intervention*. Northvale, NJ: Aronson.

Ogden, P., Minton, K., & Pain, C. (2006). *Trauma and the body: A sensorimotor approach to psychotherapy*. New York: Norton & Co.

Perls, L. (1993). *Living at the boundary*. New York: Gestalt Journal Press.

Piontelli, A. (1992). *From fetus to child: An observational and psychoanalytic study*. London: Routledge.

Racker, H. (1968). *Transference and countertransference*. New York: International Universities Press.

Renik, O. (1998). The role of countertransference enactment in successful clinical psychoanalysis. In S. J. Ellman & M. Moskowitz (Eds.), *Enactment: Toward a new approach to the therapeutic relationship* (pp. 111–128). Northvale, NJ: Aronson.

Rizzolati, G., & Sinigaglia, C. (2008). *Mirrors in the brain: How our minds share actions and emotions*. New York: Oxford University Press.

Rustin, M. (1988). Encountering primitive anxieties: Some aspects of infant observation as a preparation for clinical work with children and families. *Journal of Child Psychotherapy, 14*(3), 15–28.

Rustin, M. (1998). Observation, understanding and interpretation: The story of a supervision. *Journal of Child Psychotherapy, 24*(3), 433–448.

Rustin, M. (2002). Struggles in becoming a mother: Reflections from a clinical and observational standpoint. *Infant Observation, 5*(1), 7–20.

Rustin, M. J. (2002). Looking in the right place: Complexity theory, psychoanalysis, and infant observation. *International Journal of Infant Observation, 5*(1), 122–144.

Schore, A. N. (1994). *Affect regulation and the origin of the self*. Mahwah, NJ: Erlbaum.

Smith, E. (1985). *The body in psychotherapy*. Jefferson, NC: McFarland.

Solms, M., & Turnbull, O. (2000). *The brain and the inner world: An introduction to the neuroscience of subjective experience*. New York: Other Press.

Sossin, M. K. (1987). Reliability of the KMP. *Movement Studies, 2*, 23–28.

Sossin, M. K., & Birklein, S. (2006). Nonverbal transmission of stress between parent and young child: Considerations and psychotherapeutic implications of a study of affective movement patterns. *Journal of Infant, Child, and Adolescent Psychotherapy, 5*(1), 46–69.

Stern, D. B. (1995). Unformulated experience. *Contemporary Psychoanalysis, 19*, 71–99.

Stern, D. B. (1997). *Unformulated experience: From dissociation to imagination in psychoanalysis*. Hillsdale, NJ: Analytic Press.

Stern, D. B. (2010). *Partners in thought: Working with unformulated experience, dissociation, and enactment.* New York: Routledge.

Stern, D. N. (1977). *The first relationship: Infant and mother.* London: Fontana/Open Books.

Stern, D. N. (1982). Some interactive functions of rhythm changes between mother and child. In M. Davis (Ed.), *Interaction rhythms: Periodicity in communicative behavior* (pp. 101–118). New York: Human Sciences Press.

Stern, D. N. (1985). *The interpersonal world of the infant.* New York: Basic Books.

Stern, D. N. (1995). *The motherhood constellation: A unified view of parent-infant psychotherapy.* New York: Basic Books.

Thelen, E. (1984). The relationship between physical growth and a newborn reflex. *Infant Behavior and Development, 7,* 479–493.

Thelen, E. (1995). Motor development: A new synthesis. *Journal of the American Psychological Association, 50,* 79–95.

Thelen, E., & Smith, L. (1993). *A dynamic systems approach to the development of cognition and action.* Cambridge, MA: MIT Press.

Tortora, S. (2006). *The dancing dialogue: Using the communicative power of movement with young children.* Baltimore, MD: Paul H. Brookes.

Totten, N. (2003). *Body psychotherapy: An introduction.* New York: Open University Press/McGraw Hill Education.

Totten, N. (2005). *New dimensions in body psychotherapy.* New York: Open University Press/McGraw Hill Education.

Trevarthen, C. (1979). Communication and cooperation in early infancy: A description of primary intersubjectivity. In M. Bullowa (Ed.), *Before speech: The beginning of interpersonal communication* (pp. 321–348). Cambridge, UK: Cambridge University Press.

Trevarthen, C. (2004). Intimate contact from birth. In K. White (Ed.), *Touch, attachment, and the body* (pp. 1–16). London: Karnac.

Tronick, E. (1989). Emotions and emotional communication in infants. *American Psychologist, 44,* 112–126.

Tronick, E. (2005). Why is connection with others so critical? The formation of dyadic states of consciousness: Coherence governed selection and the co-creation of meaning out of messy meaning making. In J. Nadel & D. Muir (Eds.), *Emotional development* (pp. 293–315). New York: Oxford University Press.

Tronick, E. (2007). *The neurobehavioral and social-emotional development of infants and children.* New York: Norton.

Tronick, E., Als, H., & Adamson, L. (1979). The structure of early face-to-face communicative interactions. In M. Bullowa (Ed.), *Before speech: The beginning of interpersonal communication* (pp. 349–370). Cambridge, UK: Cambridge University Press.

van der Kolk, B. A., MacFarlane, A. C., & Weisaeth, L. (Eds.). (1996). *Traumatic stress: The effects of overwhelming experience on mind, body and society.* New York: Guilford Press.

Yontef, G. (2001). Relational gestalt therapy: What it is, and what it is not. Why the adjective "relational"? In J. Robine (Ed.), *Contact and relationship in a field perspective* (pp. 79–94). Bordeaux, France: l'Exprimerie.

Yontef, G. (2002). The relational attitude in gestalt therapy theory and practice. *International Gestalt Journal, 25*(1), 15–36.

Index

Lightning Source UK Ltd.
Milton Keynes UK
UKHW03f2236010518
321952UK00001B/58/P

9 780415 876407

I Don't Believe in Astrology

Believe in

Astrology

A GUIDE TO THE
LIFE-CHANGING WISDOM OF THE STARS

DEBRA SILVERMAN

bantam

TRANSWORLD PUBLISHERS

UK | USA | Canada | Ireland | Australia
India | New Zealand | South Africa

Transworld is part of the Penguin Random House group of companies
whose addresses can be found at global.penguinrandomhouse.com.

Penguin Random House UK,
One Embassy Gardens, 8 Viaduct Gardens, London SW11 7BW

penguin.co.uk

Penguin
Random House
UK

First published in Great Britain in 2025 by Bantam
an imprint of Transworld Publishers

001

Printed and bound in Great Britain by Clays Ltd, Elcograf S.p.A.

Designed by Steven Seighman
Interior art by Freepik

The authorized representative in the EEA is Penguin Random House Ireland,
Morrison Chambers, 32 Nassau Street, Dublin D02 YH68.

A CIP catalogue record for this book is available from the British Library

ISBNs:
9780857505743 hb
9780857505750 tpb

Penguin Random House is committed to a sustainable future
for our business, our readers and our planet. This book is made from
Forest Stewardship Council® certified paper.